THINK
BLACK

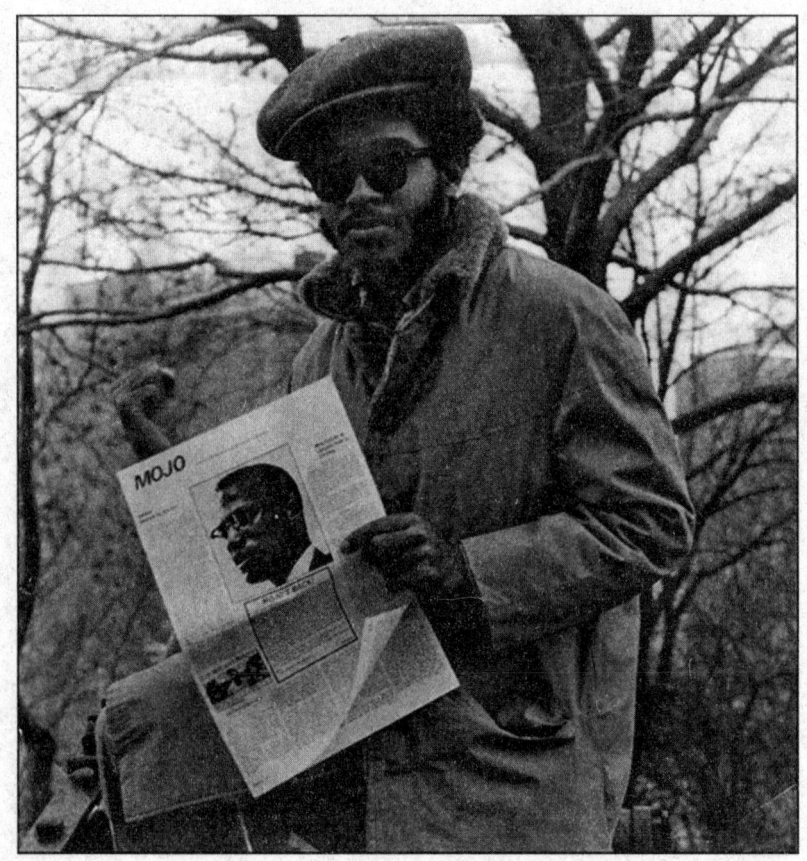

The author in the late 1960s, just prior to entering IBM.

THINK BLACK

A Memoir

WITHDRAWN

CLYDE W. FORD

Amistad
An Imprint of HarperCollinsPublishers

HarperCollins books may be purchased for educational, business, or sales promotional use. For information, please email the Special Markets Department at SPsales@harpercollins.com.

FIRST EDITION

Designed by Joy O'Meara

Library of Congress Cataloging-in-Publication Data has been applied for.

ISBN 978-0-06-289056-6

19 20 21 22 23   LSC   10 9 8 7 6 5 4 3 2 1

To my sister, Claudia Jeanne Ford:

With much love

The author's father in the mid-1950s with his IBM colleagues.

CONTENTS

AUTHOR'S NOTE

While writing this book, I faced a challenge that many memoirists face: How do I relate an important story or account for which I have no firsthand recollection and for which no factual documentation exists? I did not want to deceive the reader by suggesting that I was knowledgeable of, present at conversations with, or had insights into the motivations of individuals mentioned in the book, when such knowledge, presence, or insights on my part were just not possible. Since so much of this memoir centers on my father's career at IBM, I wrote to the company requesting his employee records and mine. I contacted IBM many times before reaching the conclusion that the company would not release this material to me. There are, of course, other sources of corroboration that I did use. Books, newspaper accounts, articles in magazines and on websites, and the few source documents I found among my deceased father's effects. I documented my reliance on these sources in notes for each chapter.

In writing this memoir, I relied heavily on discussions I had with my father over many years. Dialogue is not written to represent word-for-word documentation; rather, I've retold conversations in a way that evokes the real feeling and meaning of what was said and the mood and spirit of any given event. In some instances, I used my understanding of a person I knew well, like my father or my grandmother, to suggest how they would have responded in a given situation. In other instances, I described the actions of individuals as told to me by my father using words that clearly convey my description as a secondhand account.

For the purposes of narrative coherence and in consideration of the privacy of individuals still living, some names have been changed and some details relating to events and characters have been modified. At times, I have collapsed several characters into one.

Finally, *memoir* derives from the French word *memoire*, which means "memory." Memory, as has been shown so often, is fallible. I stand by any mistakes, gaps, and failures of memory, given in this book, as my own.

Clyde W. Ford, March 2019
Bellingham, Washington

THINK
BLACK

First Days

I held fast to an overhead bar as the elevated train I rode in swayed side to side, rocketing into Manhattan from the Bronx. When it dove beneath the Harlem River, everything outside the car went dark, and I caught a reflection of myself in the window: a ballooned Afro, pork chop sideburns, a blue zoot suit with red pinstripes, a fire engine red turtleneck, a trench coat with its collar turned up.

A half hour later, I strutted from the subway through the light rain hanging over Wall Street, humming the theme song to the film *Shaft*, which I'd seen the night before. I fancied myself as the movie's Black hero, about to engage in battle with the White troops of injustice arrayed before me. I entered one of the skyscrapers squeezed into the Financial District and took an elevator to a higher floor. There, stenciled in blue, the sign on the glass doors read IBM, and beneath it in white: NEW YORK FINANCIAL OFFICE. I grasped the door handle but paused, catching another glimpse of myself in the glass door pane. I shook my head, unsure of what to make of this decision, unready to push through those glass doors, uncertain of what fate awaited me on the other side of the threshold.

On that fall day in 1971, I was young and Black, defiant and angry, and more than ever determined not to be like my father. Yet there I stood, about to report for work at IBM, where he'd worked for twenty-five years.

When I finally pushed through the double doors, conversation stopped. The *whiz-peck-whiz* of Selectric typewriters fell silent. Many heads turned toward the teenager with the huge Afro, who now stood inside their doors. For an instant, I held hostage some fifty men in white shirts and ties, cradling telephone headsets, and a dozen female secretaries with their fingers perched on typewriter keys. I scanned the room for Black faces, but found only three: two men immersed in a sea of White faces at the center, and a young woman at work as a secretary to my left.

Art Conrad, the branch manager, stood abruptly when I entered his office. He embodied what I came to call the IBM "manager's look"—a man who could have played football in college, tall, broad-shouldered, square-jawed, solidly built, and White. He reached down to shake my hand.

"IBM dress code," he said.

I didn't reply.

Conrad trained an intense stare on me. But I held my silent ground and returned his stare. At last, he seemed to finally relent.

"I'm supposed to give you this."

He handed me a small, open box containing a silver pen and pencil set nestled in cotton.

"Thanks." I headed toward the door.

"Ford."

I spun back around.

"Take any empty seat." He pointed toward the open floor. "You won't be here long."

"Excuse me?"

His devilish grin now seemed to be payback for my previous silence. "Class," he said. "You'll be in class for the better part of a year."

I can only imagine his first entries in my employee file.

I took a seat partially hidden by one of the large pillars that supported the floor above. I had not been seated long when my telephone rang.

"I like the way you look," the female voice said. She hung up.

I swung around to the secretarial pool, but no one looked back.

Soon after, a Black man casually made his way to my desk. He sat on the edge and leaned over.

"Name's Harold," he said. "Harold Brown."

"Clyde Ford."

"Listen, Clyde. You want to do well in this company? Take some advice. Suit? Lose it! Get a plain suit, dark blue or gray. Normal length. No wide lapels. Wear a white shirt, maybe light blue shirt. Red or blue tie. You want to be different? Try a three-piece suit, a button-down shirt, or a dotted tie."

Harold pulled up a pant leg. "Dark socks. Black or dark brown shoes."

He looked at my Afro and pork chop sideburns, ran a hand through his crew cut, and smoothed the sides of his face. "Man, I don't know what to tell you about all of that hair. It's embarrassing. You just don't get it, do you? You're working for IBM now."

Harold made his way back to his desk, shaking his head.

In fact, it was Harold who didn't get it. I may have been nineteen years old, still a teenager, that first day at work, but nothing about my dress or my demeanor was unconscious or unintentional.

———

A generation earlier, in 1947, my father also gazed across a similar threshold, into an IBM office in New York City. He was a member of the Greatest Generation and had been a first lieutenant in the famed Black 369th Infantry Regiment of the US Army. From the photographs I saw of my father as a young man, at twenty-seven years old he cut a handsome figure in his dark gray suit, red striped tie, and wide-brimmed hat with a satin band. But instead of defiance, he masked diffidence; instead of anger, he displayed anticipation; instead of determination not to be like his father, he stood ready to prove to everyone, including his father, that he deserved to be the first Black systems engineer to work for IBM.

It was the late 1940s, post–World War II America. Anything was possible! Duke Ellington swung jazz. Jackie Robinson swung a big-league bat. *Brown v. Board of Education* swung through the courts. Nowhere were new possibilities and promises felt more deeply than in Harlem, which was then Black America's gravitational center. In a City College classroom on the edge of Harlem, an accounting professor invited one of her students to dinner. The Black GI arrived at her swanky apartment dressed to the nines, and Thomas J. Watson Sr., founder of IBM, stepped from the shadows. Watson offered my father a job, and a Branch Rickey–Jackie Robinson moment ensued: the start of an unknown chapter in the history of modern-day computers.

As a staunch Dodgers fan, thoughts of Jackie Robinson could not have been far from my father's mind as he crossed the threshold into IBM. Less than two years before, on October 23, 1945, Wesley Branch Rickey signed Jackie Robinson to the Montreal Royals, a farm team of the Brooklyn Dodgers, thereby breaking the "color line" in Major League Baseball and ending decades of segregation. In the postwar Black community of New York City, as around the world, Jackie Robinson came to symbolize change and a long-fought, long-sought victory for racial justice. Though Robinson would wait until the spring of 1947 for his at-bat debut as a Dodger, by the time my father entered IBM in early 1947, Jackie Robinson had already taken "first"—not first base but the status as the first Black ballplayer in Major League Baseball. And in this important regard, my father and Robinson played for the same team.

My father was not the first Black man hired by IBM. That distinction belonged to T. J. Laster, hired less than a year earlier. But Laster was hired as a salesman, making my father the first Black man hired to work as a systems engineer. And just like Robinson, hired by Branch Rickey, the head of the Dodgers' organization, my father was hired by Thomas J. Watson Sr., the legendary president and founder of IBM.

From the military to academia, politics, the media, and entertainment, postwar America was a time of "firsts" for Black men and women. Many had risked their lives on the battlefields of Europe, Asia, and Africa. They had experienced a world where bravery, not skin color, determined their fate. Then they returned to America, to hatred, to Jim Crow, and to lynchings. Something had to give. A similar push for change after World War I stalled in the wake of mounting violence by White mobs. But this time, after World War II, a few Black men and women pushed, or were catapulted, past America's discrimination.

Robinson's fabled career had yet to unfold in 1947, but Black Americans had already elevated him to near hero-like status; his role as a symbol far overshadowed his everyday life as a man. Les Matthews, a legendary sportswriter at the Black-owned *Amsterdam News*, captured the prevailing zeitgeist in the Black community as he described how pastors spoke to parishioners contemplating attendance at Dodgers games where Robinson might come to bat. "This is a very critical time for us, because not only is Jackie Robinson being judged, we're all being judged by how we behave at the ballpark," Matthews reported the clergy saying. "So we're asking you, please contain yourselves, act like ladies and gentlemen, wear proper attire, please do not drink or make any derogatory remarks. As Jackie goes, we all go. We're all going to rise or fall together."[1]

Like Robinson, my father had also stepped into a role elevating him as a symbol much larger than his individual self. At this "very critical time," my father believed that not only would he be judged at IBM, but all Blacks to come in the high-technology industry would be judged by how he behaved. He sat in the bleachers at Ebbets Field on April 15, 1947, along with a mostly Black crowd. The sportswriter Ed Silverman recalled the scene: "The women were all well coifed. Many wore lovely dresses and light coats. The men were all nicely attired. It was more like going to church than to a ballgame."[2] The Brooklyn Dodgers faced off against the Boston Braves. With a paddle-wheel arm crank and the words "Play ball," the home-plate umpire began the first Major League Baseball game with a Black man in the starting lineup.

No arm cranks or fanfare accompanied Thomas J. Watson's words to my father in 1946. That Branch Rickey–Jackie Robinson moment came at the invitation of his accounting professor at City College in New York City. Recently returned from the US Army, my father went to college on the GI Bill. His professor, a White woman, invited him to dinner at her apartment.

My grandmother, Grandma Tena, apparently expressed her alarm. "Lordy" is how she usually began. I can imagine the scene that followed.

"What's a White woman want with my baby? You can't go. You know that, Stanley, don't you? You can't go."

His teacher. Her invitation. Something he couldn't turn down.

My father, never one to shy away from confrontation, would have stood his ground.

"Lordy," I can hear Grandma Tena saying again. "So what if she's your teacher? That's all she is and all she ever can be. And that's all the more reason you can't go. A Colored man going to a White woman's home for dinner? Don't care if this is New York City, White man'd lynch you for that."

But my father had fought in World War II. He'd been to Europe. He'd had a young British woman as his girlfriend. He'd seen a new world, where a Black man and a White woman could be together.

Still, that would not have placated my grandmother.

"Hmmph. Like hell it's a new world! You think 'cause you've been to war and seen Europe that suddenly everything's different? May be a new world over there, but it's the same old 'Keep the Colored man down' world here. And if you know what's good for you, you'll tell Miss Whatever-her-name-is 'thanks but no thanks.'"

My father left for dinner anyway. Over the years, I heard the rest of the story from him many times.

He arrived at his professor's swanky Manhattan apartment, dressed up but extremely nervous. She ushered him in for dinner, informing him there was someone she wanted him to meet.

Suddenly, a tall, gaunt man with thinning white hair emerged from the shadows and reached for my father's hand.

As they shook, he introduced himself. He asked if my father knew who he was.

My father recalled stammering, before replying that of course he knew the president of IBM.

Then, my father told me, Watson delivered a line that stayed with my father throughout his life. "And I'm the only damn person in this company who can offer you a job."

Watson reportedly grilled my father about IBM's business.

When my father replied that the company's business was typewriters and tabulators, Watson sternly rejected his response. So my father served up other answers. But Watson swatted them away as well. Perhaps it was out of desperation that my father finally offered that IBM was in the information business.

Only then did Watson smile.

When my father's turn came, he questioned why Watson would offer him a job. After all, my father was an accounting student, not an engineer.

Watson let him know he had plenty of engineers and could get plenty more. His company needed smart people from all walks of life. People to learn these new information machines and take them as far as possible. Watson also informed my father that he'd have to pass the IBM entrance examination. If he didn't pass, Watson couldn't hire him.

My father stated his readiness to take, and to pass, the exam.

Finally, Watson let him know it wouldn't be easy for the first Black systems engineer at IBM, that apart from IBM's dress code, there'd be a separate "color code" for my father to follow, much like the "color code" that Jackie Robinson faced in Major League Baseball.

What would he do when someone called him "Boy" instead of "Mr. Ford"? How would he handle a manager who thought Negroes had no place in a corporation like IBM? Would he fight back when a group of engineers sought to foul a project to make him look bad?

My father told me he listened to Watson, then responded with a single word, "Think." Then, after a moment, he went on to say that as a chess player, he won by outthinking his opponents.

As dinner ended, Watson reached into his jacket pocket for a business card. He handed it to my father with instructions to call with his reply. My father kept that business card as a memento of his meeting with Watson. It's a card I still have in my possession.

My father had not sought a job with IBM. He did not think of himself as an engineer. A reluctant technologist at best, my father would have been much happier further developing his substantial musical talent—playing violin in a symphony orchestra for the beauty, playing slide trombone in a jazz band for the fun, singing lead in a church choir for the spiritual fulfillment—all the while working as an accountant for the decent living. Yet, much like Robinson, my father passed into a realm beyond such mundane possibilities by saying "Yes" to Watson. He'd become a symbol, and symbols do not always get to choose a path, or a life, of their own.

My father already knew about symbols. Watson's offer was not the first Branch Rickey–Jackie Robinson moment in my family. That moment came in a previous generation, in early 1924 on the Winsted Express, in a well-appointed coach of a New Haven Railroad train steaming south along the eastern seaboard from New England. There, Robert Malcolm Keir, a professor of economics at Dartmouth College, slipped into an easy conversation with John Baptist Ford, the Pullman porter in whose coach he rode. "We talked about life and death, what they meant to us," my grandfather recalled.[3] By the time the Winsted Express pulled into Grand Central Station in New York City, Keir had invited my grandfather, an uneducated cotton-picker from South Carolina, to lecture to his economics class at Dartmouth.

Fast-forward to my grandmother, her youngest son now about to follow a trail blazed by her husband. She no longer voiced admonitions but aspirations, her own and also those of the larger community. "Of course you're going to work for IBM," she declared. "What other choice do you have?"

News traveled quickly through my father's tight-knit Black community in the Bronx. Like many others, Lena Rogers, a childhood friend, expressed both amazement and pride.

"Thomas J. Watson offered you a job?"

Whenever Lena's name surfaced in conversation, my father deftly changed the subject. While she may have been a cousin, as he sometimes claimed, their relationship always seemed to me more like one between "kissing cousins."

Growing up, I soon came to understand why others, including my mother, referred to my father as a "ladies' man." While walking with him on the streets of the Bronx or Manhattan, he'd tip his hat, then nod and smile at the attractive women we passed. As we rocked back and forth on the wicker seats of the Third Avenue elevated line, which ran near our Bronx home, he'd stare intensely at a woman until catching her gaze. Some women would sheepishly look away. Others would determinedly stare back. Often my father would flirt with these women through gestures and eye contact without ever saying a word. My father liked women, but even more, he liked getting a rise out of other people.

When I was old enough to ask, he told me that his favorite date involved rowing on the lake in Central Park while a setting sun painted the city's skyline in shades of apricot and orange. Of course, I also wanted to know what happened after the lake. He'd smile and say, "You're too young" or "Someday you'll find out."

My father was guarded about the work Lena did and why she did not have children. My mother, however, was more direct, simply calling her, with considerable disdain, "that floozy." So it takes little for me to envision my father pulling at the oars of a rowboat, while Lena sat in the bow facing him, her long, straight black hair falling past her shoulders. A cigarette dangling from her deep red lips. Her sexy voice, deep and husky from years of chain-smoking. I can picture her leaning in toward my father, then whispering of the IBM she knew, of the men who came through her doors and revealed to her the corporate secrets forbidden even to their wives, men in white shirts and dark suits seeking an hour of her time for relief and release from the stress of a company that extracted their loyalty and sacrifice.

Lena, who called my father "Stan," would have used the phrase "our first" in describing his new position. I heard that phrase repeatedly in reference to him and the other Black pioneers of his era, as though their accomplishments had been achieved by an entire community. She might also have slipped in a scriptural reference to my father as Daniel. Those I recall speaking in such biblical terms about Blacks in never-before-held positions, like my maternal grandmother, often stopped with that simple comparison and left dangling the image of Daniel thrust not of his own choosing into the famed lions' den.

———

Postwar racial codes swirled around my father as he walked into IBM's headquarters on Madison Avenue. Heads snapped to attention, tracking him as he parted a sea of White faces on his way to the elevators. Unaware of his presence, a few people stepped into the elevator car with him, then looking up and seeing him, they suddenly stepped out. Some already inside hurriedly exited. Others hesitated at the car's threshold, peered at my father and the Black man at the elevator's controls, and waved the car on.

During the years that I taught at IBM's New York Advanced Education Center, Thomas "Tommy" Barnes sat all day at a small desk just to one side of the elevators on the eleventh floor. Tommy always had a joke ready, greeted those who stepped from the cars, held the doors open for us, reached inside to push buttons, and could suggest the best restaurant for lunch.

A tall, well-built Black man in his late fifties, with a mustache and graying black hair, Tommy also had a uniform: dark pants, a short-sleeve white shirt, and a dark blue tie. When not acting as the Education Center's concierge, Tommy buried his head in books on Greek mythology and esoteric philosophy. Give him some time, as I often did, and he would regale you with stories of Zeus, Ariadne, Sirens, and nymphs or tales of Atlantis and Lemuria.

Tommy, who lived in Brooklyn, watched over a threshold between a world "out there" and a world inside IBM. And he made that sometimes hostile world of IBM more welcoming for me.

"How you holdin' up, my man?" he'd whisper as I stepped off the elevator.

I'd nod. He'd wink. Then he'd nod back.

Sometimes, Tommy would pop his head through a classroom door or take a seat at the back for a little while, just to see for himself how the young Black kid with the big Afro was actually holding up.

Managers, instructors, and students all took to Tommy. Part guard, part greeter, part guide, Tommy's position was never fully clear to me. Did he work for IBM or the building's management? Electronic controls had long since made elevator operators obsolete, though in his younger years Tommy had been an elevator operator himself.

Now, much like an old fisherman who still went down to the docks early every morning to watch the fleet leave the harbor, and returned in the late afternoon to see it come in, or like a retired porter sitting in a station or by the side of the tracks, awaiting the arrival of memories that rolled in with each train, Tommy seemed at peace, sitting by the side of his elevators.

Tommy and my father knew each other, although Tommy never once talked about my father to me. I do not know if Tommy ever carried my father in his car, but Black men like Tommy surely did ferry my father between floors. As a younger man in the late 1940s, dressed in a dark blue double-breasted uniform with gleaming brass buttons, white gloves, and a cap with a black patent leather brim, Tommy Barnes, the elevator operator, would surely have reminded my father of his father dressed in his Pullman porter's uniform.

And I can hear Tommy say matter-of-factly, before sliding the doors closed on my father that first day of work, "Sir, do you know where you are going?"

"To work at IBM."

"Hot damn!" Tommy would have whispered, loud enough for my father to hear. "One-one. I'm playin' the numbers today, yes . . . I . . . am. . . . First Negro on his first day at work for IBM. Now that's a sign. A sure sign."

My father crossed the threshold of his IBM office to the din of voices, the ringing of telephones, and the clacking of typewriter keys. But the voices suddenly hushed. The typewriters fell silent. THINK signs stood quiet sentry on top of desks. Only the telephones continued to ring. My father slipped off his hat and held it nervously to his side, unsure of where to go, who to see, or what to say. He just stood there inside the doors for a moment, and he stood out—to the men clustered in the middle of the large open space, and to the women gathered to one side in the secretarial pool.

When a secretary rose to offer my father assistance, another layer of racial codes quickly set in. It did not matter that she was young and attractive or that she smiled at him. She was White, my father was Black, and the entire office stared at them. He dared not smile back. Instead he nodded and simply thanked her for pointing him to a manager's office.

My father's first walk across that IBM office floor to his manager's office must have felt like Robinson's first walk from the Dodgers' dugout to take a stance at home plate. The air my father passed through was thick with the same taunts and jeers and racial epithets that Robinson heard, but muttered in silence behind closed lips.

My father knocked on his manager's door, and upon being invited in, he met a tall man in his late forties with chiseled features, wide shoulders, and a graying crew cut. The man hammered down his phone, then pointed to it, barking at my father his displeasure to have just received a call from the Old Man, as employees called Thomas J. Watson, inquiring whether my father had arrived, whether he was situated, and what the manager's plans were for him. He uttered something about the Old Man breathing down his neck, then made a point of telling my father not to "fucking screw up," because if he did it would cost not only my father's job, but his as well. He then dismissed my father and ordered him to go find a suitable desk.

Outside of his manager's office, my father stopped at the desk of a young man about his age. He reached out to shake his hand, but the man barely lifted his head, and he did not reach back. He nodded over his shoulder and mumbled something about a desk "back there for you." My father walked toward the lone empty desk at the back corner of the floor, in an aisle just before the secretarial pool. Once there, he noticed that someone had placed his lacquered THINK sign upside down in its base. He took his seat and stared at the wooden sign before him. He slid it out, righted it, and slid it back into its stand. Then he looked over the IBM office floor before him. With desks arranged in orderly rows, the floor brought to mind a large chessboard. White always moved first, before Black had a chance to counter.

———

My earliest and fondest memories of my father came from the home we lived in at 760 East 221st Street in the Bronx. John Baptist Ford, my grandfather, had purchased the home not long after he migrated north from South Carolina and began working as a Pullman porter. His wife, my grandma Tena, lived downstairs, even after he died in 1947. I was born in 1951, when our family occupied the entire second floor.

As a child, I'd anxiously await my father's arrival home from IBM each day and greet him at the apartment's front door. When he stepped into our apartment, I'd step atop his shoes, my right foot over his left foot, my left foot over his right foot, and wrap one arm around each leg. With my father at six feet, my head rose just above his knees. He'd walk me around the house for five or ten minutes that way. I learned to explore the world by walking in my father's footsteps.

As a child of a similar age, my father had the nickname Buster. But my mother rejected that name for me; instead, she named us Big Bub and Lil Bub, and between the ages of three and five, Lil Bub is what I was called within our family.

Mythic tales of the father quest abound, spanning all continents and all ages. The Greek goddess Athena visited twenty-year-old Telemachus and said to him, "Young man, go search for your father," that father being none other than wandering hero Odysseus. Slayer-of-Monsters and Born-of-Water, the Navajo twins, traveled north in quest of their father, the Sun. Horus, the Egyptian falcongod, set out to avenge his father, Osiris. Dionysus, born from his father's thigh, descended into the underworld on a quest sanctioned by his father, Zeus. Jesus, in the biblical account, was given of a father, then willingly sacrificed himself to return to that father.

Psychotherapists speak of an unavoidable Oedipus complex, pitting father against son for the love of the same woman—as wife or as mother. I do not know if my mother was the unconscious source of my conflicts with my father, but I do recall the intensity of our skirmishes.

At the height of his career at IBM, my father escaped New York City with his family for a suburban life north of the city. Our Rockland County home sat at the end of a cul-de-sac, on a large tract of land with a view of the rolling hills along the west side of the Hudson River. We'd spent more than a year looking at homes north and west of New York City. But the acreage of this plot seemed to close the deal for my father. We fled the Bronx for a split-level home, fruit trees, a large lawn, and a garage. We moved to Rockland County in the spring of 1966 and became one of the few Black families in our town.

At six feet tall and slightly overweight, with a pipe clenched between his crooked teeth and blue smoke curling up from his lips, my father dominated the space in front of our kitchen window. He pulled the pipe from his mouth and pointed it out the window to our large backyard. In his deep baritone voice, he called my mother, Vivian, my younger sister, Claudia, and me over.

"There. There. There. And There."

In the air, he'd marked a rectangle's corners, sixty feet long and twenty-five feet wide.

"We'll put in a pool."

My mother smiled. I did not.

As a child heading to Virginia for family summers, I recalled a pervasive fear that settled over our family as we entered the South; laws forced us to change to a "Coloreds Only" bus and forced me to swim in a "Coloreds Only" pool. My father recalled that fear too. He saw his pool as an antidote for such injustice: as a testament to all the values and freedoms he had fought for in World War II, all the racism and bigotry he'd fought through in his career at IBM, and as a status symbol that would finally allow him to leapfrog ahead of his older brother, Gene.

We would be the first in our family to have the luxury of an in-ground pool. Being first, however, held risks. That, I knew. As the first all-Black family in our Bronx co-op apartment, I regularly ran a gauntlet of rocks hurled by other kids in the six blocks to the subway station on my way to and from school. I endured the repeated taunts of "Nigger" from Irish and Italian youth who lived in our building and "Schvartze" from the yentas who rode the elevators (as if masking the slur in Yiddish somehow hid their disdain). As a family, we learned not to trust our neighborhood mechanic's shop, where once, a flat tire resulted in a gas tank filled with sugar and an astronomical repair bill.

A secluded home along the Hudson's Palisades promised my father a peaceful paradise to escape the racism we'd known, a confirmation that he'd achieved the American dream, and a tribute to his accomplishments as the first Black systems engineer at IBM. Except, the world beyond the Palisades experienced no peace. Civil rights battles set cities ablaze; a war in Vietnam vaporized human flesh; and in two years, King would step fatefully onto a balcony in Memphis.

"Build your pool," I said. "But don't expect me to ever swim in it. It's nothing more than a monument to you finally becoming part of the Black bourgeoisie."

———

As a child walking around on my father's shoes, I had unconsciously begun my father quest, which unfolded through my conflicts with him. Then I continued this quest by going to work for IBM myself.

Several years ago, as I started to write this book, I contacted IBM's Employee Records Department with a request for my father's employee records and also my own. IBM had positioned itself as a leader in Open Human Relations, and I assumed this would translate into open access to personnel files, particularly for a former employee, like my father, who'd been hired seventy years ago and retired almost forty years ago.

Furthermore, Diane Gherson, IBM's chief of human resources, had recently announced, "Our job in HR is to create that connected, transparent, mobile, personalized, searchable and 24x7 universe through our workplace and our tools. It means investing in new technology and reinventing all our processes through the lens of the employee."[4]

When several weeks passed without a response, I contacted them again. This time, I received an email informing me that I had not included enough information with my previous request and that employee records were provided only to actual former employees or to those with power of attorney granted to them by actual employees. It seemed not to matter that I was a former IBM employee.

My father passed away in 2000, and as the executor of his estate, I had been granted absolute and enduring power of attorney for any matters related to him and his affairs. I also offered proof of my identity by photocopying my Washington State driver's license. I re-sent the request for my father's records with this new information. When I did not hear back from IBM after several weeks, I contacted them again by email and by fax. After three similar requests for these records went unanswered, I realized my efforts would not bear fruit.

IBM's silence on the matter now raised its own set of questions. What information lay in those personnel records? What did the company not want me to see? I had heard of other investigators into IBM's past facing similar corporate roadblocks in seeking information. I just could not imagine anything in my father's past, or mine, that warranted stonewalling on IBM's part.

But then I pieced together the stories my father told me about his early years with the company; I recalled my own experience working at IBM; and I dug deeper into the shadows of IBM's corporate history to unravel the tale that lay there.

When I went to work for IBM, I risked following the thread of my father's path into the very corporate behemoth that nearly swallowed him whole. And where I had thought to find a contented man reaping the benefits of good fortune to build a comfortable life, I found a troubled soul battling both inner and outer demons arrayed against him; where I had thought to find a man quietly accepting of his place, I found a man covertly working to bring about change; where I had thought to find a company awakened to social justice, I found a business blinded by corporate greed; and where I had thought to come only to a deeper understanding of my father, I came also to a deeper understanding of myself.

A Sacrificial Pawn

Liebesträume No. 3, the rich tone poem for piano by Franz Liszt, scores many of my earliest memories of my father. He and my mother had an arrangement, whereby she stayed at home with my sister and me, while he earned an MBA in the evenings from New York University, and he watched us on those nights when she worked toward her master's in education from Hunter College. For dinner, my father almost always made one of his signature dishes, Hungarian goulash, which he spun as his own secret, special recipe but which was, in reality, cans of whatever the pantry offered dumped into a single pot. After dinner, he'd put us to bed and then sit down at the piano, and I would drift off to melodies of *Liebesträume.*

As classically trained musicians and vocalists, my parents left little doubt about the role of music in my future. "From any instrument," my father pronounced, "you should be able to produce a reasonable sound." It's an expansive belief that has stuck with me to this day.

Lessons began at age four. My father insisted I study the piano with his teacher, Carmen Silva, a stern older woman who lived not far from us in the Williamsbridge neighborhood of the Bronx. Stepping down into Miss Silva's basement felt like a descent into hell, where two monstrous, gleaming wooden guardians—a grand piano and a bass piano—snarled with their pearly white teeth. Miss Silva, mistress of the monsters, insisted I play with my fingers bent at ninety degrees to my palms. She sat on the piano bench next to me holding a ruler with which she rapped my knuckles whenever my fingers lost their required form.

To make matters worse, Carmen Silva delivered each syllable of a word, overannunciated and accompanied by a fine spray of spittle. She also substituted a *u* for an *a* in any word ending in -*able*. So, *vegetable* sounded like "veg-ge-tubble" and *comfortable* like "com-for-tubble." The whole experience of being with her felt alien and did nothing to endear me to the piano. None of this seemed to faze my father, who recalled his own difficult time with Miss Silva as though shared torture might strengthen a bond between us.

Then came time for Miss Silva's annual music recital, where each of her students played onstage in front of an audience of adoring family and friends. My father's excitement grew even as my enthusiasm plummeted. I pleaded not to perform. He insisted. I yelled. He told me not to worry. I cried. He ignored me. He had to perform, and so would I. I may have been only four, but in the face of his intransigence and insistence came my first inkling that he saw himself in me, perhaps more so than he saw me. Pleading and crying would do no good. So I stopped. But I did not stop my planning for Miss Silva's recital.

When the day of the recital came, my father had me dress in a dark blue suit and bow tie. He and my mother also dressed up for the occasion. They stepped from our upstairs apartment before me, and I told them I'd forgotten my music in the living room. I calmly walked back into the living room, closed myself into the closet, stuck a skeleton key into the lock from the inside, and turned it, locking the closet and keeping the skeleton key in place so that no one could open the door from the outside without first breaking it down.

Now came my father's turn to plead and to yell. He insisted I open the closet, which I steadfastly refused to do. He banged on the door. I did not budge. He threatened me with all manner of corporal punishment. It did not matter. I had quite a simple plan: stay locked in the closet until the recital was over. After that, I'd take any punishment he meted out.

This standoff between my father and me lasted for some time until finally my mother intervened. If I'd taken to locking myself in a closet, she reasoned with my father, maybe I really didn't want to perform, and maybe they shouldn't force me. So he bargained.

"If you come out of the closet, you won't have to perform at Miss Silva's recital."

I hung tough. "No more music lessons with her."

Silence descended on the other side of the closet door. Finally, my father relented. "Okay, no more lessons. Now come out."

But I had a plan, and by God I was sticking to it. An hour later, when my mother said, "It's too late to go to the recital anyway," I unlocked and opened the closet door. She hugged me. My father angrily stormed off. In truth, he'd only backed away in strategic retreat.

Not long after Miss Silva's recital came another of my father's pronouncements, one he repeated often. "A man needs only three things for happiness: a good pipe, a good game of chess, and a good woman." He enjoyed parenting through such pithy sayings, cribbed from others and then refashioned in his own words. A serious gaze, without a hint of self-deprecation, accompanied this pronouncement. Although originating in a comedy sketch by George Burns, when reformed and restated by my father, it became a philosophy of life.

The sweet aroma of his cherry-blend pipe tobacco would waft through the air as he'd unfold a spindly legged card table, open a chessboard, and begin stamping down pieces on the board. I'd move. He'd pull his pipe from between his teeth. I'd hear his rolling baritone voice.

"Sure you want to move there?"

By then, it was already too late. He'd glimpsed many moves ahead to certain checkmate.

My father lived for, lived by, and lived through chess. Never just a game, chess served as a way to apprehend and manipulate his world. He saw average people as pawns with limited moves at their disposal, and he believed intelligent people to be rooks, knights, bishops, queens, or kings in possession of more sophisticated means.

"If you're going to succeed you have to think three or four moves ahead. Where will I move? What will the other person do if I move there? Back and forth like that," he said. "Life's a chessboard, and you have to think like a chess player if you're going to win."

Chess and IBM have long been connected. Secret IBM efforts were often code-named Project Chess. IBM poured millions of dollars into developing Deep Blue, a chess-playing computer that defeated the world chess champion Garry Kasparov in May 1997. And IBM employees, like my father, relished the game. IBM also realized that the public could better comprehend computers if they were associated with a well-known game like chess. If a computer could succeed in tackling the complex problem of two people playing chess, it could certainly take on any other problem humans faced.

My father was a member of the IBM championship chess teams of 1957 and 1959. Even before IBM, he played correspondence chess, from the 1940s through the 1960s, with moves sent back and forth on postcards. A special code recorded the game: For example, "e4 e5 Nf3 Nc6" meant that White had opened with its King pawn played to column e, row 4. Black responded by moving its King pawn to column e, row 5. White then moved a Knight to column f, row 3, and Black played a Knight to column c, row 6.

Through numbered rows and lettered columns, through single-letter abbreviations for chess pieces (lowercase for pawns, uppercase for other pieces), this code condensed a world of limitless possibilities. If you understood the code, you saw beauty, imagination, creativity, and daring. If you understood the code, you peered into the mind of your opponent. If you understood the code, you communicated your own deep thinking with regard only to the color of your pieces, not the color of your skin. If you understood the code, you lived in a world inhabited by others who also understood the code. My father understood this code, and before he even began working with computers, he understood the power of any code to create, shape, and transform the world.

Manipulation. Deception. Feigns. Gambits. My father studied winning chess moves and found great comfort in understanding himself in the rigid Black and White terms of chess—a respite, I'm certain, from the fluid color terms of race and racism that he also knew.

"If you're White, you're all right. If you're Yellow, you're mellow. If you're Brown, stick around. If you're Black, get back!" goes a ditty handed down from slave master to slave, now enshrined in the beliefs of many Americans, Black and White.

Standing on the banks of the James River in Virginia in 1712, Willie Lynch, a plantation owner from the West Indies, offered a group of fellow slave owners his advice.

"Gentlemen," Lynch began, "in my bag here, I have a foolproof method for controlling your black slaves."

Lynch went on to discuss treating slaves as chattel and breaking them as one would a horse. But he returned often to a favorite theme: sowing divisions.

> *Don't forget you must pitch the old black male vs. the young black male, and the young black male against the old black male. You must use the dark skin slaves vs. the light skin slaves, and the light skin slaves vs. the dark skin slaves. You must use the female vs. the male. And the male vs. the female. You must also have your white servants and overseers distrust all Blacks. . . . Gentlemen, these kits are your keys to control. Use them. Have your wives and children use them, never miss an opportunity. If used intensely for one year, the slaves themselves will remain perpetually distrustful of each other.*[1]

My father described himself as the "black sheep" of his family, which he meant quite literally. In the 1800s, my great-grandfather Thomas McLeod of South Carolina, who had Scottish ancestry and was perhaps a slaveholder or the child of a union between a slaveholder and a slave, fathered children with my great-grandmother Abbie Davis. From that union came several generations of my father's family, some fair enough to "pass" for White. My father believed that his darker skin placed him at a disadvantage. It also made him perpetually distrustful of others.

Skin color conveyed intelligence for him. Lighter skin meant greater intellect, darker skin the opposite. My father read widely of such racist views in books and articles by authors such as Arthur Jensen and Charles Murray, and he did nothing to counter what he read.

Jensen sat on the board of the German neo-Nazi journal *Neue Anthropologie* (New Anthropology) published by the Society for Biological Anthropology, Eugenics, and the Study of Behavior. His work, which set the tenor for many articles published in the journal, is often quoted by White nationalists today. Jensen worked actively and closely with American scientists and business leaders to oppose and reverse efforts to effect school integration and affirmative action. His statements are chilling:

> *There are intelligence genes, which are found in populations in different proportions, somewhat like the distribution of blood types. The number of intelligence genes seems to be lower, over-all, in the black population than in the white. As to the effect of racial mixing, nobody has yet performed experiments that reveal its relative effect on I.Q. If the racial mixture weren't there, it is possible that the I.Q. differences between blacks and whites would be even greater. I think such studies should be done to lay this uncertainty to rest once and for all.*[2]

It has been shown that *The Bell Curve*, coauthored by Charles Murray, relied on "tainted" sources linked to eugenicists, White supremacists, and Nazi sympathizers.[3] Yet Murray still stands by his equally chilling racist and misogynistic findings, though couched in a scholar's lofty language:

> *The professional consensus is that the United States has experienced dysgenic pressures throughout either most of the*

century (the optimists) or all of the century (the pessimists). Women of all races and ethnic groups follow this pattern in similar fashion. There is some evidence that blacks and Latinos are experiencing even more severe dysgenic pressures than whites, which could lead to further divergence between whites and other groups in future generations.[4]

Even with the theories of these authors debunked, and their reasoning shown to be corrupt, my father argued in their favor, despite all the contrary evidence of his own substantial intellect and his many fine accomplishments. His vociferous support of this self-inflicted racial wound was a constant source of friction between us.

When I was in high school, a typical afternoon would find me parked in New York City's Schomburg Library, devouring books on Black history. I savored the accounts of men and women whose greatness had not found its way into the texts forced on me at school. Then I'd come home to a man lamenting being born with dark skin.

My father even ranked my sister's children—his own grandchildren—by the color of their skin, whispering to each a selective message of their inferior or superior intellect. Such internalized racism, as Willie Lynch understood in 1712, is not difficult to instill in long-oppressed people.

Although personal genetic testing was not readily available during my father's lifetime, I wanted to better understand our ancestry, in part because of his wide embrace of these racist ideas. So a few years ago, I spit into a small test tube, which I sent off for DNA testing. When my results arrived, they seemed wrong!

A map showed four principal genetic "hot spots," when I'd long assumed there would be five, if not six. One large hot spot, and the only one in Africa, showed ancestry from the Angola/Congo region, which came as no surprise. I had long suspected African origins in Angola, in part because, before Alex Haley's *Roots*, I'd traced my mother's side of the family back to a slave named Scipio in the Tidewater region of Virginia along the banks of the James River, where my DNA test also revealed a hot spot. In 1974, after several summers searching through the Virginia State Archives and the Surry County courthouse, I actually found the deed of manumission that freed Scipio from his slave master, Thomas Bell. Scipio Brown, born in 1762, married a woman named Amy Johnson, apparently born free.

The Johnson name among free Blacks in this area is very old and hints of a lineage dating back to the first "20 and odd Negroes" who arrived in the Virginia colony aboard the English ship the *White Lion* in late August 1619. English sailors had captured those Africans from the Portuguese slave ship the *São João Bautista*, whose captain, Manuel Mendes da Cunha, had boarded them in Luanda, the present-day capital of Angola. These first Africans were sold by the English for food and bought by colonists who later turned around and resold them in Jamestown—not into slavery, as most suggest, but into indentured servitude. Many eventually worked off their indentures, took anglicized names, and married. Among them in 1628 were Anthony and Amy Johnson, whom I suspect were relatives of Amy Johnson, who married Scipio Brown.

One explanation for the lack of a second genetic hot spot in Africa is that my father's ancestry is also traceable back to precolonial Angola/Congo, which would not be surprising, since the Angola/Congo region gave up many sons and daughters to the horrendous trade in human beings.

My European ancestry really shocked me. I knew that I had European roots on both sides of my family, but instead of two

European hot spots—one for each parent's lineage—I found only one major hot spot in Europe.

Even now, my hair and beard, both with more gray than black, show streaks of red, especially after time under the summer sun. I call these red hairs my "Nancy's hairs," after Nancy Campbell, my Scottish grandmother, several times removed on my mother's side. In the middle of the nineteenth century, she, along with other White women, fled to the South to escape the prejudice and bigotry toward Scottish and Irish immigrants in northern cities like New York. There they married Black men freed from bondage or those still in chains, whose freedom they then secured.

I found another hot spot in South Carolina, where I knew my father's side of the family originated, but it seemed odd that there wasn't at least one more major European hot spot on my father's branch of the family tree, since he had so many light-skinned relatives. With all the major hot spots of my genetic makeup accounted for, where did this obvious Caucasian ancestry enter my father's side of the family?

As I pondered this conundrum, I was contacted by a woman who'd been notified by the DNA testing company of the high probability that we were related. When Edna Messick and I compared notes, the family name McLeod kept coming up. My paternal grandmother's maiden name was McLeod. I had often heard my father identify himself as a McLeod. On my father's side, the McLeod branch of my family tree had roots in the same region of Scotland as the Campbell branch, on my mother's side.

My test results showed only one major European hot spot because my family on both my mother's and my father's side had roots in the same Scottish Highlands. Clan McLeod (originally MacLeod), my father's side, with its tartan of black lines running over yellow and red squares, squabbled with Clan Campbell, my mother's side, with its tartan of black lines over blue and green squares. Eventually, both clans intermarried and joined forces against Clan MacDonald over several centuries of Scottish clan wars beginning in the 1300s. Friends and enemies, allies and adversaries—that is how one might describe both my parents and their respective clans.

3

The Bones of the Machine

As far as machines go, it looked unremarkable. *But, then, so did that Ethiopian gully where Donald Johanson made his remarkable archeological find.* A card reader, a converted typewriter, a door at the far right end, all housed in a plain gray frame. *A humerus, some vertebrae, the back of a skull, all lying on a slope above the gully. One by one, Johanson and his graduate student, Tom Gray, picked up the bone fragments, piecing them into a skeleton named Lucy, which told an astounding story of the dawn of the human race.*[1] One by one, smartphones, laptops, notebooks, the internet, social media, crowdsourcing, Apple, Microsoft, Google—fragments of our digital era—can all trace their stories back to that unremarkable machine at the dawn of the Digital Age.

While many specialized computers had been built before, no programmable computer had been mass-produced or was commercially available until IBM introduced the model 407. In fact, there's still some debate over whether to call the IBM 407 the first true computer or the last programmable accounting machine. Just as Lucy had characteristics of both modern-day humans and apes, the IBM 407 had characteristics of both modern-day computers and older accounting machines. Still, it's a safe bet to trace the origins of modern humans at least as far back as Lucy. And it's a safe bet to trace the origins of modern digital technology at least as far back as the IBM 407. IBM announced the model 407 in 1949, not long after my father began his career. The company trained him to operate and program the machine. So it's safe to say that my father was present at the dawn of the Digital Age.

You can swipe or type to enter data into your smartphone or laptop. But the only way to enter data into an IBM 407 was through punch cards, read at 150 cards per minute by a card reader built into the machine. The smartphone you're carrying contains at least 8 gigabytes of memory. The IBM 407 had none. Still the idea of memory could be found within the model 407: punch new cards to store the data required, and then load that new deck back into the machine.

Today, we take for granted being able to view the results of a spreadsheet computation on a monitor or video display. With a model 407, you had to wait for a clackety line printer to slowly spit out results, line by line. But that line printer—essentially a typewriter connected to a computer—was, in itself, a revolutionary advance in information processing. Until the advent of the 407, the best typists could produce one hundred words a minute. Along came a machine that could compute, and produce results, much faster than any human could type. Line printers, capable of printing customized text at one hundred lines a minute, rather than one hundred words a minute, bridged this gap between the information a machine could produce and the information a human could understand. Printers were the window into the mind of the machine. The 407 produced output that a line printer could print and humans could read. In that humble beginning lies the foundation of much of our modern-day human-machine interaction.

Vestiges of the 407's line printer are still with us today. Modern-day operating systems, such as Windows, possess an LPR command (short for *Line PrinteR*) that sends output to a printer, and modern-day software developers describe their output in terms of "lines of code," hearkening back to a time when line printers produced a single line of print for each written line of code.

At more than several tons, including supporting equipment, an IBM 407 often occupied its own separate room. By modern measurements, the all-electromechanical IBM 407—with no solid-state devices, no transistors, and not even vacuum tubes—was ancient and primitive. Yet in its day, the model 407 represented state-of-the-art digital technology, and it was the first of many IBM machines my father mastered.

To an untrained eye, the fully wired control board of an IBM 407 looked like a jumble of wires or a woven basket; systems engineers at the time even called the practice of wiring control boards "basket weaving." Patching sockets together controlled how one internal circuit communicated with another and therefore governed how the machine added numbers and printed results. Software had not yet been invented. Long before HTML, BASIC, Java, or C#—modern-day software languages used to program computers—my father hard-wired control boards.

My father brought home an IBM 407 control board in 1957. After dinner, he placed it on our kitchen table and pulled out a bag of patch cords. He set down a list of written connections, which he read to my sister and me, while supervising which hubs we pushed the ends of the patch cords into. At six years old, I was programming a computer. At three years old, Claudia was a bit too young to do much more than play with the colored wires. As usual, a pithy quote accompanied the lesson.

"Computers will control your life one day," he said. "Better if you learn how to control them first."

We wound up with a dense jumble of colored wires arcing between holes on the control board. My father sent us to bed with his thanks. That next evening he told us our control panel had worked perfectly and had caused the 407 to do exactly what he needed, though I imagine we'd left him with much to rewire.

Fifteen years later, I was the only Black systems engineer in my class at IBM's New York Education Center for a lecture on the history of programmable machines. After presentations on the punch card programmable Jacquard loom of the early 1800s and the wizardry of Herman Hollerith in the 1900s, an older IBM employee stepped to the lectern, holding a model 407 control board. Like a long-forgotten photograph, the sight of that board opened a floodgate of memories.

"Anyone know what this is?" he asked.

Only I raised my hand. "It's an IBM 407 control board."

He nodded with surprise and then held up a patch cord.

"How was this used?"

Again, my hand shot up. "It's a patch cord used to connect two different hubs on the control board."

If my answer seemed matter-of-fact, his rapid-fire questions surprised me. He shook a fully wired control board in my direction.

"And this?"

"It's a program, a hardwired program used to control the operation of the 407."

"I suppose you've programmed a 407 as well?"

"I have."

A "gotcha" expression flashed across his face. "The 407 was introduced twenty years ago. You're only twenty now. So how could you have programmed a 407?"

After I explained my father's job and those evenings at the kitchen table, the instructor conceded checkmate. At the time, I may have been the only Black systems engineer in my class, but I was far from the only Black systems engineer in the company. In the generation since my father, more Blacks had entered IBM, some thanks to him. I found it easy to stand up to this instructor. But I also understood that my father had struggled far more in establishing his credibility in an IBM classroom.

My father's IBM report card shows he began his education on the model 407 in late 1952 and completed the class, with honors, in early 1953. Here is where he encountered the wonders of this modern machine and the wrath of colleagues convinced that a Black man should not be among them.

In these early years of computing, few understood how to tame an electromechanical behemoth like the model 407, and even fewer understood how to teach that skill. Peter Hauptmann, an immigrant from Germany, was that rare individual who instructed others on the arcane art of programming an IBM 407. Hauptmann, who worked at Columbia University's Watson Research Laboratories, filled classes with students from around the world who came to sit at the feet of a master. He also taught internal classes for IBM employees, like the class my father completed.

Hauptmann may well have been one of the first nerds. In his late twenties, he had a boyish face and dressed in a slightly crumpled dark suit. A tie uneven and just off-center. Wire-rimmed glasses. A cleft chin jutting out. Dark hair slicked back. Photographs from that period show Hauptmann in front of a blackboard stenciled with what appears to be several cribbage boards drawn side by side. An IBM 407—five feet wide, four feet tall, and three feet deep—

stands to one side of Hauptmann. Punch cards are stacked in a hopper on the left side of the machine. The truncated top of a typewriter sits in the middle. From a door at the far right, a large handle protrudes.

The model 402 had preceded the model 407, and before the 402 had come the model 405. 405, 402, 407. A joke circulated that a company that produced counting machines could not itself count sequentially. One can imagine how this naming sequence might have rubbed the sensibilities of an engineer like Hauptmann the wrong way, and how he might have attempted to tell this joke as an icebreaker, only to have it fall horribly flat.

Less than twenty years after my father entered his first computing class at IBM, I entered mine, fortunate that men like Hauptmann still taught. I heard essentially the same message my father had, though refined by years of classroom instruction; it began with the systems engineer's mantra, "Input. Processing. Output."

Hauptmann would have touched the left, center, and right of the 407 as he delivered that slogan. That's how a 407 was designed: an input section read data from punch cards, an output section printed numbers and words on a typewriter converted to a printer, and a processing section performed additions.

"Input. Processing. Output," my father intoned countless times over the years. "These are the basic stages of any computer."

Sitting in class, my father would have seen Hauptmann move to the right side of the 407 and grab the large handle to pull the door down and open, revealing a control board with many holes and a dense patchwork of colored cords: the same board stenciled on the blackboard behind him. I can imagine the drama as Hauptmann popped out the board, held it overhead, and waved it in front of the class, as many of my IBM instructors did. Systems engineers like my father became intimately familiar with plugboards, as these control boards were also known, and with the colored patch cords connecting the sockets, or hubs, on them.

No doubt Hauptmann used the word *program* to describe a completely wired control board, for that was the original meaning of the computer term. And while the 407 could execute only one program at a time, it was possible to have multiple control panels wired and ready. Instead of writing results to a printer, each intermediate program would punch its results to a new card deck. A new control panel would then be inserted, and a new card deck would be read, as many times as necessary, until the final program sent its results to the printer.

My father used the knowledge Hauptmann imparted to do his job, to design and wire programs to meet IBM's customer needs. After a day's class, his colleagues would often gather over dinner without inviting him. He would sometimes visit with Lena Rogers.

———

I never visited Lena's apartment, but apparently my father often did. I have only vague recollections of hearing that she lived in a studio, perhaps within a hotel, on Manhattan's West Side with an impressive view of Central Park.

I have no doubt that my father and Lena were drinking and smoking buddies. I smelled booze and tobacco on her breath whenever I was in her presence, and on his when he returned from seeing her. I believe they were probably more. I also believe that my father unburdened himself with Lena in ways he could not with my mother, much like the other men that Lena entertained.

Perhaps it was from pride or shame that, after a few drinks with Lena, my father opened up about his difficulties in class. How when Hauptmann stopped drawing colored chalk lines representing patch cords on the blackboard and began handing out real patch cords and real control boards, suddenly there were not enough supplies for my father. How when my father raised his hand for a question, Hauptmann often never got around to calling on him. And how when it came time to step up to the classroom's 407 for a demonstration, my father found himself at the back of the line, farthest away from the machine.

I have also long wondered how my father rationalized this friendship, or affair, with a woman who seems in hindsight to have been a high-end call girl. For all of his mastery of deception, my father was also a creature of habit. His preferred parry when I brought up Lena was to shift to a wartime story, one that I suspect he also told her.

"For almost a year, I was a quartermaster for the Army Air Corps, the 339th Fighter Group, stationed at an airfield just outside of London," my father recounted. "I met Winifred McAllister, an English girl who bicycled to the field each day to help care for our wounded airmen. When we had free time, we'd take long walks, talk for hours. She brought me home once, to meet her parents.

"Then one day she didn't show up at the base. When she didn't show up the second day, I bicycled into town to find out why. Her mother answered the door and fell into my arms, sobbing. Winifred had been killed two nights earlier in a German bombing raid."

My father, who rarely showed his feelings, would pause, his voice choked with emotion. But to be honest, he was also a master of manufacturing emotions on cue, so it was hard to know whether, after so many retellings, he had choked up for real or simply felt the story required this of him.

"Her mother said to me, 'Stanley, Winnie told us she'd met a man she was falling in love with, and she didn't give a damn about the color of his skin. And we didn't either, just as long as our Winnie was happy.'

"I never got to tell her how I felt about her. Never got to hold her. Never got to kiss her. She was there one day, then she was gone forever the next."

With Lena, I can also hear my father adding a coda. "So, no, I don't judge any man, or woman, for needing or finding love and companionship when, where, and how they can. Life is too short."

———

IBM's classes for systems engineers ended in examinations, usually a practical test of skills rather than a written test to be turned in. Often a class was split into teams that faced off against each other over the challenge of designing the best solution for a hypothetical customer's needs.

Peter Hauptmann would have designed the final examination for my father's 407 class. A typical customer problem in those days concerned the production of financial statements from the data a company kept on punch cards. So, for example, Hauptmann would have instructed my father's class to create a profit-and-loss statement and a balance sheet for a fictitious XYZ company using data he supplied to them on a stack of punch cards.

IBM final exams were rigorous and competitive. Each set of punch cards required its own set of instructions. But the instructions for one set of punch cards would not work with another set, which made such exams rife for sabotage. One team could secretly manipulate the instructions or card deck of another team in order to secure an advantage.

Depending on its size, my father's class might have been split into two self-selected teams, with a different set of colored punch cards supplied to each. From what I gathered, no team in his class wanted a Black man, which left him with two choices: join a team where he was unwelcomed, or become a team of his own. He chose the latter.

Years later, when my IBM class was given a final exam of creating a balance sheet for a fictitious company, I chose to be a team of one battling for a grade against several teams populated with four or more systems engineers. Each team's data already lived inside the computer's memory, but we punched our programs into cards to access and manipulate that data.

I understand what it must have been like for my father to pencil in patch cord connections on a printed sheet of control board templates rather than drawing them on a blackboard diagram because there was no space left for him at the board. And I know what it felt like to need machine time to test his program, when others had occupied all the available slots.

Like my father, I too showed up early for class right before my final exam to grab machine time to test my program in the absence of other students. I dropped the cards containing my program into the computer's card reader. *My father swung open the doors of the 407 and dropped his control board in, then fed the card deck containing his data into the machine's hopper.* My cards zipped into the computer. *The 407 consumed his more slowly.* Lights blinked on the computer in front of me. *Relays clacked and circuits hummed on the 407 in front of him.* In both cases, a printer sprang to life, spitting out the results of our labor. And when we tore the pages from the printer, I have to believe we both had the same sinking feeling in the pit of our stomachs. Nothing worked!

Here our stories diverge because I do not believe I encountered the same racial animosity that my father did. One of my instructors, a young White man, once stepped in to help me when he could have let me fail. But in telling the story of how he succeeded against the bigotry he faced, my father acted more like a reporter protecting his sources. He refused to name those who'd helped him for fear, I believe, that it might threaten their jobs at IBM. But I also believe a White woman in the education department's secretarial pool, perhaps a woman he'd secretly flirted with, had typed the instructions for those card decks. That would have been a common practice. Upon recognizing his plight, she may have also interceded at the last minute to provide him with a correct set of instructions, giving him, at least, a fighting chance.

Tommy Barnes knew. Whether it happened behind the closed doors of a classroom or a manager's office, he knew. Some spoke to Tommy as though it didn't matter. Others conversed in front of him as though he weren't there. Tommy, as far as I could determine, was a shrewd but unobtrusive observer who, from decades conducting the public floor to floor, could read volumes behind the slightest change in facial expression, stance, or gait.

Before I stepped into an elevator car, he might whisper, "Don't worry. It's gonna be okay."

The seer. The soothsayer. The sage. Most failed to recognize the wisdom, insight, and encouragement available daily. But this lack of recognition never seemed to bother Tommy. He focused on the few of us who'd gladly miss an elevator to hear whatever he had to say, especially the few of us who were Black.

My father would have readily laid down his burdens while riding in Tommy's car. To which I can hear Tommy reply, "I'll say a prayer for you, Stan. Miracles happen every day."

4

The Book of Changes

My mother, Vivian, began practicing yoga in the late 1950s as part of a modern dance class she attended. Few in the West had even heard of yoga at that time. My father would often get confused, telling other people his wife was "doing yogurt," which I recall bringing about a smirk from those who heard him, followed by a swift rebuke and correction from my mother.

In my twenties, even as I worked for IBM during the day, in the evenings I taught yoga at the Integral Yoga Institute in New York City. Through Integral Yoga, I'd also become a student of Swami Satchidananda, the yoga master from India who'd opened the Woodstock Festival during the summer of 1969. My father viewed these eastern metaphysical practices and teachings as a sharp fall from the grace of his Christian upbringing. He'd long given up on influencing my mother, but he lamented that her actions had also damned my sister, Claudia, and me.

I found this very strange, since modern computing is predicated on the very eastern metaphysics my father eschewed. Digital technology based on binary arithmetic, the computational mathematics of 1s and 0s, can be directly traced back to a three-thousand-year-old Chinese divination system known as the *I Ching*, or the *Book of Changes*. The *I Ching* begins with a question about yourself, your life, or something meaningful to you at the moment. Write that question down. Then toss six coins and randomly arrange them top to bottom. Let heads represent a solid line; and tails, a broken line. You'll end up with a hexagram of six lines. Now, look up that hexagram in the *Book of Changes* to determine the answer to your question.

From left to right, the hexagrams shown above in the illustration represent the aspects of Force (*qián*), Innocence (*wú wàng*), and Humbling (*qiān*). The *Book of Changes* interprets each hexagram with additional commentary. The hexagram representing Force, for instance, is described, in part, in the *I Ching* as follows:

> *The power represented by the hexagram is to be interpreted in a dual sense in terms of its action on the universe and of its action on the world of men. In relation to the universe, the hexagram expresses the strong, creative action of the Deity. In relation to the human world, it denotes the creative action of the holy man or sage, of the ruler or leader of men, who through his power awakens and develops their higher nature.*[1]

But if a solid line is assigned the value 1, and a broken line the value 0, the three hexagrams shown in the illustration can also be represented, top to bottom, in binary arithmetic as 111111, 111001, and 000100 (63, 57, and 4 in decimal). With six lines and two possible states for each line, that makes the 2^6, or 64, hexagrams that form the *I Ching*. Gottfried Wilhelm Leibniz, the seventeenth-century German philosopher and mathematician, the father of calculus, translated the *I Ching* system of divination into a system of binary arithmetic, the basis of today's digital technology.

It's an equally interesting observation that the current IBM logo, designed by Paul Rand in 1972, bears such a striking similarity to three *I Ching* hexagrams, although with eight lines instead of six, each letter would technically be an octagram.

While this metaphysical backstory is fascinating, it is actually more useful to trace the history of modern-day computing technology back just to 1888, when a German-born engineer named Herman Hollerith won a competitive bid hosted by the US Census Bureau to create a mechanized way to tabulate census results.[2]

The Census Bureau greatly needed an automated system because it took nearly eight years to complete the 1880 census by hand, leaving little time to prepare for the 1890 census, which, with the nation's population growth, some feared would not be completed until after the 1900 census had begun. But by 1890, Hollerith's system was in place. It relied on punch cards to categorize and collect census results, and on punch card readers to tabulate the results from those cards.

Constructed out of heavy paper stock, punch cards have a fixed number of rows and columns where rectangular or circular bits of paper can be punched out, leaving a hole. Punch card machines for sorting, tabulating, and printing "read" these cards by mechanically passing them between brushes and a metal surface. If a brush completes a circuit with the metal, it has passed over a punched-out row and column hole. If a brush does not complete a circuit, then it has passed over a row and column for which no hole has been punched out. Yes or no. On or off. Punched out or not punched out. One or zero. Punch cards and the equipment that reads them operate on the binary logic of 1s and 0s, the same binary logic of computers.

Early in the life of punch card technology, many sizes and formats existed. Hollerith, a shrewd inventor, engineered his machines so they were compatible only with the cards made by his company, the Tabulating Machine Company, which later became part of IBM. For the 1890 census, Hollerith's punch cards had twenty-two columns with eight punch positions in each column. By 1928, IBM had settled on an eighty-column, twelve-row card that remained in use well into the twenty-first century.

As a storage device, an eighty-column, twelve-row punch card is capable of storing 80 times 12 binary digits of information, or 960 bits (*bit* is shorthand for *binary digit*). Modern-day computer storage is measured in bytes, and there are usually 8 bits to a byte. So, an eighty-column, twelve-row punch card can store 120 bytes of information. Put into perspective, it would take roughly 80 million punch cards to store as much information as a typical 8-gigabyte smartphone stores today. That's a stack of cards eight miles high. Set end to end, the cards would span the distance between Los Angeles, California, and Cape Town, South Africa.

Punch card equipment (sorters, tabulators, printers, etc.) can process twenty-five thousand cards per hour, which equates to roughly six cards per second, or 6 kilobits per second. A solid-state drive (SSD) on a modern laptop computer can process data at rates of up to 6 gigabits per second, which is about 1 million times faster.

Punch card equipment, also known as unit record equipment (URE), was in use throughout the later part of the nineteenth century and much of the twentieth century, prior to the advent of electronic computers. The IBM 407 is a prime example of a transitional machine with aspects of both the older electromechanical digital technology and the newer electronic digital technology. My father needed to learn both technologies, and when I went to work for IBM, so did I.

Astute businessmen do not necessarily arise from brilliant engineers, and Herman Hollerith embodied that notion. Obstreperous, pugnacious, and litigious, Hollerith lost his Tabulating Machine Company's main client, the US Census Bureau, in 1905, owing to his intransigence. Infuriated and paranoid now that he'd been displaced by a competitor, Hollerith sued for the right to automate the 1910 census. Ultimately, he took the US government to court in an attempt to stop the census from taking place unless his machines did the counting. Needless to say, he lost.

In 1911, Charles Flint, an arms merchant who'd amassed a fortune selling weapons to all sides of brutish nineteenth-century wars, saw an opportunity to buy not only Hollerith's faltering company but three other seemingly unrelated concerns: International Time Recording Company, which manufactured time clocks for recording workers' hours; Computing Scale Company, which produced retail weighing scales; and Bundy Manufacturing, which produced key-actuated time clocks and also owned prime real estate in Endicott, New York. Flint rolled these diverse businesses into the Computing-Tabulating-Recording Company, otherwise known as CTR. Though Hollerith's Tabulating Machine Company was the largest of the four, Flint refused to allow Hollerith to run the firm. Instead, he turned to one of America's rising corporate rogues, and a once-indicted felon, Thomas J. Watson. With a reputation for ruthlessly crushing rivals and stealing their business, Watson became CEO of CTR in 1924, and he changed the company's name to IBM, short for International Business Machines.

As Watson swelled to power in these early years of the twentieth century, a Black Tide swelled north. Fleeing the racism and brutality of the Jim Crow South, millions of Black Americans joined this Great Migration, seeking relative freedom and greater opportunity in cities like New York. A "new civilization of sidewalks, churches, and the most beautiful country ever"[3]—that's how the Williamsbridge neighborhood of the Bronx was advertised at the turn of the twentieth century, attracting many southern migrants, like my grandfather John Baptist Ford, to the farms and the pastoral setting this area afforded well into the mid-twentieth century. My grandfather purchased a home at 760 East 221st Street, where my father grew up and where I spent the first ten years of my life.

Trinity Baptist Church, on East 224th Street, served the growing number of upwardly striving Black families in Williamsbridge. Our family belonged to the church, as had my father's family. In part, my father insisted that his children go to Trinity Baptist Church because his father had insisted on his own Christian upbringing. Working as a porter, my grandfather slept on his train car and had but four hours a day to spend with his family—and most of those hours, his three children were at school. Still, on Sundays, my grandfather visited church twice. "I go to church from eleven to twelve Sunday morning and take my children to Sunday school from one to two in the afternoon," he told *Collier's Weekly* in 1924. "If I knew there wasn't any heaven or hell, I'd still say that the Christian religion was the best thing for us all to follow."[4] My grandfather's funeral was held at Trinity Baptist Church.

As a child, I found Trinity Baptist Church, with its open baptismal pit sitting just behind the altar, terrifying. The preacher laid a board across the pit, upon which he stood to deliver fiery sermons. And when the preacher wasn't preaching, the Women's Auxiliary took over to raise money for new construction, scholarships, and the Bible camp and to serve as a liaison between the church and the Williamsbridge community. The auxiliary was an outgrowth of the Community Circle, begun by women in the early days of the church.

I'd just turned five when my reputation as a lost member of Trinity's flock took flight. My Sunday school teacher rapped twice on her desk and asked the class what the knocking meant. She was, of course, fishing for Luke 11:9 or perhaps Matthew 7:7: "Knock and it shall be opened unto you."

But instead, I shot my hand into the air and blurted out, "Knock, knock for Knickerbocker Beer!" Knickerbocker Beer, a popular brand in New York City at the time, featured television commercials with a hand knocking on wood.

Word of my transgression spread quickly. Unsure whether to spank me or to burst out laughing, my father fretted over my faith. He vowed to read the Bible with me more often, to correct my waywardness. For a time, our family gathered in our upstairs living room to kneel in front of our couch. With eyes closed, we recited together the Psalm of David, "The Lord Is My Shepherd."

Throughout his life, my father professed being a devout Christian, though I could never reconcile his love and understanding of science and technology with his love and understanding of an anthropomorphic God. I often thought that maybe his religious devotion was a way he sought to hedge his bets.

Williamsbridge, and community bulwarks like Trinity Baptist Church, never failed to show pride in their prominent Black sons and daughters. When I was a child, my father constantly introduced men and women to me by saying, "He's the first to work for a prestigious law firm" or "She's the first to graduate from this college" or "He's the first to be promoted to captain in the New York City Fire Department." Thomas J. Watson's job offer catapulted my father into these lofty ranks, where failure was simply out of the question.

———

Finally in possession of instructions that matched his punch cards, my father was not in possession of time. With his project due soon, my father turned to Trinity Baptist Church for help. I don't believe it was for spiritual guidance when what he really needed was his 407 control boards programmed and ready to work. I believe he may have asked for assistance from the Women's Auxiliary. If he did, it would have been a masterful stroke of genius, or the trenchant insights of a chess master bent on winning with whatever pieces remained. Over many years, I witnessed him as both that genius and that chess master.

Imagine twenty older Black women gathered in the basement of a small but proud neighborhood Baptist church, the pastor among them. Beneath the gaze of a painted crucifixion, my father had placed one model 407 control board on each of two long fold-up tables that normally held fried chicken and potato salad. He'd stripped each board clean, and arranged several baskets of patch cords nearby. Diagrams of the control boards with his penciled-in connections also rested on the tables. He raised his arms to ask for quiet.

Then he let the women know that in a short period of time he must teach them how to program an IBM 407 from the control boards and patch cords sitting in front of them, and from the diagrams of those boards and the instructions he'd written out. He began to describe how to read an instruction and make a connection between two sockets, when an older woman named Gladys raised her hand but did not wait, and interrupted my father with a high-pitched, staccato burst of her voice.

To my father's surprise, she described perfectly how to find one socket, take one end of a patch cord and plug it in there, then find another socket and plug the other end there. She then volunteered that she had been a switchboard operator during the war, who used patch cords and control boards for years. When my father asked if anyone else had worked as a switchboard operator, several women raised their hands. They all received instant promotions to supervisors of the other women's work, and Gladys got promoted to be the supervisor of the supervisors.

Eight women worked to a control board. Four primary programmers, four looking over their shoulders. Supervisors walked around checking and rechecking everyone's work. Those not at the boards helped by serving food and drinks to those who were.

As the Trinity Baptist Women's Auxiliary sprang into action, hummed spirituals floated through the air. Women reading diagrams called out control board socket names and patch cord colors. Others pushed and pulled patch cords into sockets. Supervisors hovered over tables, examining the diagrams, then running their fingers the length of every patch cord. The pastor passed out lemonade and crackers.

Some women cried out that programming these machines was just like playing Bingo with two cards, only instead of Bs and Is and Ns and Gs and Os across the top and numbers under each column the row and column combinations now had highfalutin names. Others exclaimed it reminded them of pattern-knitting or basket weaving.

Gladys hushed them, with a reminder that one of Trinity's own needed their help, and there was no room for error. Meanwhile, my father worked on a third control board as the women bantered and the soft humming of spirituals continued. He watched the clock count-off time but he also watched his work getting done. When the last woman stood up from the table, Gladys examined her work and nodded.

———

IBM final examinations sometimes drew in not only students and instructors but also managers and their managers and even clerical staff, especially if a person of special interest was slated to present. As an IBM systems engineering student, I somehow had a talent for technical sales presentations, and more than once my final examinations boasted standing room only for many in the education department, most with little connection to me, who wanted to see the twenty-year-old Black kid with the huge Afro convincingly pitch a million-dollar-a-month computer system to a hypothetical customer. Thankfully, I never faced anything close to the pressure my father did as Watson's hand-chosen hire and the first Black systems engineer to complete a 407 class.

I don't know if Peter Hauptmann ran his classes the way my IBM instructors ran theirs. But if he did, he would have had the other teams present their final examinations before my father presented his. My presentations were often the highlight of the final day of class, and my instructors took pleasure in saving what they perceived as the best for last. Hauptmann may not have known what to expect from my father, and this too may have been a reason for letting him wait until the end.

Did race play a factor in these IBM final exams? I always felt it did. People packed my presentations, in part, because they had never seen a young Black kid sell the benefits of IBM's latest technology. I feel it also did for my father, simply because no one had ever seen a Black systems engineer take an IBM final exam.

Pitching the benefits of technology is much easier than presenting a program that performs correctly. There's leeway with a pitch created from a script then delivered to captivate, capture, and convince. Not so with presenting programs, which either work or don't. When you attempt to control the actions of a computer with the written instructions of a human, unforeseen consequences are frequently the result. I know. I've pitched technology and presented programs in front of IBM classes.

It's an excruciating experience to watch others present their programs before you, while inside you're questioning: Did I place my instructions in the correct card columns? Was my logic faulty? Did I remember to account for this contingency? Are my punch cards in the right order? Will the machine perform as expected? One small mistake, a missing punctuation mark or a misspelled instruction, and nothing else matters. Your program simply will not work. Before computers checked for such errors, it was left to programmers and systems engineers to produce flawless punch card code. That level of perfection is very stressful. I've felt it, as I'm sure my father did in making his final presentation.

To these questions and doubts swirling around any systems engineer, my father, when his turn came, had the added burden of standing in front of a group of men, many of whom would have gladly watched him fail, some of whom may have already had a hand in engineering his failure by providing him with instructions mismatched for his punch card deck. Furthermore, Watson's signature is on my father's report card from his 407 class, and he could have well been sitting in the classroom for my father's final presentation, watching the performance of the Black systems engineer he'd hired.

Simply making it through his final examination without a program glitch would have probably sufficed. But my father believed a Black man needed to prove his worth by being twice as good as others. When the correct result is only a set of numbers printed in the proper columns, one team's output tends to look remarkably similar to another's. How do you distinguish yourself? How did my father end up completing his 407 class not with acceptable results but with honors? Thinking like a systems engineer, like the man I knew as an exceptional programmer, I have an answer based on my father's love of pushing the limits of these early computers.

Long before today's sophisticated graphics, my father would bring home stacks of eleven-by-fourteen-inch computer paper showing graphics created using the printer's available character set. For my birthday, I'd get a set of folded pages that, unfolded, read HAPPY BIRTHDAY in large block letters, each letter created from the letter it represents—so the H would be created from Hs and the B created from Bs. Next to that saying there'd be an image of a birthday cake made of Xs and Os and other characters, complete with the right number of candles, and finally, next to the cake, I'd find my name also printed in large block letters.

For Christmas, my father would unfurl a stack of pages with an image of Santa Claus driving a sled pulled by reindeer, Christmas trees, and the words MERRY CHRISTMAS. In those days, there were no colored printers, so the images were only in black and white. Today, graphics like these are called "ASCII art" (from the American Standard Code for Information Interchange) and can often be found beneath the signature lines of emails, with plenty more examples online.[5]

When I came along with computers, as a student in high school and college, we created these graphics for fun and to boast of our prowess programming punch card machines and line printers. My father, and the systems engineers of his day, also created them simply because they could, but in the early days of computers, full-page character graphics served another purpose. They enabled programmers to distinguish the output of their program from the output of another when all outputs were stacked up in a pile of pages on the printer. This use of character graphics would not have been lost on my father as he attempted to distinguish himself from the other systems engineers in his class. I can envision the first page of his printed output with his name, JOHN STANLEY FORD, printed in large block letters, each letter created by the letter it represents, and beneath that his title, SYSTEMS ENGINEER, IBM. Surely, the Old Man would have been pleased. And if Tommy Barnes had popped his head into that room, or had a seat at the back of the class, he would have been pleased as well.

———

I have only the vaguest recollection of meeting Thomas J. Watson as a child, possibly at an IBM Christmas party in New York City, not long before his death. His name, however, I heard often: Mr. Watson, T. J. Watson, Watson Senior, or simply, the Old Man. By whatever name my father referred to Watson, throughout his life he uttered it with a reverence typically reserved for royalty. Watson loomed as large for my father as he did for other IBM employees. In fact, a cultlike atmosphere surrounded Watson, who did everything to encourage it.

Of the one hundred songs listed in the company's official songbook, *Songs of the IBM*,[6] many, like "Ever Onward," were simply odes to Watson, sung with revival-style fervor by employees at company gatherings:

> *There's a thrill in store for all,*
> *For what we're about to toast.*
> *The corporation known in every land . . .*
> *Of that "man of men" our friend and guiding hand.*
> *The name of T. J. Watson means a courage none can stem. . . .*[7]

"Hail, to the IBM," the IBM anthem written by the firm's inhouse lyricist, Fred W. Tappe, with music by operatic composer Vittorio Giannini, similarly told of Watson's glory:

Our voices swell in admiration,
Of T. J. Watson proudly sing,
He'll ever be our inspiration,
To him our voices loudly ring . . .
Hail to his honored name.[8]

By accepting a job at IBM, you became part of a family, not a company. Even in my day as an IBM employee, I heard this message often. John Baptist Ford, my father's father, died just as my father entered IBM. If my father, consciously or unconsciously, sought a surrogate to fill that void, in Watson he'd surely found one. Watson presented himself as the paterfamilias of IBM. He bestowed generous compensation packages, bonuses, vacations, health care, and country club memberships to IBM employees. Few employees questioned Watson's largesse; even fewer dared whisper that it might be a shrewd tactic to keep a unionized workforce at bay.

Anticipation laced the air on those mornings when my father left home knowing he'd receive his employee review that day. Excitement sparked between my mother, my sister, and me as we anxiously waited to learn of the pay raise hidden, it seemed, in each review. As long as my father remained loyal to IBM, IBM remained loyal to him. Watson insisted on such loyalty.

My father idolized Watson. He felt a special bond with the man, one that transcended even the bond between father and son. At the start of my father's career as the first Black systems engineer at IBM, hired directly by the Old Man, my father placed Watson on a pedestal, viewing him as a kind of boon-bestowing demigod who'd reached down from the heavens to give my father a gift he could never adequately repay.

Voices of the Dead

I first heard the voices of the dead along the West African coast. In Ghana, during the summer of 1968, the Atlantic lashed the rocks beneath the Elmina Castle, an ominous monolith of weather-beaten white stone. Built by the Portuguese in 1482, Elmina (officially, São Jorge da Mina Castle, the Castle of St. George of the Mines) was named for the mines along this stretch of coast known then as the Gold Coast. But the Portuguese, and later the Dutch, also mined human treasure at Elmina, a place where, for four hundred years, countless thousands of people began their passage into the disconsolate and treacherous world of slavery.

A wizened, slightly stooped old man emerged from the shadows of Elmina carrying an oil lamp.

He stared at me, then intoned in a high-pitched, crackling whisper, "This way."

He motioned with his finger, and I followed him across the threshold of the fortress, beginning my descent into the darkness of the abyss.

Dark, damp, and cramped, a long, narrow passageway led down to a chamber that once held male slaves. From years of walking this corridor, the caretaker's hunched back seemed perfectly matched to the shape of the tunnel. He walked slowly. His oil lamp swung. Its rusted iron handle groaned with each step. I crouched so low I was almost on all fours.

Halfway down this cramped corridor, the old man paused abruptly in front of an iron-reinforced wooden door.

"When a slave died," he murmured, "this door was opened, and his body washed out to sea."

The rhythmic pounding of waves enveloped us as we plunged deeper into the castle's inner vault, some fifty feet beneath the sea. There the old man dimmed his lamp, and when my eyes finally adjusted to the darkness, I could barely make out a window the size of my fist atop a small shaft leading up from the cave we stood in. Through that small opening came the only air and light allowed into this hopeless pit.

As I moved around to take the measure of this awful place, something crunched under my feet, like the sound of stepping on fallen leaves, only heavier and metallic. Unable to see, I reached down and groped in the dark until my fingers found their way over one, two, three links of a chain. I had walked atop the rusted remains of slave chains. The more I moved about this Neptunian dungeon, the more I felt the rusting chains everywhere underfoot.

The caretaker remained silent. Surely, he had seen this before: the sons of slaves walking on the chains of their fathers.

Finally, in a slow, measured cadence, he said, "You know, your ancestors could have been in this very room."

But I was well beyond the caretaker's words. My body had grown heavy. My feet felt shackled in place. That's when I began hearing the voices. Certain at first that it was just the roar of the sea, I listened closely and made out what sounded like the low murmur of distant conversation. The rumbling traveled closer and closer—one, then two, then three, then layer upon layer of voices; a cacophony of humans not moaning or sighing but talking in hushed tones among themselves. I strained harder to hear. Suddenly a message shot forth from the darkness! It ricocheted off the dank earthen walls, bounced back and forth over and over again in time with the rhythm of the sea.

The ghostly voices spoke in unison. "Whatever you do, my son," the voices said, "make your life count for us. . . . Whatever you do, my son, make your life count for us. . . . Whatever you do, my son, make your life count for us. . . ." Their echo slowly trailed away.

Sweat beaded my brow. Tears flooded my eyes. My heart raced. My mind failed to make logical sense of what had just happened. It felt as though I had been riveted in place for hours, when in reality only a few moments had passed.

Unsure to whom I spoke, I said to the darkness, "Yes, I know." Then I turned slowly to face the caretaker and said more deliberately, "Yes, I know."[1]

Elmina represented a moment of personal reckoning—with evil, with brutality, with the worst of human beings, but most of all with what it meant for me to be Black. One route toward this reckoning is resignation that being Black in America will always mean facing brutality and oppression, whether in chains from a slaver or cuffs from a police officer predisposed to violence against people of color. While I can never ignore or forget the brutality perpetrated in this country against people who look like me, I am not ready to define myself solely in terms of this brutality and oppression. Doing so, I believe, leads down the road of victimization.

Another available route is denial. Slavery, Jim Crow, oppression— all that happened long ago and has no bearing on being Black in

America now. At any rate, you are who you are, leave the past behind, and get on with the present and the future. My father's view of race was a variation on this theme. He was born with darker skin, and therefore, he believed, he was less capable, less intelligent, and less desirable. Though his dark skin was not his fault, it was his burden, and he simply had to make the best of it. This belief set my father and me at odds. What those who espouse such beliefs fail to recognize is that past trauma is not simply left behind. Whether trauma is passed along to subsequent generations through the child-rearing practices of those who directly experienced it, or whether trauma actually causes changes in DNA, as some studies suggest, trauma is transgenerational and cannot simply be ignored.[2]

I have long believed in a third path, a way neither laden with victimization nor lightened through denial—a way that fully embraces both our historical and our present-day struggle against racism, brutality, oppression, and violence. Instead of impediments, this way views these challenges as obstacles and trials along the long course of a heroic journey.[3] I found it personally liberating to view our collective history and present-day circumstances in such mythic terms. The weight of generations lifted from my shoulders. I could release much of the anger and despair that accompanied victimization, and the disbelief and dissociation that accompanied denial.

Viewing our collective experience in this way was also in keeping with how traditional African societies healed from the trauma of brothers and sisters, sons and daughters, mothers and fathers, ripped from their midst and sold into slavery. My father read my thoughts on these matters, even though what I wrote conflicted with his own warped and wounded self-view. However, I do recall one time when he stepped into my life as my hero.

———

"I work for IBM!"

My guidance counselor flinched and then sat upright in his chair.

"I'll be damned if my son goes to high school to become an airplane mechanic!"

My junior high school guidance counselor tamped down the air. "I understand, Mr. Ford," he said. "I understand."

The counselor motioned for me to step outside his office. Hushed tones of their heated conversation seeped from beneath the door. I could not make out what they said, but my father emerged from the counselor's office fifteen minutes later, smiling.

"Checkmate!" he pronounced. "It's all taken care of."

I swelled with pride. My father took a half day off from IBM to confront my guidance counselor. He stood up for me visibly, vigorously, and vociferously. I had not seen him do this before, and I do not remember seeing him do this again. But from that point on, no one dared mention Aviation High School as a future educational option for me.

At this time, in the mid-1960s, New York City boasted of three elite academic high schools: Bronx High School of Science, Brooklyn Technical High School, and Stuyvesant High School on the Lower East Side of Manhattan. We lived in the Bronx, so naturally my father wanted me to attend Bronx High School of Science. But I'd have none of that and insisted on Stuyvesant instead. All three schools required passing a common entrance exam for admittance, an exam that I took not long after my father met with my guidance counselor . . . and failed!

Still, by 1966, affirmative action had taken hold, and twenty-five Black and Latino boys, for whom Stuyvesant was deemed beyond their academic grasp, were given a second chance: attend ten weeks of summer school in mathematics and English, and then try to keep up with the school's rigorous classes. Twenty of us made it through that grueling summer course, and all twenty of us graduated from Stuyvesant in the top rungs of our class.

I entered Stuyvesant at fourteen, younger than many other students. After finishing my geometry homework one Sunday, I doodled with a straightedge and compass while watching a championship football game on television. Much to my surprise, it appeared that my doodles solved an age-old mathematical problem originally stated by the ancient Greeks: the trisection of an arbitrary angle (i.e., make three equal angles from any given angle) using only an unmarked straightedge and a compass.

I cleaned up my doodles and showed the solution to my geometry teacher that Monday. This man enjoyed metaphorically cracking the whip. He'd taught geometry to us students of color that summer, with an understanding, he said unabashedly, that some of us would not succeed. But he took one look at my trisection and whisked me off to see the chairman of Stuyvesant's Mathematics Department. The two men conferred in hushed tones behind closed doors before approaching me in the waiting room.

"You do realize this is Nobel-level work?" the chairman said.

Since it was mathematics, he'd probably confused the Fields Medal with the Nobel Prize, but still his voice conveyed excitement with not a scintilla of sarcasm. Stuyvesant, after all, proudly counted more than its share of Nobel laureates among former students.

"For the sake of the school, and for you," my geometry teacher said, "we think you should sit out classes for the next few days until we can determine exactly what to do."

And so Stuyvesant debated what to do with a fourteen-year-old Black kid whom many (my mathematics teacher initially among them) felt should not have been at the school in the first place, a Black kid who'd apparently just solved one of the three great unsolved mathematical problems of antiquity.

Meanwhile, in a fitting nod to antiquity, the son of an Egyptian diplomat went to work on my solution. Stuyvesant, an all-male school at the time, counted among its student body many sons of ambassadors and diplomats. This kid was one of them, and he was smart . . . really smart. Constructing an airtight geometric proof, he showed that my solution was at best an approximation, not an exact solution, but for certain angles, it was an excellent approximation.

That proved enough for Stuyvesant's Mathematics Department. Though disappointed at missing out on an international award, the head of the department concluded that any student who concocted a good approximation for a centuries-old problem belonged in Stuyvesant's top mathematics classes. They proceeded to drop me into advanced placement calculus and matrix algebra, where I found myself alongside fourteen- and fifteen-year-olds who also took mathematics classes at Columbia University because they were smarter than any of the teachers at Stuyvesant.

I felt as though someone had pushed me off the deep end of a pool before ascertaining that I could swim, and then, only once I was flailing around in the water, yelled, "Swim!" I struggled for several weeks, particularly in calculus, until discovering that New York University ran a television series called *Sunrise Semester* that taught college-level classes on-air. *Sunrise Semester*'s freshman calculus program aired at six a.m., and the curriculum matched Stuyvesant's closely, except that it was one week ahead. So each morning, I'd get up to watch college calculus on television prior to sitting in a calculus class at high school. This one-week head start provided me enough runway until I learned to "swim" on my own and gave up *Sunrise Semester* altogether.

One lesson I take from my experience at Stuyvesant is that skin color and test scores have little to do with intellect or academic performance. I also think of the many young Black kids who, in the face of America's retrenchment from affirmative action, will never be afforded the opportunities afforded me—and how a real Nobel laureate with dark skin might thereby be lost forever.

There is, of course, another equally serious side to this tale, one that cuts to the quick of the deep and abiding connection between technology and race. From my junior high school guidance counselor's office to my high school Mathematics Department office, my experience was a microcosm of the four-hundred-plus-year experience of African Americans in the face of technology, from their first contact with Europeans to the present day.

My junior high school guidance counselor could not see me. I'd completed seventh and eighth grades in a single year and had received high grades in the most advanced mathematics courses taught at the school. Still, my guidance counselor saw only a Black kid he thought ought not to be directed toward academia, but instead toward an industrial trade. Save for the intervention of my father, I would have been one of a long line of Blacks whose intellectual worth was evaluated based on the color of their skin, and found lacking.

From the earliest contacts between Europeans and Africans, starting in the fifteenth century to the present day, a remarkably consistent theme in racial relations has been that people with darker skin are perceived as less intelligent. Some have simply stated this as a matter of fact. Others have purported to prove this using a variety of pseudoscientific methods, while still others have taken to the methods of modern science to bolster this claim.

Armed with papal bulls sanctifying the slaughter and enslavement of Africans,[4] fifteenth-century Portuguese sailors, rounding Cape Verde, the westernmost tip of Africa, arrived along the West African coast and encountered people with dark skin whom many considered to be descendants of Ham, the cursed biblical son of Noah. Referring to these people as "primitives" and "savages," early tales from these voyagers told of bizarre African physical, social, and cultural traits, as seen through European eyes. Judeo-Christian-Islamic traditions already had a well-developed symbology of black and white: black was held to be evil and demonic; and white, virtuous and pure. What to make, then, of people with black skin? Surely they too were from evil, demonic stock. And in the centuries that followed these first voyagers to Africa, Europeans set out to prove just that.

As Europeans encountered other peoples around the world—Africans and people from the Near and Far East—an ordering of traits, especially intelligence, unfolded: white-yellow-brown-black, with white, of course, the most intelligent and black the least. Samuel Thomas von Sömmerring, a German physician in the late eighteenth century, dissected the cadavers of African Americans returning with the British to Europe at the conclusion of the Revolutionary War: loyalist Blacks, many of whom had been slaves in the American colonies but then fought with the British in exchange for their freedom. Von Sömmerring, employing pseudoscientific volumetric measurements of the cranial capacity of European and African skulls, claimed to show that Black Americans, with less cranial volume than Europeans and by virtue of their African ancestry, lacked the intellect of Europeans, Asians, or East Indians. Black Americans, von Sömmerring concluded, should simply resign themselves to their fate and live within a social environment of permanent inferiority.[5]

Von Sömmerring was, of course, one of many before him, and many after, who claimed that skin color determined intelligence. Since von Sömmerring's time, every decade or so some new theory emerges claiming to prove the connection between the two. The rise of eugenics in the 1920s and 1930s is an iteration of this assertion. An op-ed in the *New York Times* in 2018 resurfaced the topic again, this time purportedly based on the latest DNA findings.[6]

No matter that each resurfacing of the claim linking race and intelligence is debunked or disproven, this seems a never-ending debate with one clear effect: a majority of White Americans believe that Black Americans are lazier and less intelligent than Whites, and they believe that Blacks do little to change their dismal economic circumstances.[7] Sadly, recent polls show that the percentage of the American population holding such beliefs is growing, rather than shrinking, over time.[8]

The beliefs espoused by von Sömmerring and others like him, by eugenics and similar movements, though repulsive to many, still have currency to this day. Acting on such beliefs, people in positions of power, like my guidance counselor, even if they are well-intentioned, exact devastating consequences for young Black students who lack advocates to fight for them.

———

I do not know what tense words passed between my guidance counselor and my father that day. But I do not recall my guidance counselor ever once calling me into his office for guidance after my father's visit. I am fairly certain that one crucial aspect of race remained unstated and undiscussed between these two men, even as it loomed large over their exchange. And that is the linkage between technology and race, and the role technology continues to play in shaping the experience of race in America. Technology and my future concerned both my guidance counselor and my father. Aviation is, after all, an advanced technological field. But my guidance counselor pushed for me to become an aviation mechanic, while my father understood that the future of nearly all fields—including aviation—lay in computers and digital technology and that Black people had every right to lay claim to that future.

Anthony Walton, writing in the January 1999 issue of the *Atlantic Monthly*, lays out the case succinctly:

> *The history of African-Americans during the past 400 years is traditionally narrated as an ongoing struggle against oppression and indifference on the part of the American mainstream, a struggle charted as an upward arc progressing toward ever more justice and opportunity. This description is accurate, but there is another, equally true way of narrating that history, and its implications are as frightening for the country as a whole as they are for blacks as a group. The history of African-Americans since the discovery of the New World is the story of their encounter with technology, an encounter that has proved perhaps irremediably devastating to their hopes, dreams, and possibilities.*[9]

A natural tendency to recoil at Walton's assessment is to be expected. Technology, the common wisdom proposes, is value-neutral. What built-in evil lurks in the meshing of gears, the spinning of wheels, or the glow of a cell phone or computer screen? What inherently nefarious purpose is found in bits of silicon used for an electronic circuit, or in the electrons shuttling between those bits of silicon? How can technology ever be viewed as thwarting the aspirations of any one group, such as Blacks in America? Technology may be used in loathsome ways by certain individuals or groups, but technology itself is neither inherently good nor inherently bad. Here, the common wisdom is wrong, or at least tragically confused.

Technology may be neither inherently good nor inherently evil, but it is not inherently value-free. Technology is exploitation of natural resources, both nonliving and living, for the benefit of a segment of humanity defined by the technology makers. Those meshing gears were once metal ore extracted from the earth; the rubber on spinning wheels once ran through the veins of trees; the fuel that turns the engines that spin those wheels once lay buried deep underground or under the sea; the glow from cell phone or computer screens comes from liquid crystals fabricated from natural resources or by technology that is itself fabricated from natural resources; those bits of silicon that power so much of modern high technology originate from composite minerals found in 90 percent of the earth's crust before extraction; and our cell phones, computers, and other technology are manufactured by human beings, often working in harsh conditions in countries far removed from the technology's consumers. Technology exploits human and natural resources for the benefit of some, but not all, segments of humanity.

Along the shores of the Tagus River in Lisbon, Portugal, there stands a magnificent 170-foot steel and cement monument known as the *Padrão dos Descobrimentos* (Monument of the Discoveries). It was erected in 1960 to commemorate the death, five hundred years earlier, of Prince Henry the Navigator. Designed as the prow of a huge caravel, the principal ship construction of that age, the *padrão* features Henry standing at the bow pulpit. Behind him, along what would be the decks of this monumental ship, are thirty-three figures on the east and west sides, commemorating other significant explorers of the age. Ferdinand Magellan, the first European to circumnavigate the globe, is there. Vasco da Gama, the first to round Cape Horn and navigate a sea route to India, is there. So too is Gomes Eannes de Zurara, who chronicled the rape, pillage, and plunder of the West African coast by these early European explorers.[10]

In his hands, Henry holds a replica of a caravel or carrack, a ship whose sailing technology allowed the Portuguese to round the westernmost tip of Africa and return safely. Older, shallower ships known as cogs plied the Mediterranean for centuries before caravels, but cogs were ill-equipped for the Atlantic. Trade winds made the voyage south from Portugal to West Africa relatively easy, but the return voyage was much more dangerous because cogs had to tack far out to sea—almost as far as the coast of South America—in order to catch prevailing winds affording them a way back to Europe.

Caravels were designed from cogs but built deeper and had three or four masts and an enlarged cargo space. Caravels handled rough seas better, sailed closer to the wind, and made for shorter and safer return voyages from West Africa. Magellan, da Gama, Columbus—all of the early navigators sailed caravels.

While the term *Age of Discovery* connotes high-mindedness, these early explorers sailed under no such beneficent prime directive. *Dum Diversas* (Until Different), the papal bull issued by Pope Nicholas V to King Alfonso V of Portugal in 1452, perhaps best represents the sweeping "prime directive" of that age:

> *We weighing all and singular the premises with due medita-*
> *tion, and noting that since we had formerly by other letters*
> *of ours granted among other things free and ample faculty to*
> *the aforesaid King Alfonso*—to invade, search out, capture,
> vanquish, and subdue all Saracens and pagans whatsoever,
> and other enemies of Christ *wheresoever placed, and the*
> *kingdoms, dukedoms, principalities, dominions, possessions,*
> *and all movable and immovable goods whatsoever held and*
> *possessed by them and* to reduce their persons to perpetual
> slavery, *and* to apply and appropriate to himself and his
> successors the kingdoms, dukedoms, counties, principalities,
> dominions, possessions, and goods, and to convert them to
> his and their use and profit—*by having secured the said fac-*
> *ulty, the said King Alfonso, or, by his authority, the aforesaid*
> *infante, justly and lawfully has acquired and possessed, and*

doth possess, these islands, lands, harbors, and seas, and they
do of right belong and pertain to the said King Alfonso and his
successors.[11]

Caravel technology, which enabled the Portuguese to reach West Africa, was designed to extract the human and natural resources of the continent. Little wonder, then, that caravels, with their large holds, carried gold and other precious metals but also enslaved Africans, first to work in Portuguese colonies and then for sale in far-flung ports, notably in the Americas. Caravels ruled the slave trade until replaced in the seventeenth and eighteenth centuries by galleons, which were even better equipped for their mission as slavers.

From cog to caravel to galleon, Western technology progressed in almost direct proportion to its devastation of progress in racial relations. Western technology in Africa stood at the forefront of slavery in other ways as well. Reporting on his travels in 1591 to Angola, Portuguese writer Duarte Lopez noted that "one cavalry soldier is equal to a hundred negroes, who are greatly afraid of horsemen, and, above all, of those who fire the guns and pieces of artillery."[12] A page later, Lopez observes with surprise that Angola "is peculiarly rich in mines of silver and copper, and there is a greater abundance of various metals than in any other country in the world."[13]

In a vicious cycle, African and Arab slavers traded captured human beings for the advanced Western technology of the day: textiles, metal products, and firearms. In turn, they used the superior firepower they obtained against other tribes they wished to vanquish and whose members they then captured as slaves.

In the cotton gin lies a similar story of technological progress presaging retreat in racial relations. By the late eighteenth century, the agrarian economy of the southern United States, built on slave labor, the human technology of the age, lay faltering, and the economic wisdom of slavery lay in question. For reasons of geography and the economics of production, cotton, tobacco, sugar, indigo, and rice, the principal cash crops of the South, all required increasingly more money to produce and returned increasingly less profit to southern planters. In particular, cotton plantation owners found themselves paying more and more for the upkeep of their slaves, with less and less returned from the sale of their cotton. This economic equation changed dramatically with the introduction of a new technology—the cotton gin—in 1793, to which Eli Whitney lay patent claim.

Whitney's gin could process fifty pounds of cotton lint a day, separating cotton fibers from seed. What southern planters now needed was an inexpensive way to grow and pick cotton to feed the hungry, new machines, which would produce the raw materials for northern textile mills, which then exported their textiles worldwide. For that labor, the South turned once again to the sale and purchase of slaves. Suddenly, cotton became wildly profitable, and a technology some hoped would save labor and thereby reduce the South's reliance on slavery had just the opposite effect. The 1790 census recorded approximately 700,000 slaves in the South. By the 1860 census, that number had increased to nearly 4 million human beings held in perpetual bondage.[14]

An advance in technology led to yet another retrenchment in race relations. But cotton's techno-racial roller coaster did stop there. With Emancipation and the advent of automated cotton-picking machines in the later nineteenth century, the need for a huge cotton labor force dwindled. Blacks, eager now for new opportunities and an escape from the brutality, headed for northern cities en masse. Yet again, an advance in technology resulted in a decay in race relations as these internally displaced people often traded the overt racism of the South for the subtle, yet equally devastating, racism of the North: lack of housing, lack of educational opportunities, lack of health care, lack of jobs—the very same issues that plague race relations to this day.

To Speak of Rivers

My grandfather John Baptist Ford died at home on March 2, 1947, four years before my birth. His body lay in the parlor room of the family home on 221st Street so family members and friends could pay their final respects prior to his funeral at Trinity Baptist Church on March 8. Before being called a "living room," the parlor was known as the "death room" precisely because it received the body of deceased family members. As a child, I lived upstairs with my family, and hearing stories of my grandfather's body lying downstairs terrified me. I believed his ghost haunted the first floor of our house, where my grandmother lived, and I cried whenever my parents left me downstairs in her care.

But all paths in quest of my father lead through a better understanding of my grandfather. And to understand my grandfather, I need to speak of rivers, as the poet Langston Hughes so eloquently wrote.[1]

"History is a great river," said Vincent Harding.

The late Vincent Harding—my mentor and longtime friend, Martin Luther King Jr.'s speechwriter, and an esteemed scholar of Black history—often pointed out that history, while bound by time, does not flow like time in a straight line from some long-ago source to the present and then forward into the future. Instead, like a river, history follows a serpentine course of twists and turns, bends and back channels. Tame and constrained at times, wild and free at others, it moves inexorably toward the sea.[2]

Vincent explored many of the backwaters and unnamed places along the river of Black history to tell the stories of the people who lived along those shores and how their lives and strivings contributed to that mighty river's unstoppable flow. The lives of Black men like Tommy Barnes, sage of the elevators, can be situated along the shores of those backwaters, so too the life of my grandfather John Baptist Ford. The impact of these unknown men, as Vincent never failed to point out, was as important as the lives of men whose names we know, such as Booker T. Washington or W. E. B. Du Bois, for the efforts of the lesser-known among us also altered the course of that mighty river forever.

The flow of the stories of men like my grandfather and Tommy Barnes begins upstream from the present day—indeed, very far upstream. It goes at least as far back as the fifteenth century, when Black sailors were not an uncommon sight on European quays. From there, it passes on to the caravels that carried early Europeans around Cape Verde to plunder mineral and human wealth along the West African coast. The popular version of history then tells of millions of souls—some 60 million or more—ripped from Africa's shores, transported across the Atlantic through the horrendous nightmare known as the Middle Passage, and sold into slavery to feed the unquenchable economic and social appetite of a growing American nation.

This popular version of African American history is not wrong; it is just not complete.

Even as European technology first met race—and gained the upper hand—from the eighteenth century until Emancipation, enslaved and free Blacks figured significantly in the Atlantic maritime industry. These "Black Jacks," as they were known, helped shape the future course, and speed, of the river of Black history.[3]

By the early 1800s, Black men worked at 18 percent of all American seafaring jobs,[4] a remarkable number when the 1800 census also recorded Blacks as just over 18 percent of the total American population.[5] Black Jacks endured the owners, the captains, the whips, the fears, and the general privations and hardships of being sailors, while also enduring the brutality and racism they encountered being Black and being at sea. In exchange, they enjoyed the adventure, the relative freedom, and the autonomy of a sailor's life. Aboard ships, they worked as cooks and deckhands, as first mates, and, in some cases, even as captains.

Many held tightly to their Seamen's Protection Certificate, issued by the United States beginning in 1796, which identified them as citizens under the protection of America both abroad and at home, regardless of race. An anomaly to be sure, yet this was one of the first official documents declaring free Blacks to be citizens of this country. Black Jacks returned from sea not only with these documents, but with good news and good hope. Black seamen, slaves and free, saw a world of promise beyond slavery, and they returned to Black communities throughout the United States with just such news, helping to agitate and organize for change.

"Worldly and often multilingual slave sailors regularly subverted plantation discipline," notes nautical historian W. Jeffrey Bolster.[6] A Black seafaring captain, Paul Cuffee, helped foment the largest slave rebellion in South Carolina history, led by Denmark Vesey. Frederick Douglass used his skill as an enslaved ship's caulker, and his extensive maritime knowledge, to deck out in sailor's garb and borrow a Seamen's Protection Certificate from a free Black sailor. Then on September 3, 1838, he slipped away from Baltimore to Philadelphia by train, blending in unnoticed among other free Black Jacks. From Philadelphia he traveled to New York City and, ultimately as a free man, to the shipbuilding town of New Bedford, Massachusetts.[7] Blacks also filled the ranks of pirates, led by men like Edward Teach, also known as Blackbeard, and William Lewis of the Flying Gang.[8]

When they were paid, Black sailors made good money for their travails. They provided for families on land and helped build institutions such as churches, which became the pillars of Black communities across the nation. More than one Black sailor slipped effortlessly from the pulpit of a ship to the pulpit of a church, where they could preach and teach from real-world experience, planting seeds that would one day flower into a mighty river's roar for freedom and justice.

―――

The Triangular Trade, a euphemism for the Atlantic Slave Trade, is actually misleading. This trade was not three-sided: from West Africa with humans, to the Americas to sell humans for goods, to British ports to sell those goods. In fact, is was quadrilateral: from Africa to the West Indies, to North America, and then on to Britain. Black sailors, some slave, some free, went to sea on every leg of these transatlantic routes.

Briton Hammon's seafaring autobiography, *A Narrative of the Uncommon Sufferings, and Surprizing Deliverance of Briton Hammon, a Negro Man,*[9] is astonishing on many accounts. It stands among a half dozen Black autobiographies, all published in English before 1800, all written by Black mariners, as the first salvo in two genres of uniquely African American literature: slave narratives and Black maritime sagas, a genre to which several of my books, including this present one, directly trace their literary ancestry. Hammon's work, while thin, reads like a short-form, thirteen-year, Odyssean epic.

In 1747, Hammon negotiated with his slave master, General John Winslow of the British army, to leave the relative safety and security of Massachusetts "with an Intention to go a Voyage to Sea." He signed on to a thirty-day journey from Plymouth to Jamaica to pick up a load of bloodwood and then return. But a poorly navigated ship left Hammon and his crewmates stranded on a reef off Cape Florida, where a band of Native Americans slaughtered all but him. They either sympathized with his plight or recognized his greater barter value alive. Hammon escaped on a Spanish schooner to Cuba, only to be captured by a press-gang for service aboard a ship bound for Spain. But Hammon refused and instead was sentenced to five years in a Havana dungeon. Upon Hammon's release from the dungeon, the Spanish governor of Havana claimed him as his slave. After two failed escape attempts from Cuba, Hammon managed to escape with the help of an English lieutenant aboard the *Hercules*, bound for London. Wounded in a battle with a French warship, in ill health, and destitute in London, Hammon signed aboard a slaver bound for West Africa. In 1759, just prior to the slaver's departure, a chance meeting with General Winslow on a London street enabled Hammon to abort his voyage to West Africa in favor of a return journey to Massachusetts.

Hammon's tale, while it may have been the first of only a handful published by Black sailors, hewed closely to the lives of many Blacks who went to sea in the Age of Sail. From the West Indies to the Americas to Europe and even to Africa, these mariners, slave and free, sailed to every corner of the Black Atlantic community, where they met and interacted with all manner of individuals. They transported more than just the cargo in the holds of their ships. As newsmongers, Black seamen networked the Atlantic, conveying information to widely disparate points of the African diaspora. Their efforts helped knit together conglomerates of African people into cohesive communities of color. As world travelers, Black Jacks began the arduous task of forging a new identity for the people of these communities, one based neither on the Africa they had been ripped from nor the America that despised and enslaved them, creating a unique dual identity somewhere betwixt the two.

Then Emancipation occurred.

After 1863, steam had freed ships from the vicissitudes of the wind, and the Emancipation Proclamation had freed slaves, in theory, from the sting of the master's whip. The dance of technology and race moved on yet again. And as before, with an advance in one came a decline in the other. Under steam, fewer ships were required, and those that did sail were larger, requiring fewer hands on deck. Under Jim Crow, a vicious new form of oppression arrived, and Blacks could no longer find work at sea as those dwindling positions became almost exclusively the prerogative of Whites. Besides, with the cotton gin, southern White planters desired more hands in their fields, rather than on decks. The era of the Black Jack had finally crossed the bar.

Still, the dance continued.

A new technology rose, transporting the field of adventure from the sea back to the land, atop a lattice of parallel iron strips hammered into the earth. A multitude of trains began crisscrossing the land, as a multitude of ships had once traversed the sea. By 1865, thousands of miles of track had been laid in America, much of it by slave labor.

By 1900, mechanical cotton-pickers prowled white fields, while men in white hoods prowled dark nights. But boats with white sails no longer prowled the seas. At seventeen years of age, my grandfather could neither read nor write. "This was not my fault or that of my parents," he told Robert L. Duffus, then a reporter for the *New York Times*, in 1924. "I worked for $5 a month and my board and saved money to pay my way in school . . . so that I could learn to read and write."[10]

My grandfather left South Carolina with the Great Migration north. In New York City in 1908, after a three-month apprenticeship, he set forth on his journey as a Pullman porter, sailing across the country by rail to San Francisco and St. Louis and points in between. I believe Briton Hammon and all those Black Jacks who had gone before the mast would have well understood the travels and travails my grandfather faced, though they might have chafed at the sight of white smoke billowing from the stacks of locomotives rather than white sails billowing in the wind.

Most of the memories I have of my grandfather come from pictures I've seen of him. And all the pictures I've seen show him dressed in a Pullman porter's uniform. There's an image of him with my father on his lap, my uncle and aunt as children to his right, and my grandmother sitting to his left. That picture, taken in the early 1920s, captured a moment in time when my grandfather held celebrity status for many Blacks and Whites, with reports of his activities being sent around the world by the news media.

———

What IBM was to my father, being a Pullman porter was to my grandfather. Many Whites called any Pullman porter George, a derisive name hearkening back to slavery when male slaves were simply called by the first name of their masters, now referring specifically to George Mortimer Pullman. From his headquarters in Chicago, Pullman first hired newly freed slaves en masse shortly after Emancipation to fulfill his dream of creating a luxury railroad experience for White Americans, whom he believed would feel most comfortable being attended to by subservient Blacks in uniform.[11]

Along the track, as before the mast, a porter faced many challenges. Like Black sailors, they ran a gauntlet of racial insults and indignations from White passengers and White railway crew. They worked exceptionally long hours away from their families, for exceptionally low wages. Pullman expected them to get by on tips. For many years, my grandfather worked the Winsted Express, which ran between New York City and Winsted, Connecticut. Though it placed him closer to his home, he still served the commuting needs of wealthy Whites who traveled between Connecticut and New York City, as Duffus reported:

> *Every night Ford sleeps on his car at Winsted. At 6:45 in the morning he starts for New York, where he arrives at 10:23. If he is lucky he gets home by 11:30. Four hours with his family and he leaves again, to take his car back to Winsted on the 4:25. Such is his life—a pretty useful one, according to those who have occasion to travel between New York and stations on the New Haven line.*[12]

Within the Black community, Pullman porters, like Black sailors before them, retained a vaunted position of admiration and respect. Many Pullman porters were highly educated, even if they were not highly respected by those for whom they worked and served. By some estimates, 30 percent of Black medical school graduates first served as Pullman porters.[13] In 1924, my grandfather told the *New*

York Times, "I was studying to be a minister, though I'm past that now.... I know a couple of doctors—brothers—who stayed ten years in the service [as Pullman porters] after they'd taken their degrees. They were saving money all the time. When they'd got enough they set up in practice."[14]

With Pullman porters, the informal news gathering begun by Black Jacks decades earlier became a formal relationship with Black newspapers throughout the country. As my grandfather told *Collier's Weekly* in 1924, Pullman porters served as the news reporters of their day:

> *I have carried many of the big men of this country. They are just like other people. Mr. John D. Rockefeller, senior, was just a nice old man. Mr. J. Pierpont Morgan just a quiet gentleman. Former [New York State] Governor Whitman, the same. If some one hadn't told me President Coolidge was in my car, I would never have known it.*[15]

Pullman porters had unfettered and unparalleled access to presidents, politicians, tycoons, sports stars, and celebrities, and prominent Black newspapers capitalized on the information this access provided. The *Chicago Defender*, *Pittsburgh Courier*, and *New York Age*—several of the principal Black newspapers of the early twentieth century—built a robust business around Pullman porters who provided daily information and occasionally scoops, wrote columns, and even surreptitiously delivered newspapers by tossing them off their trains at designated pickup spots in Black communities.[16]

Pullman porters symbolized the subservience that Black men needed to survive slavery and Jim Crow, and that White Americans desired, but they also represented a New Negro, to use a term popularized by Alain Locke, a writer and philosopher of the Harlem Renaissance. Having fought and died to save democracy in World War I, Black American soldiers returned to a country that had not changed much with regard to race relations. Black Americans who bled on the battlefields of France were still lynched in the cotton fields of the South. Educational, political, economic, and social opportunities were still placed beyond their reach. So, in 1919, when White American mobs attacked Black communities in more than two dozen cities across the United States, Black Americans fought back.[17]

A Pullman porter first broke the story of a White lynch mob attacking a Black community in North Platte, Nebraska, driving hundreds of Black men, women, and children from their homes. As a result of this early news, reported by the porter to a local branch of the NAACP, the organization contacted the governor, the mob's advance was stopped, and the Black community was allowed to return safely home.[18]

Famed Black poet and author Claude McKay, also a member of the Harlem Renaissance, captured the essence of this new militancy for social justice in his 1919 poem "If We Must Die," in which he exhorted Blacks to "face the murderous, cowardly pack, pressed to the wall, dying, but fighting back!"[19] McKay, a former Pullman porter, wrote his first book, *Home to Harlem*, during his breaks along the rails.[20]

Pullman porters tapped A. Philip Randolph to lead them in forming the Brotherhood of Sleeping Car Porters (BSCP), a union targeting higher wages and better working conditions for the men. Despite moles planted by the Pullman company at organizing meetings, in 1925 Randolph successfully formed the BSCP, the first predominantly Black labor union. Although the BSCP never enrolled a majority of Pullman porters as members and never received full recognition by the American Federation of Labor (AFL), it won its first labor contract with the Pullman company in 1937.

The union served for many years as a training ground for future Black leaders. Randolph spearheaded the movement to desegregate the US military and organized the first March on Washington in 1941. E. D. Nixon, while still working as a Pullman porter, masterminded the 1955 Montgomery Bus Boycott, which vaulted Rosa Parks and Martin Luther King Jr. to fame. Malcolm X, a Pullman dinner car waiter, wrote about his observations of race relationships between Pullman porters and customers on trains.[21] Gordon Parks, the first Black photojournalist for *Life* magazine, found a magazine with Dust Bowl images of poor women and children while working as a Pullman porter, which spurred him on to a legendary career in photography and filmmaking.

Count my grandfather John Baptist Ford also among the ranks of Pullman "firsts," even though he was not a union man. In February 1924, my grandfather met Robert Malcolm Keir, PhD, a professor of economics at Dartmouth College's famed Amos Tuck business school. *Collier's Weekly* reported my grandfather's account of what happened next:

> *On one of my trips into New York a gentleman got talking to me, as many do. We talked about life and death, what they meant to us, and at New York he said he would see me again. When he did see me again I was his guest, through the courtesy of the Pullman management, at Dartmouth College.... I wasn't nervous because I didn't have anything to say but what I knew, and I thought what I might say might help someone else. I was made to feel among friends, although the students did fire a lot of questions at me.*[22]

Clearly impressed by this sophisticated Black porter who lacked a formal education, Keir invited my grandfather to give three lectures to his Economics 22 class at Dartmouth on March 25, 1924.

His first lecture that day was so successful that his second pulled students and professors away from classes throughout the campus to fill a standing-room-only hall.

"DARTMOUTH TO HEAR PARLOR CAR PORTER: John Baptist Ford, Negro, Will Give Lecture Tomorrow to Transportation Class," a March 24, 1924, *New York Times* headline read. Two days later, the paper printed the story, "PULLMAN PORTER LECTURES: Ford Makes a Hit in an Address to Students at Dartmouth." The *Times* continued to report on my grandfather in its April 13 issue of that year: "PULLMAN PORTER WINS AS COLLEGE LECTURER; John Baptist Ford, Who Made Four Hundred Dartmouth Students Look at His Profession with New Eyes, Talks of Traveling Public."

My grandfather was one of the few Black men to speak at Dartmouth since Booker T. Washington. In the spring and summer of 1924, reports of his lectures appeared in the pages of more than forty newspapers around the country—the *New York Age*, the *Pittsburgh Courier*, the *Detroit Free Press*, and the *Portsmouth Herald*, to name a few.

"This Ford's a Pullman Porter" read the title of a feature article on the cotton-picker-turned-college-lecturer in the July 5 issue of *Collier's Weekly*. The article began by favorably comparing my grandfather to Henry Ford. In his many interviews, my grandfather never failed to mention his family, insisting that while he may have been invited to speak at a prestigious university, all of his children would be graduating from one.

Although my grandfather met professors, bankers, moguls, and presidents in his railway car, I cannot say for sure if he ever met Thomas J. Watson. I strongly suspect that he did. Watson had a summer home in New Canaan, Connecticut, during the years when my grandfather worked as a Pullman porter on the Winsted Express. To get to New Canaan from New York City in those days, you either drove, a long and harrowing journey that wealthy men like Watson did not make, or you rode in a well-appointed train car on the Winsted Express—a far more appealing option for men like Watson. Stamford, Connecticut, would have been the stop at which Watson disembarked, to ride to New Canaan either by car or perhaps by train.

According to a 1924 feature article in the *Sunday New York Times*, with the exception of Henry Ford, my grandfather "hauled" most of the famous millionaires of that age on his train; Watson was most likely among them.[23]

My father was not wholly unaware of the tides of history that he rode into his first meeting with Thomas J. Watson. More than once, he spoke to me in hushed tones of his previous membership in the American Communist Party (ACP) in the late 1930s. He knew A. Philip Randolph, who was also involved in the ACP. Though my father never spoke of it, I can well imagine the conflicts that arose between him and his father, who disapproved of the Brotherhood of Sleeping Car Porters, which Randolph organized and led. I can imagine the political and rhetorical battles that took place inside the family home, when my grandfather returned from his job on the rails to confront my father returning from a meeting of the ACP.

During the McCarthy hearings, afraid that any hint of a communist past might derail his career, my father gradually became vociferously anti-communist, pro-American, and one of the few Black Republicans at the time.

If Pullman porters like my grandfather helped America stretch from sea to sea, then elevator operators like Tommy Barnes helped America stretch from sea to sky. Elevators allowed buildings to grow taller, and operators allowed elevators to convey passengers safely to these higher floors. Dressed in snazzy uniforms, like Pullman porters, elevator operators were witness to the interchange between presidents, politicians, tycoons, sports stars, and celebrities. And like porters, elevator operators were meant to be invisible—serving and subservient to the White passengers they transported.

In 1917, before founding the BSCP, A. Philip Randolph formed a fledgling labor union of elevator operators. By the time my father was hired at IBM, tens of thousands of primarily Black operators worked elevators in buildings etching the New York City skyline.

Enter the rise and fall of technology and race once again.

Cars operating over interstate highways made suburbs, once accessible only by train, more convenient extensions of urban centers. Trains, once the preferred mode of transportation for the wealthy, gave way to airplanes or simply became commuter conveyances rather than luxurious palaces on rails served by elegantly uniformed porters. By the mid-1950s, the era of the Pullman porter was closing, as digital technology was similarly shutting down the era of the elevator operator. Passengers traveling upward could now control their journeys by pressing buttons, rather than relying on operators to pull levers and swing gates.

Tomorrow's technology eclipses today's, which surpassed yesterday's. And in this way technological progress is characterized by a smooth, steady, ever-upward march of science and innovation, unlike progress in race relations.

Examples abound of the difference between progress in technology and race relations. Take the automobile. With each new model year, manufacturers add new features, enhance existing ones, or in some way improve aspects of a car's performance or style. Contrast this with the history of African Americans: captured and sold into slavery (retrenchment), freed from slavery through the Emancipation Proclamation (renewal), and soon after subjected to draconian Jim Crow laws (retrenchment).

Then there are smartphones. With each new model, processor

speeds increase, screen quality is enhanced, memory capacity grows, and camera resolution is improved. But consider the ups and downs of voting rights for Blacks, once specifically written out of the US Constitution: during slavery, none; during Reconstruction (a brief period after Emancipation), an increase; with the advent of Jim Crow, a decrease; with the struggle leading up to the Voting Rights Act of 1965, an increase; with the nationwide attack on voting rights in the twenty-first century, a decrease.

As described earlier in this chapter, the interaction between technology and race can be profound. Often it begins with the introduction of a new technology, which brings with it decreased progress in racial relations but also the seeds of a renewal of progress as marginalized people adopt and become proficient with the new technology. And then, when an even newer technology arises, the cycle begins again.

Honeypot Traps

When I was ten, my father called me in from playing to sit me down at the kitchen table for the Big Talk. "Someday you'll go to the bathroom and it will come out milky white instead of yellow," he said. "Then you'll be a man."

Without another word, he released me to resume playing. I guess he was satisfied with the CliffsNotes version of puberty. It didn't matter. It was already too little, too late. By six, my parents had schooled me in the use of the library and the encyclopedia. Whenever I questioned anything, they said, "Just look it up." By nine, I had a lot of questions about sex, and instead of asking them, I looked it up. By ten, my classmates looked to me as the go-to person on sex, especially when they also got the CliffsNotes version at home. By thirteen, I received the best sex education class a teenager could ever hope for, and that education happened, at all places, in church.

After realizing that I'd probably never make a good Christian, and nor would she, my mother yanked my sister and me from Trinity Baptist Church and took us on a pilgrimage that my father saw as a certain road to hell. Each Sunday, we visited another alternative church in New York City: Unity, Religious Science, Ethical Culture. Afterward, my mother would debrief us, and generally we gave those churches a "thumbs-down." That is, until we found Community Church on 35th Street and Park Avenue. One of the largest Unitarian-Universalist churches in the city, Community Church welcomed spiritual outcasts like my mother and her children.

During the sixties, under the leadership of the Reverend Donald S. Harrington, Community Church was a hotbed of liberal thought and liberal action. Young people from the church went south to work in the burgeoning Black freedom struggle. Bar mitzvahs, bas mitzvahs, Shinto services, Buddhist services, Islamic services, Hindu services—in Sunday school, we studied one of the world's great religions each month. But in New York City, we could also attend a worship service from these different religions and find a restaurant that served foods related to any of these faiths. For the first time in my life, I looked forward to Sundays, when I learned as much as I did in school during the week.

My father, however, hated our newfound spirituality, which was so diametrically opposed to his own. Community Church helped young people develop their own definition of their religion. Our Sunday school class collectively determined that religion was not what we believed in, but how we lived our lives. And since sex was part of living, sex also became part of our religious education.

One Sunday, a group of us teens peppered our religious education teacher with questions about sex and sexuality. The next Sunday, one of the heads of condom-maker Schmid Laboratories in Little Falls, New Jersey, who was also a member of Community Church, arrived at class armed with life-size, detailed plastic replicas of the male and female reproductive systems, condoms, and other birth-control devices. His in-depth, no-holds-barred presentation was decidedly not the CliffsNotes version. We sat in awe, and afterward we discussed what we would do with our newly obtained knowledge. What better place than church to help teenagers learn about sex and sexuality, and to talk about how they would integrate them into their lives? The presentation thrilled my mother even as it confirmed my father's belief that Satan ran roughshod at Community Church.

The Sexual Revolution. Feminism. The Summer of Love. Woodstock. Sex was laid bare in the midst of the sixties, even for my father. In the top drawer of his blond-wood dresser, my father kept a gold key to the New York City Playboy Club. In the upper left-hand drawer of a small desk in our downstairs living room, which doubled as his office, under a stack of typewriter paper lay an iconic photo of that age. In the photo, my father is sitting at a table with several White IBM coworkers, and above him stands a White Playboy waitress. She is holding a tray full of drinks and cigarettes, while the tips of her breasts, shaped conically by her bunny outfit, point to the grin on my father's face. Surely that grin rose from titillation. I suspect it also rose from vindication. Yet even as he sat in the newly opened Playboy Club in New York City, a similar expression of a Black man's pleasure in the overt sexuality of a White woman would be grounds for lynching in places like Mississippi.

My father, a concert baritone, loved Billie Holiday's smooth voice. She recorded "Strange Fruit," with its powerful images of southern lynchings, in 1939, when my father had not yet turned twenty and was, by his account, a member of the American Communist Party. News of southern lynchings dominated the pages of northern Black newspapers and galvanized movements by Blacks, and by the American Communist Party, to bring them to a halt.

These lurid, horrific images and Billie's lilting, haunted melody could not have been far from my father's mind that day in the late 1940s when he hailed a yellow and black checkered cab.

My father often told me the story of how, early in his career, some of his IBM colleagues had attempted to entrap him by arranging a business meeting that instead was a rendezvous with a prostitute. They hoped that capturing him in such a compromising situation would force his ouster from the company. He told me that his suspicions mushroomed the moment his taxi deposited him at a familiar hotel, which seemed an unlikely place to meet an IBM customer.

He also told this story not with anger but with pride at how he had outsmarted his colleagues and eluded entrapment, but he refused to reveal just how. Although I've long suspected it had something to do with Lena Rogers, his deftness at avoiding this "honeypot" trap revealed a side of my father that few knew or even suspected. Underneath the veneer of a well-manner IBM employee lay a scrappy, streetwise kid from the Bronx.

My father recognized the dark side of life and was unafraid to descend into its depths. When my sister or I got in trouble with the law, my father had no compunctions about determining whether a bribe given to the right person would remedy the situation. I once got into a rock fight with a group of Italian kids who lived a few doors down from our Bronx home. I flung a rock that hit a kid named Johnny in the kneecap, and he went down screaming. Johnny vowed to get me in big trouble by telling my father. When he did, my father listened dutifully and then closed the door and turned to me.

Behind the closed door he waved Johnny off. "Ahh. Got into plenty of rock fights with his father."

When my father told the story of stepping out of that cab for a sham IBM business meeting, I never once heard anxiety or fear. Instead, his reaction reminded me of the man I knew playing chess, who'd already glimpsed many moves in advance and had a response waiting for any move his opponent could make. Still, it must have come as a surprise to realize his colleagues had conspired against him. And it must also have brought some relief to know they'd unintentionally shifted the game onto terrain he knew far better than they imagined. This is where I suspect Lena fits into the puzzle.

My father's recognition of the hotel where he was being set up suggests that he'd been there before. A prostitute? A hotel? An attempt to shift the story to something else? This tells me it may also have been the hotel where Lena lived. Under pressure, my father often acted as that proverbial "cool customer." So it doesn't take much to envision him in business attire, swinging a briefcase, while walking casually into a place where he was on a first-name basis with everyone from the doorman to the concierge to the front desk clerk, or that instead of taking an elevator to the meeting room, he took an elevator to Lena's studio.

When she flipped aside the peephole cover and then flung open her door, I can hear the shock in Lena's gravelly voice before whisking him inside. "Stan, what the . . . ?"

And when he told her about his suspicious meeting, I can also see Lena placing a reassuring hand on my father's shoulder with the words, "Stan, stay here. I'll be back in a jiffy," and then returning with the news that someone had paid one of the other girls a lot of money to lure my father into bed but leave the door open so a photographer could slip in and capture the scene.

———

"I want you," the woman whispered.

Her calls always came at night, near bedtime, in the years before cell phones and caller ID.

"I need you," she said. "You can't hang up."

I didn't. Instead, I danced with her in a drama that played out over many weeks. Three or four nights each week my telephone rang. She spoke with a deep, husky, even sexy voice.

"Hi, Clyde."

"Hi. What's your name?"

"In time, Clyde. All will be revealed in time."

"But I don't know what to call you."

"My name's not important. You're important. You're important to me. I was very hurt last night. I called and you didn't answer."

"I was out."

"Where?"

"At a restaurant."

"Which one?"

"I don't remember. Near my work. One near where I work."

"With whom?"

"Friends."

"With another woman?"

I said nothing.

"Is one of them your girlfriend?"

I did not answer.

"I would be very hurt to discover you had a girlfriend, when I know we are meant to be together."

"And you know that because . . . ?"

"Because we are soul mates."

"Tell me again how you know this?"

She sighed. "Do you enjoy that?"

"What?"

"Hurting me."

"No."

"Have you heard anything I've said?"

"Yes."

"Then, please, don't ask me again how I know that we're meant for each other."

"And if I don't feel that way?"

"Trust me, you will."

"Do I have a choice?"

"Do you believe in destiny . . . fate?"

"Perhaps."

"Well, I do. And we are destined to be together."

"Which one gave you my telephone number?"

"What?"

"Destiny? Or fate?"

"You're mocking me. Hurting me again. Do you enjoy being cruel?"

"I do not."

"Then why ask? Besides, I not only have your telephone number, I know where you live and where you work."

My mind raced. How did she know where I lived, and where I worked?

Soon her calls took an ominous turn.

"I'm tired of playing this game," I said.

"What game? This is my life. Our lives. My heart. Our hearts. You're completely insensitive to call it a game. I want you. I need you. I love you."

"You can't love me. You don't even know me."

"Don't you dare! Don't you dare ever tell me who I can or can't love. I love you. We're meant to be with each other. My life would not be worth living without you. I'd sooner take my own life if we can't be together."

"Take your own life? You can't be serious."

She slowly annunciated each word. "Obviously, you do not understand the depth of my feelings." Her voice rung with a plaintiff wail. "Yes, I'd rather kill myself if you didn't want to be with me."

She must have sensed a weakness that she could exploit. Our conversation now teetered on this macabre balance: love me, or I'll take my own life. I kept answering her calls, talking with her, afraid of the consequences of hanging up.

One day, after weeks of these chilling late-night calls, I sat at my desk, head down in a flowchart, when I heard a woman from the secretarial pool speaking on the telephone. "I'm sorry, sir," she said. "Perhaps you do not understand that Mr. Benson is not in today. I can take a message for him if you would like."

I didn't turn around. But what she said, "you do not understand," and how she said it, played over and again in my mind. I knew those words. I knew that voice. They belonged to Michelle Johnson, a Black woman who worked behind me.

I left work early that day and sat on a bench across the street from my building, where I had a clear view of the workers heading home. Shortly after five, Michelle Johnson walked out. I stood up and followed her from behind. She flowed in a sea of humanity pouring around the corner and swarming down the stairs to await the #2 train to Brooklyn. I hid behind a pillar at the far end of the station. The subway train screeched to a halt. I peered around the pillar as Michelle stepped into a forward car. I waited until the doors were about to close before pushing my way into the last car. I lurched backward as the subway left the station, balancing on one foot while fighting to maintain my spot at the door. Our train rocked from side to side as it sped under the East River. On the Brooklyn side of the river, at each station, a crowd of people overwhelmed me, pushing me backward out of the car, onto the platform. I turned to see if Michelle had stepped out, and then hustled to get back into the car and fight, once again, for my spot at the door.

Pushed out, again, into the station at President Street, I saw Michelle exiting her car and being swept along with a mass of people toward an escalator leading up toward the street. On the escalator up, I turned to face down until I felt the stair treads flatten out and solid ground slide under my feet. Four staircases led up to the street from the escalator landing. I looked but could not see which one Michelle had taken. I stepped quickly toward the stairs opposite the escalator and joined a line of people plodding upward.

Aboveground I realized I'd chosen incorrectly. Catercorner, across the street, I saw Michelle disappearing down the block. The traffic light changed, but not in my favor. I held up my hand to oncoming traffic, dashing between cars whizzing by. I couldn't risk losing her. A half block ahead of me, Michelle strolled down President Street, crossed over Kingston Avenue, and took a left on Carroll Street. She opened a gate midway down the block. I ran toward her, calling out.

"Michelle!"

She walked quickly to her front door, shoved a key into the lock, turned it, then opened the door. With her front door partially opened, she looked back with a mixture of horror and disdain.

"Whaddya want?" she snapped.

"Why?" I asked.

"Why what?"

"The deception. The telephone calls. Threatening to kill yourself."

"I don't know what you're talking about."

"Did someone put you up to it?"

"Up to what?"

She ducked inside, then slammed the door closed behind her.

I never had a late-night caller threatening suicide again.

———

In the early 1970s, when I worked for IBM, I also taught yoga at Aquarius, a four-floor brownstone on 148th Street between

Amsterdam and St. Nicholas Avenues in Harlem. Long since defunct, Aquarius, named after renowned Black yoga teacher Maxine (Daya) Quander, herself an Aquarian astrologically, featured a natural foods store in the basement, a natural foods restaurant and music venue on the first floor, a yoga studio on the second floor, and a sauna and massage studio on the third. A throwback to the days of Harlem rent parties and in-home restaurants, Aquarius carried these notions into a new age.

At one of Aquarius's famed all-night Saturday parties, I met a young woman named Kisi. Though born in America, like many, she had taken an African name. Her Ghanaian name meant "a girl born on Saturday." My Ghanaian name, which I received during a traditional naming ceremony in Kumasi, Ghana, was Kojo, which meant "a boy born on Monday." Kisi and Kojo. An epic match so it seemed.

Kisi claimed to be an aspiring actress, which allowed her to blend in well with the many actors and actresses, working and aspiring, that frequented Aquarius. Kisi also seemed very intrigued with me, which I found flattering. Where did I work? What did I do? Did I like my job?

I drove a VW camper at the time, which I used to escape from New York City as often as I could. A Black guy camping seemed an endless source of fascination for Kisi.

"Camping? Whaddya do out there?"

"Nothing."

"Got a television?"

"No."

"Bathroom?"

"No."

"You're kidding?"

"No."

"You really do nothing?"

"Maybe hike. Relax. Read."

"Grizzly bears and cougars?"

"It's western New Jersey!"

"I gotta see this for myself."

And one weekend we did.

Not long after we returned, my manager called me into his office.

"Ford," he barked. "While you were in class last week a woman came to visit me." He raised his right arm. "About five-five. Slender. Maybe attractive." He chuckled. "Couldn't tell under all that makeup and that wild Afro everywhere." He shook his arms back and forth, palms facing each other on either side of his head. "Know her?"

"Maybe." I perched in a chair in front of his desk.

"Maybe? She said you two were together. About to get married."

"Did she."

"She said she wanted to meet 'Clyde's manager,' which is why she came to see me. Look, your personal life is your own business. But when your personal life steps into this office, it becomes your professional life, and therefore it's my business. She dressed like a cheap hooker. Denim skirt frayed at the edges. Way too short. Up to her ass. Hairy legs, no stockings. Sandals. Huge earrings. Even huger sunglasses. Wide, floppy hat like she was at the beach. Nice tits—I'll give her that. You get the picture?"

"I do."

"Here's the thing, Ford. I can't tell you who to marry." He pointed away from his office out onto the office floor. "But I can tell you she'll never fit in. She's just not IBM material. If I were you, I'd value my job more than that . . . that gal. I'd sooner see you lose her than lose your position with us."

As I stepped from my manager's office, it felt as though I met a sea of smirks from the floor. Something also felt familiar; like I'd been here not long before. That night I called Kisi.

"You came unannounced to my office and met with my manager? And you didn't even think to tell me?"

She said nothing.

"You told my manager we were getting married?"

Still nothing.

"What were you thinking?"

She hung up.

I called back but she didn't answer. I tried calling the number I had for her several times, but I only got another woman who claimed she'd never heard of Kisi. I was at Aquarius many times—to teach yoga, take a sauna, or have a meal. I did not see Kisi again.

I'll never know why these women did what they did, never know if it was from some warped romantic sensibility or if someone else put them up to an involvement with me. Yet, as I've pondered the honeypot trap that my father escaped during his early years at IBM, I've long wondered if I also escaped my own honeypot traps in my early years with the firm.

Twice as Hard

When I was nine, we moved from our home on 221st Street to a co-op apartment at 1950 Hutchinson River Parkway, in the Pelham Bay section of the Bronx. Ours was the first co-op in the Bronx, and we were the first all-Black family in the co-op. Co-ops were a novelty in 1960. The apartments in this co-op had been leased quickly, and none were given to all-Black families, although one mixed-race family lived a few floors below us. My father had applied several times for one of the few vacancies, and each time he was turned down until only one apartment remained, 13C, an exclusive corner apartment on the building's top floor. This time, my father went to the building's management agency, but instead of filling out an application, he called aside the man leasing the apartments and asked how much it would take to secure apartment 13C. My father slipped the man several hundred dollars and walked away with a lease.

Of course, with a new address came a new school: PS 102 in the Parkchester neighborhood, where my mother also taught kindergarten. Excitement filled me as I entered a special fifth- and sixth-grade class devoted to music, where each student could choose the instrument they wanted. But I walked into class that first day to find that my music teacher was none other than the mistress of the monsters, my former piano teacher and nemesis, Carmen Silva.

We lined up to select instruments. When my turn came, I picked up a flute. Miss Silva smiled devilishly and snatched the flute from my hands.

"The flute's a girl's instrument," she snarled. "Here." She thrust a clarinet at me. "You'll play clarinet instead."

"But—"

"There are no *buts* in my class, young man. You're a boy, not a girl. You'll make yourself com-for-tubble with the clarinet, and that's that."

Even years before Miss Silva's rigid insistence that musical instruments somehow aligned with gender, I'd overheard my father more than once whispering to my mother his fears about my being gay because I never took to baseball, even though he tried his best by taking me to games at Yankee Stadium. Terms like *geek* and *nerd* had not yet entered the popular lexicon, so he found himself in a bind when I bounded with joy at the prospect of accompanying him on a trip to IBM World Headquarters to help with the latest computer but failed to display a similar "manly" enthusiasm when Mickey Mantle or Roger Maris, baseball greats of the era, stepped up to bat.

One Saturday morning in the late 1950s, I accompanied my father to 590 Madison Avenue to help him and a group of systems and field engineers[1] perform a memory check on an IBM 705, recently installed in the basement of the world headquarters building. Heading south into Manhattan from the Bronx, the #2 train rocked and rolled. My father leaned in to deliver a now-familiar line.

"Computers will control your life one day. Better if you learn how to control them first."

At the time, the IBM 705, a successor to the IBM 407, was one of the world's most advanced commercial computers, with a processor capable of 0.04 MIPS (millions of instructions per second), disk drives able to store 60 kilobytes of data per drive, and 20 kilobytes of memory. I walked through the doors of the data-processing center holding my father's hand. My head reached just above his waist, while above and around me, seemingly endless tape drives jerked, disk drives whirred, and vacuum tubes glowed. With the machine's housings and covers removed, men scurried between rows of the 705's electronic guts.

My father, thoroughly trained on the IBM 705, sat me down at the operator's console with very specific instructions: An engineer would call on the rotary-dial telephone sitting next to the console and tell me which of the many switches to set and which of the many buttons to press in order to activate specific memory locations. A group of engineers would then hustle over to the vacuum tubes managing those memory locations and ascertain that all the filaments glowed. Tubes would be replaced as needed. Then I'd receive another call with instructions to activate a new memory location, and the cycle of inspection and replacement would repeat.

As much as I loved the feeling of power that came with flipping switches, punching buttons, and sending a group of adults running around a room, it turned out to be grueling work for an eight-year-old. With 1,700 vacuum tubes glowing, and electricity running through miles and miles of wiring consuming 70 kilowatts of power, a full IBM 705 system easily weighed 16 tons, generated 250,000 Btus of heat, and required the equivalent of 1 ton of ice per day to cool. Needless to say, the room housing the 705 felt frigid. With the sprawling size of the 705, I experienced long periods of boredom as my father and the other engineers walked long distances to inspect and replace tubes.

It helps to put the 705's specifications into perspective. If you consider that the smartphone you are carrying has at least 8 giga-bytes of memory to store pictures and music, a 705 with 20 kilobytes of memory had roughly 1/500,000 the memory capacity. And that smartphone's 8 gigabytes of memory fits into roughly the same physical space as 1 bit of memory on the 705, less the vacuum tube circuits to control that bit of memory. In other words, the memory of a 705 would occupy the physical space equivalent of the tip of a pin when compared to the memory of your smartphone. A 705 had a processing speed of approximately 0.04 MIPS. Your smart-phone's processing speed can easily reach 71,000 MIPS, an almost 2-million-fold increase.

While vacuum tubes performed the processing logic on an IBM 705, they could not function as memory: turning on and off power to the machine turned on and off power to the vacuum tubes, and hence no tube could retain its state. So the IBM 705 had an array of tiny ceramic and iron donuts called ferrite cores, one-quarter of an inch or less in diameter. Each core had several wires threaded through it—directional wires and sense wires. Directional wires magnetized the core in either a counterclockwise or clockwise di-rection (on or off, 1 or 0), while sense wires determined the direction of magnetization. Once a core was magnetized in a counterclock-wise direction (representing a 1, for example) it would retain that magnetization even if the machine lost power, hence core memory was nonvolatile.

My work at the operator's console—flipping switches and punch-ing buttons—helped to isolate bits of memory that the engineers could inspect. Today, a check on 8 or 16 gigabytes of memory in a smartphone or a laptop happens in a few milliseconds, but in those days a memory check on a model 705 might take all weekend. When my father and I left for home that day, the 705's memory check still had not been completed. Yet whatever I'd accomplished at the operator's console met some unspoken benchmark set by my father. Even though I was not yet ten years old, on that day a more formal tutelage in computers began.

It started with binary arithmetic.

Holes punched or not punched in card columns; switches set on or off on a control panel; logic circuits buzzing with electricity or silent; core memory magnetized in one direction or another; pixels illuminated or dark on a screen—all digital technology centers on the duality of being and not being, of existence and nonexistence, of here and not here. Punched, on, buzzing, counterclockwise, and illuminated can be represented by 1s. Not punched, off, silent, clockwise, and dark can be represented by 0s. In this way, 1s and 0s are mathematical shorthand for describing the state of any collection of digital devices.

In an office entered from the front corner of our living room on 221st Street in the Bronx, an IBM THINK sign stood sentry over my father's large wooden desk. He set his pipe in an ashtray, though the smell of his cherry-blend tobacco lingered, and tapped a blank sheet of paper with his pencil.

"Count," he commanded. His baritone voice had the power to make me tremble.

He wrote down the first three binary numbers—000, 001, 010.

"Zero. One. Two," I said.

At eight years old, I thought the binary numbers looked strange, more like 0, 1, 10.

"Now the next three," my father said.

He wrote down 011, 100, 101.

"Three, four, five," I said.

"And the final two."

He wrote down 110, 111.

"Six and seven."

"Good."

But it wasn't good. I knew how to count in decimal and had simply repeated the numbers from 0 to 7 without really understanding the relationship between those numbers and the strange way they now appeared. My father also knew that, so he flipped the page and wrote down a random binary number, 101.

"What's this?" he asked.

I hesitated.

"Count," he said.

"I'm confused," I said.

"First position on the right represents a one. Second position on the right represents a two. Third position on the right represents a . . ." He paused.

In a weak voice, I answered. "Three?"

"Wrong," he said. "Four." He tapped each digit with his pencil. "One is on. Two is off. Four is on. One plus four is?"

"Five?"

"Right. In binary, 101 is five."

"It looks like one hundred and one," I said.

"But in binary it's only five," my father said.

"It's confusing."

"Try this." He wrote down 011.

I studied the number, then guessed, "Two?"

He tapped each digit with his pencil, beginning on the right side. "One is on. Two is on. Four is off. . . . One plus two is?"

"Three," I said, though I still didn't really get it.

"This is the math I use all day at work," he said.

It went this way when my father came home from work and on weekends. I'm not certain that I ever really understood binary in those days, but I did get really good at recognizing any binary number between 0 and 7. I even tried out binary on a classmate. I scribbled 101 in my notebook.

"What's this number?"

"Hundred one," the kid said.

I smiled. "Nope."

"Is too," he said.

"Is not."

"Okay, what is it?"

"Five."

"Five? Is not."

"Is too." I fumbled through an explanation of columns and digits and 1s and 0s.

The kid waved me off. "I'm tellin' you, it's a hundred one. No five anywhere. And if you think it's five, you're weird."

My smile drained away as the kid walked off.

At our next lesson, I told my father about my experience teaching binary. He laughed. "That's good."

"Good?" I mumbled.

"You know something. They don't." He tapped the side of his head. "You only need to be sure of what's up here. Doesn't matter what anyone else thinks. Doesn't matter if they call you weird or any other names." He tapped the side of his head again. "Only matters what you know. So, whatever you think you know had better be right."

For Christmas 1960, my father bought me a personal computer. Though hardly a computer by today's standards, the Lego-like contraption had a register—a white plastic piece that slid in and out. Pull the register out, then push it in, and on the front of the machine, three binary digits showed a 1 or a 0, counting from 000 to 111 (zero to seven) in binary.

Meanwhile, my father proceeded with instruction in simple binary multiplication and division. Multiply by 2? Add a 0 to the right of a binary number, and treat it as though it had four digits. Thus, 101 binary times 2 became 1010 binary, or 10 in decimal. Divide by

2? Lop off the farthest digit to the right and add a 0 on the far left. If a 1 is lopped off, treat it as a remainder. Read the binary number, and add the remainder if needed. Thus, 111 binary divided by 2 became 011 binary remainder 1 (7 divided by 2 equals 3 with a remainder of 1). If this is confusing, imagine how it scrambled my young mind.

Nineteen sixty also marked our move from the family home on 221st Street to the thirteenth floor of the newly built co-op apartment in the Bronx. As the only Black kid in an accelerated seventh-grade class, I felt trapped between dualities—Black and White, decimal and binary.

At school, students would gather in a tight circle behind combatants, segregated by skin color. A heated, singsong cheer went forth.

"A fight. A fight. A Nigger and a White."

I knew only to avoid such melees, for there were no students of any color behind me.

At home, our family was trapped between being seen as the only all-Black family in the building and not being seen at all.

"I know what you are," a kid said.

He sat inside one of the large concrete barrels in the building's playground. I stood outside.

"My parents told me you're an eegro."

He'd mispronounced the word. Still, a white-hot flash of embarrassment shot through my body. I drifted away as the kid chanted, "Eegro, eegro. You're an eegro."

I tried playing sandlot football but grew tired of hearing kids say, "I mean no offense by this." Everyone would look at me. "But the Niggers have challenged us to a game."

The last time I played with the kids in our building, a game of ring-a-levio turned savage. Ring-a-levio is a special variation of tag, originating on the streets of New York City. We'd split up into two teams. One team hid while the other tried to capture them. Captured players were thrown in a "jail," perhaps our playground barrels or some other defensible area. Prisoners could be sprung from jail by tagging them and shouting, "Olly olly oxen free," at which point all captives were released and had to be recaptured. Ring-a-levio ended when one team captured all members of the other team, or when one team conceded defeat.

That day, I was still free, and it seemed as though the game had changed and all the kids on both teams now hunted me. They were all White. I peeked around the rear bumper of a car and spied the mob of kids a block away. I took off running. They saw me. I ran. They yelled, "Get him! Get him!" I ran harder. They chased me. My heart pounded as I bounded up the steps of an elevated subway station. I popped a token in the turnstile, pushed through the wooden arms, and, still running, leaped into a subway car. I rode the subway several stops, got off, and raced down the steps. I kept running. The mob of kids was long gone, but I did not stop running. I ran out of my body. I ran back through time. I ran as though my life depended on it. I ran as though I were running for every Black person ever chased by a crazed White mob. And when I stopped running, I found myself on the far side of that binary divide between Black and White. I never played with the White kids in our building again.

———

Soon binary arithmetic proved insufficient to meet the needs of ever more sophisticated computers and the humans who programmed them. Strings of 1s and 0s grew too long and too complex for humans to easily grasp. One thousand and eight, for example, while readily expressed in decimal (1,008) became cumbersome in binary (001111110000). Systems engineers initially adopted octal numbers to curb the excesses of binary numbers. Octal arithmetic (octal meaning "eight") is a base-8 system, where one counts from 0 to 7 and then moves over a column to the left and starts counting again. By comparison, decimal is a base-10 system, where one counts from 0 to 9 and then moves over a column to the left and starts counting again.

Not long after extolling the virtues of 1s and 0s and insisting that I learn binary, my father switched to octal, which had displaced binary at IBM. He made the switch to keep up, and therefore in my father's mind octal was now the best way to represent the innermost workings of digital technology. Out came new blank sheets of paper, and new numbers were scribbled with a pencil, as "Learn octal" became the new battle cry for him. Fortunately, octal and binary are intimately related. Take the number 1,008, represented in binary as 001111110000. Now make groups of three digits, and you have 001 111 110 000. If you represent every three binary digits as a single digit between 0 and 7, it yields 1760. So, 1760 in octal is 001111110000 in binary and 1,008 in decimal.

Still, for a ten-year-old, deriving 1,008 decimal from 1760 octal is no easy feat. I struggled under this new mathematics and the relentless insistence of my father to come up with the right answer. Just as I seemed to make some headway with octal, it too proved insufficient.

Along came hexadecimal. Hexadecimal, or simply hex, is a base-16 numbering system, as the name implies. One counts from 0 to 15 and then moves a column to the left and begins counting again. However, there's a catch. What do you do after the digit 9? Base-10 arithmetic counts from 0 to 9, and there is a single character for each digit. But in hexadecimal, you run out of single digits after reaching the character 9, so letters of the alphabet are used for digits between 10 and 15. Hence, in hex, the count is 0, 1, 2, 3, 4, 5, 6, 7, 8, 9, A, B, C, D, E, F.

Confusing? Yes, it is. Especially for a ten- or eleven-year-old kid who was still mastering plain old decimal math. Again, out came the blank paper and the penciled numbers, and my father pontificated that hex was the latest, greatest, and ultimate digital numbering system that I needed to learn. From decimal 1,008, represented as binary 001111110000, create groups of four digits, yielding 0011 1111 0000. Now use a single hexadecimal digit to represent each group of four binary digits, and what results is 3F0—1,008 decimal equals 001111110000 binary equals 1760 octal equals 3F0 hexadecimal. While I may have been confused when I first attempted to decode a hexadecimal number, time has proved my father right. No other numbering system has yet surpassed hexadecimal in representing the underlying logic of digital devices. Hex is in widespread use today.

This transition from binary to octal to hex came at a time when I transitioned from junior high school to high school to advanced placement within high school, and each transition was more difficult than the previous one. I left behind friends as rapidly as I made them, with my father's voice always close, reminding me that I didn't need them anyway.

This transition also came at a pivotal moment in the maturation of computers. To be more useful, computers needed to be "human-friendlier." Machines needed to interact with people in a manner more easily understood by humans: they needed to understand human language. In the early days of computers, this did not mean voice recognition or handwriting recognition, which are so common in smartphones and digital devices today. It meant that humans should be able to program computers using English-like languages.

Around this time, IBM bifurcated itself into scientific and commercial computing and designed machines specifically to handle the different computational needs of the scientific and business communities. IBM promoted the IBM 704, for example, as a scientific computer, while featuring the IBM 705, which my father knew intimately, as a business computer. Thus IBM created scientific and business computer languages. FORTRAN (short for *FORmula TRANslation*) became the first widely used scientific computer language, and COBOL (short for *COmmon Business Oriented Language*) was the first widely used commercial computer language. IBM assigned my father to the maintenance and propagation of COBOL.

Prior to FORTRAN and COBOL, computer programming relied on a set of arcane skills. By the middle 1950s, my father no longer performed "basket weaving," as he had on the IBM 407, to control the internal logic of a computer. Instead, he typed instructions into designated columns of punch cards. Those punch cards were read by a computer that decoded the instructions and, in turn, enacted the logic they contained. Instructions had an extremely terse syntax, making it difficult, even for the humans who had written them, to later trace the flow of their execution. For instance, the instruction **A ANSWER,=X'0A'** actually means, "Add 10 to a number in storage." Now, imagine thousands upon thousands of lines of such nearly unfathomable nomenclature. That's what early written computer programs were composed of, and programs written in this way are still described as machine code, or assembly language, because the instructions are so very close to what the actual machine circuitry does.

Clearly, a better way to program computers had to be found, and the quest for this better way gave rise to computer languages and the notion of computer software. If hardware represents the physical circuitry of a computer, software represents the instructions that, when decoded, cause a computer's physical circuitry to behave in unique ways that perform the tasks described in the software.

So, in FORTRAN, that strange line of code might read **ANSWER = ANSWER + 10**, and in COBOL it might read **ADD 10 TO ANSWER**. In both cases, these statements are manifestly easier to understand than the original statement. FORTRAN had a very crisp, human-readable syntax. COBOL had a long, meandering set of divisions to describe each aspect of a program, such as an Identification Division, a Data Division, an Input Division, an Output Division, a Procedure Division, and a Printing Division.

For obvious reasons, many considered COBOL, the brainchild of famed computer scientist Rear Admiral Grace Hopper, to be too verbose. Defenders of COBOL claimed that its wordiness made it self-documenting. Regardless, by 1970, COBOL had become the most widely used computer language in the world.

My father maintained the Data Division of the first IBM COBOL compiler. He had the responsibility of identifying and correcting errors, or bugs, found in the way the IBM COBOL compiler managed the memory of an IBM 705. Especially in early computers, a complex program like a compiler, which takes English-like instructions and translates them into assembly language statements for execution by physical circuitry, could contain many errors despite the best efforts of diligent programmers to create error-free code. Often, those errors were encountered only when the COBOL compiler was running in a customer's real-life production environment.

An error could surface in many ways. For example, a card reader might stop suddenly in the midst of reading a COBOL program from a stack of punch cards; once a program card deck was read, lights on the IBM 705 operations console might flash with an error code and halt the program. Or a program might produce garbled results. If it involved the Data Division of the early IBM COBOL compiler, such an error frequently landed on my father's desk. He'd return home with a thick stack of pages called a "core dump," staying up late in search of "bugs."

Bug and *core dump* are buzzwords from the dawn of computing that are still used today. Grace Hopper is credited with elevating the term *bug* to prominence in the late 1940s, when she reported finding a moth lodged between the contact points of relays, preventing them from closing. But frustrated engineers in pursuit of glitches and gremlins in their creations had used the word many decades before her. "'Bugs'—as such little faults and difficulties are called," said Thomas Edison, "show themselves and months of intense watching, study and labor are requisite before commercial success or failure is certainly reached."[2] Origin aside, by the late 1940s, the term *bug* stuck in reference to any computing error, hardware or software.

Core dump, on the other hand, originally referred to printing out the status of computer memory at a time when that memory was composed of the small ferrite cores described earlier. Today, and even in my father's time, a core dump is any printout of a computer's memory.

Core dumps, by their very nature, are messy. My father was handed as many as several hundred folded, printed pages containing line after line of numbers and letters, and then instructed to "find the bug" within that massive hexadecimal sea.

Locating a bug in a core dump is a little like following clues in a hexadecimal treasure hunt. One hexadecimal memory address often contains a pointer to another address that contains a pointer to yet another address, and so forth. In this way, the state of the computer at the time of the error can be traced and the bug, hopefully, found.

Pipe in hand, blue smoke curling up, THINK sign above his core dump, my father would hunker down at his large wooden desk in our apartment in Williamsbridge. When we moved from the 'Bridge to Pelham Bay, and there was no space for his desk, he'd unfold a card table and hunker down over a core dump in the living room of our thirteenth-floor apartment, THINK sign close by. When we moved from the city to Rockland County, he'd hunker down over that same spindly legged card table in the basement entertainment room of his dream home, the THINK sign not far away.

Regardless of where he hunkered down, I recall a man consumed by the search for elusive bugs; a man unavailable for family vacations, outings, or playtime, precisely because he was hunkered down; a man burdened by his determined quest for the errors created by others; a man in relentless pursuit of perfection. My presence as a young child walking into his office, or standing beside his card table, seemed to cause painful questioning of these trade-offs and choices. More than once, he lifted his head from a core dump to answer a question I never asked.

"A Black man has to work twice as hard to be considered half as good as Whitey."

I grew to deeply resent this notion, even as I learned to accept its truth.

Then I went to work for IBM and had my own core dumps to plow through. I'd been assigned to IBM's New York Financial Office; my team's only customer was the Federal Reserve Bank of New York. Once a week, I'd report to my IBM home office at 1 Wall Street. The other days, I'd simply commute directly from my apartment in the Bronx to the Fed. At twenty-one, after a year and a half of IBM education and training, I had my own office in the bowels of the fortresslike Federal Reserve Building, which occupies the entire block between Liberty, William, and Nassau Streets and Maiden Lane, in the Financial District of Manhattan.

COBOL programmers lined up at my office, their outstretched arms laden with heavy core dumps. Like anxious supplicants bearing gifts for some worshipped idol, embarrassed parishioners slipping into confessionals, or wounded children with skinned knees running to their mother, one by one they dropped stacks of pages on my desk with the universally uttered demand, "Fix it!" The Fed, after all, paid several millions of dollars a month to lease our computers and expected attentive IBM service in return, even from the kid with the big Afro.

Bruce, an IBM colleague, also had an office at the Fed. I considered

Bruce a wizard of the dumps. Pencil in hand, programmer hovering over him, Bruce would tear through a core dump, circling a hexa-decimal number, drawing an arrow to where in the dump that number pointed, examining the data at that next address, and using that data to point to yet another address—over and over until he got to a place where what he expected at a location in the dump did not match what he found.

"Here's your problem," he'd announce. He'd tap the address, then double-circle the error, sending the happy programmer back to his cubicle with a thoroughly marked-up dump.

I wanted to learn from Bruce, who freely offered me his insights into navigating this hexadecimal swamp. But the more I circled addresses and penciled in arrows, the more frustrated I grew. I did not want to end up like my father, whom I'd seen spent by the process. So I developed my own technique for reading core dumps, one based on the Socratic method, which meant I never even peered at the pages programmers plopped on my desk.

I looked beyond the core dump, directly at the programmer, and asked, "What was your program trying to accomplish?"

I'd nod while listening to the programmer's answer, even if I did not fully understand what the program was meant to do.

"How did you go about doing that?"

A short moment of silence preceded the programmer's next answer. Like a sympathetic psychotherapist, I kept nodding my understanding and approval.

"And why did you choose that method of accomplishing the task?"

The silence grew longer, and I continued to nod.

"I'm wondering if there was a better way of going about this?"

It rarely took more than four questions before the programmer would snap his fingers, point at me, and say, "That's it! That's what I did wrong!"

Though I frequently never knew what had actually gone wrong, I'd say, "Wow, we found the bug."

"Thank you, so much," the programmer would say.

By this time, he had already grabbed the core dump from my desk. Like a priest, I'd reach out to touch the dump, bless his discovery, and send him back to his cubicle, smiling, with a stack of unmarked pages.

———

Binary, octal, hexadecimal mathematics, core dumps, computer programs. For the untrained eye of the uninitiated, examining computer software is much like a nonmusician viewing the score of an orchestral arrangement. Lines, marks, symbols, squiggles everywhere. But what do they mean on their own? More important, what do they mean taken together?

Music, anyway, is not a bad analogue for computer software. Music is a written code that, when executed correctly, causes a physical device to perform in an expected way. It's one reason my father loved both, as did many early systems engineers. It's also one reason my father insisted that I learn not one or two instruments but many.

Before I landed in Carmen Silva's fifth- and sixth-grade class, my father pushed me to study the accordion, even though I could barely lift a full-size instrument or see around it to the music on my stand. My father was a classically trained violinist, and for a few brief moments I tried learning the violin under his tutelage, until we both agreed that such an arrangement would never work. He bought us both recorders, an alto and a soprano, and we practiced duets together.

When my sister made her way into Carmen Silva's music class, my father's dream of a family quartet could finally be realized. We would get together for family music time with my mother on the piano, my father playing the violin, my sister on the flute, and me playing clarinet. A special bond exists between members of an ensemble, and those times playing music stand out as some of the closest I felt to my family.

Then I discovered the guitar.

It happened one summer at camp, about the time I first held hands with a girl named Betsy Schwartz. I loved everything about the guitar—how its shape reminded me of the female form, how it was cradled while being played, how one's fingers moved over the strings in a sinewy, sensuous way. I feel in love with the guitar, and for a time with Betsy Schwartz too.

But a guitar in the early 1960s also stood as a powerful symbol of political protest and social change. Odetta, Bob Dylan, Joan Baez, Richie Havens, Phil Ochs, Pete Seeger, Leon Bibb, Dave Van Ronk, and all the other marvelous folk singers of the 1960s wielded their guitars almost as weapons accompanying voices that rose to demand a new order, rebuke the existing order, and ask how long the oppressed must wait.

In the early 1960s, when I was twelve or thirteen, New York City flourished as a center of music and social unrest. Community Church, which I attended regularly, fostered it. At one Sunday's service delivered by the church's youth, I played my guitar and sang Dylan's epic song "The Times They Are A-Changin'."

My father, however, would have none of it, and it caught him in a bind. He loved music and expressed some satisfaction that I'd finally found an instrument that spoke to me. Yet he detested what the protest music I loved stood for—a strong stance against the war in Vietnam and a soundtrack for urgent and direct action on civil rights for Blacks in America. He dismissed me, and anyone who played this music or participated in the protests and actions it in-spired, as just a "bunch of commies."

As my relationship with my father began to fray, other signifi-cant male figures came into my life. Sitting in the balcony of Community Church one Sunday morning, I spotted Pete Seeger in a pew down below. As the service ended, I made my way over to Pete, a tall, gaunt man, tugged on his sleeve, and handed him a church program, which he autographed with his signature draw-ing of a banjo. He leaned over to speak with me. His graciousness in those few brief moments profoundly touched me. Many years later, toward the end of his life, I had a long telephone conversation with Pete, in which I thanked him for that day and for serving as a role model for me.

Immediately after our youth service, a church member, Charles E. Wilson, pulled me aside. "The world hates a smart-ass kid" were his first words. And with that began our years-long relationship. "C.E.," as he was known, showed me how to channel my youthful exuberance, enthusiasm, and anger to create meaningful social change. Education was one of C.E.'s abiding concerns. He worked tirelessly, fighting the New York City Board of Education, to establish IS 201 (independent school district 201) in Harlem. He served as the district's first admin-istrator, and I worked as his part-time, unpaid assistant throughout my high school and college years. C.E. introduced me to a world of Black radicalism and intellectualism tethered to pragmatism. He also served as an unseen mentor to other radical Black movements in New York City, like the 1968 uprising at Columbia University.

As I began spending more time with this man, and as my respect and admiration for him grew, my mother asked me, "Would you rather have Charlie as a father?"

Her question came on the verge of her divorcing my father, and I wisely sidestepped the answer.

Around the time I met C.E., I also had my first experience of truly independent social and political thought. Unitarian-Universalist teenagers throughout the country organized weekend regional conferences that featured speakers during the day and dancing to the latest music at night. Paul Krassner, a comedian, social critic, and founder of the *Realist* magazine, spoke at the first conference I attended. I was thirteen. I recall sitting at the back of a meeting room in a Unitarian church on Long Island as, late in the afternoon, Krassner spoke about America's involvement in Vietnam.

I huddled with a group of friends afterward, most of them two or three years older.

I stammered with excitement. "I got what he said."

"So?" a kid name Danny replied.

"I mean, I understood his words, all of them, individually and together."

Danny squinted, then shook his head.

"Least you're not some kind of idiot."

No doubt, it helped my receptivity to Krassner's message that an hour before he spoke, I'd had my first real slow, deep kiss with a girl in the coat closet at the rear of the meeting room. Later that night at the dance, that girl, Susan, grabbed my hand and dragged me off into a corner of the dance hall. We passed Danny on the way there. He nodded his approval as we walked by.

The muffled voices of the Drifters crooned "Under the Boardwalk," as I rambled to Susan, in a stream of consciousness, about understanding every word and idea that Krassner spoke; about years of my father drilling me on chess and binary math, salted with the message that I should think for myself; about years of watching him work twice as hard as others in the relentless pursuit of perfection.

She smiled as though she understood and then pulled me in for more kisses. In this coming-of-age moment, I not only had the experience of my first kiss, but I also had the first experience of myself as an independent being who could think on his own. I could not turn back from this awakened sense of self, even as it set me further on a collision course with my father.

For Black Americans in postwar America, arranged marriages were also a vehicle for overcoming the opportunities denied the partners because of their race. The calculation, if not romantic, was certainly straightforward: the reduced opportunities afforded one member of the couple, in a given field, were compensated for by the opportunities available to the other member of the couple, in a different arena.

Where my father's career was thwarted because of the racism he faced at IBM, my mother's career as one of the first Black principals with the New York City Board of Education helped to make up for a portion of my father's reduced wages. Similar considerations, still common among upwardly striving socioeconomic groups, contributed to the rapid rise of a postwar Black middle class.

As in more traditional arranged marriages, the families of the bride and groom had some say in the matter. My grandparents on both sides, only a few generations removed from slavery themselves, approved of my parents' marriage precisely because they recognized that my parents might be able to advance beyond them economically and socially. And they disapproved of anyone who might not afford such advancement.

What's love got to do with it?

In his upper desk drawer at our Rockland County home, beneath the picture with his IBM colleagues at the New York City Playboy Club, my father kept a photograph of a young Ruby Dee. It was signed, "To Stan. With Love, Ruby." Growing up, I dismissed the wistfulness that accompanied his mention of her name as the infatuation of a young man for a beautiful young starlet. Then I read Ruby's autobiography and later spent many hours with her over several years, only to have her confirm everything my father said about their relationship and hint at much that he left out.

After her family moved to New York City from Cleveland, the legendary stage, film, and screen actress Ruby Dee (née Ruby Ann

Wallace) grew up in the Williamsbridge section of the Bronx along with my father and my mother. She spoke of my father throughout her autobiography, which was written with her husband, the equally legendary Black actor Ossie Davis.

My father, she said, introduced her to a world "outside the all-girl cocoon"[1] and also to her acting career, which began at the American Negro Theatre:

> I had heard about the American Negro Theatre from Stanley Ford, one of the boys who met with Mother's approval and who often came to call on Sunday afternoons when we girls were allowed to have company. His sister, Ruth, was a member of the group and knew of plans to mount the first production, a new comedy by Abram Hill called On Strivers Row. She told Stanley, who suggested that I audition for Cobina, the debutante and leading love interest. Mother and Daddy thought it was a good idea, so I took a chance.[2]

That chance turned into a stunning seventy-five-year-long, award-winning career.

Ruby performed her one-woman show, *My One Good Nerve*, at Seattle's A Contemporary Theatre (ACT) in 2000. After one performance, I met her backstage, introducing myself as Stan Ford's son and Ruth Ford's nephew. Ruby wagged her finger at me, then spoke in her trademark husky, breathless voice.

"Why'd you wait until after my performance to come backstage and say 'hi'? You know I wouldn't be here if it weren't for your father, and for Ruth."

I told her my father had passed away a month earlier, but with others now waiting in line to greet her, we said little else. She squeezed my arm as I left.

Years later, I met Ruby again, this time around a table in the living room of Morgan Freeman's palatial estate in Charleston, Mississippi. Myrna Colley-Lee, then Morgan's wife, had recently started the SonEdna Foundation to bring the performing and literary arts to the Mississippi Delta. Myrna invited me to be a founding board member. Hasna Muhammad, Ruby and Ossie's daughter, also sat on the board. Ruby signed on as a foundation adviser. Among the many other luminary Black film and stage figures sitting around that table were Roscoe Orman, who played Gordon on *Sesame Street*; playwright Ifa Bayeza; critic and scholar Karen Baxter; and Pamela Poitier, Sidney's daughter.

I spent the weekend with Ruby, and at one point she pulled me aside. With the same wistfulness I'd seen in my father, she said, "Stan would pick me up from my house, and we'd take the subway to Central Park. We'd get a rowboat, and he'd row me around the lake for hours. We'd talk and all, then he'd bring me back." She let go with a lusty laugh.

Writing to her friend Carlotta, a young Ruby recalled a vacation spent with my father and his family on Long Island: "Did you get my card from Nassau where I spent a whoopin' good time with Stanley under the guard and guidance of his whole family?"[3]

But then a Shakespearean tragicomedy unfolded in which my father's desire to marry Ruby was thwarted by his sister's untimely love affair and a chance encounter with my mother.

My aunt Ruth graduated magna cum laude from Hunter College in New York City in 1931, and after graduation she fell in love with a man whom she was determined to marry. My grandfather, who would have no such fate befall his brilliant young daughter, reckoned her lovesickness an insanity and committed her to Rockland State Hospital, an institution for the mentally ill. After suffering through rounds of electroshock therapy and high doses of antipsychotic medication, Ruth actually did become mentally ill and remained in Rockland State Hospital for most of her life.

In the early 1940s, mental illness stigmatized a family, predisposing all members and their offspring, the reasoning went, to a similar condition. Even if children refused to accept this diagnosis, parents often stepped in to seal their children's fate. Whether my grandparents, or Ruby's parents, objected to the union, or whether my father was simply embarrassed by his sister's plight, I do not know. But he never married Ruby. She went on to marry the blues singer Frankie Dee Brown in 1941, divorced him in 1945, and then married a dashing young actor named Ossie Davis, with whom she remained for the rest of her life.

My father first saw my mother on a subway heading into Manhattan from the Bronx, while he rode to his job at IBM and she to school at Hunter College, where both Ruth and Ruby had also graduated. Though they lived just around the corner from each other, my parents had not met before. My father came home to say he'd just seen his next girlfriend. My mother, determined to finish her degree, came home to say she'd seen a man on the subway whose stare frightened her to death. Apparently, she got over my father's stare, and he found someone new to row around the Central Park lake.

My father then told of riding a double-decker bus with my mother. Just at the moment he leaned in to ask for another date, the bus hit a bump, obscuring the end of his sentence, which began "Will you . . ." When my mother replied, "Yes, I will marry you," he felt duty bound to comply. My mother told a similar story, only, in her telling, it happened on the subway, when the train's wheels screeched around a curve, obliterating my father's words. At any rate, they married on December 23, 1950, two years after Ruby married Ossie Davis.

Now on life's stage are two wedded couples with a mélange of emotions between them. My father never got over Ruby. What Ruby felt for my father I can only infer from what she wrote in her auto-biography. My mother remained cool to Ruby, as did Ossie toward my father. In their joint autobiography, Ruby and Ossie both freely admit to having an open relationship in the early part of their marriage:

> *It occurred to us, from observation and from reasoning, that extramarital sex was not what really destroyed marriages, but rather the lies and deception that invariably accompanied it— that was the culprit. So we decided to give ourselves permission to sleep with other partners if we wished—as long as what we did was honest as well as private and that neither of us ex-posed the family to scandal or disease.*[4]

This period did not last long, but Ruby also wrote of Ossie's later bringing up my father in a fight that erupted between them. Ossie asked her if she wanted a divorce and said, "You know what? Maybe you should have married Stanley."

To which Ruby replied indignantly, "What made you bring up Stanley? I never loved Stanley, and you know it. What's Stanley got to do with you and me?"[5]

When I asked my father for more insight into his relationship with Ruby, he told me he would take those details to his grave. When I asked Ruby, she simply let go an alluring, husky laugh. Through-out his life, my father periodically visited Ruby at her New Rochelle home.

An arranged marriage is the best way to understand my parents' relationship, but it was not arranged in the traditional sense of two families brokering a deal regarding their children. My father's marriage proposal, while comedic if not bordering on the absurd, came at a time when both he and my mother felt the pressure of prevailing social customs and conventions, especially for upwardly mobile Blacks.

My mother was the first in her family to advance beyond high school. She received her master's in education from Hunter. She spoke fluent German and Spanish and ultimately received her doctorate from the University of California at Berkeley, after time at Heidelberg University, for a thesis on the relationship between music, reading, and mathematics. My father graduated from City College, and not to be outdone by my mother, he got his master's in business administration from New York University while working at IBM. Both my parents were uncommon, highly educated, intelligent people, though not immune to common human temptations.

During the early years of their marriage, each of them had paramours. My mother blamed her dalliances on the lack of attention she received from my father. My father blamed this lack of attention on his need to work twice as hard as a White man to maintain his position at IBM, while fighting off the attempts of managers and coworkers to engineer his failure. I believe they both suffered from AMS (arranged marriage syndrome), characterized by love that grows based on mutual respect, admiration, and shared support of each other's life goals, yet lacks an essential passionate spark.

"It surprised me how inexperienced your mother was." My father grinned, winked, nodded. "Know what I mean?" He winked again.

But my mother told my sister, "Men expected to marry virgins. . . . And, oh, by the way, I simply faked it. Your father never knew the difference!"

Deceit and deception characterized their relationship from the very start.

Williamsbridge, where my parents grew up and where they lived when first married, is not far from Pelham Bay Park, which is home to Orchard Beach, otherwise known as the Bronx Riviera.

The mile-long, U-shaped Orchard Beach began as a marvelous illusion, created in the 1930s by dumping garbage, politely called landfill, to connect several islands off the Bronx coast to the mainland, and trucking in millions of cubic yards of sand from New Jersey and Queens. A majestic, curved pavilion housing thousands of lockers stood just before the faux beach.

As children, my sister and I often spent summer evenings at Orchard Beach with our mother, sometimes in the company of men clearly not our father. It surprised me, then, when one such humid summer evening my father showed up at the beach, having left IBM early, briefcase in hand, suit jacket slung over his shoulder, tie loosened, and shirt collar opened. A determined gaze set into his eyes. My sister and I licked the last of our ice cream sundaes from our spoons. Leonard Williams, who went by the name of Lonnie, a deacon at Trinity Baptist Church who shared our blanket, dropped his sundae as my father marched over. My mother, head down, licked an empty spoon.

My father threw down his briefcase in the sand before Lonnie, as though he were a knight laying down a gauntlet before another knight. Then both men faced off as if vying for the hand of a waiting dark queen. At seven years old, I could not fully comprehend the words that flew between them. I remember only that those words had something to do with my mother. Their heated argument grew to the point where I remember thinking, *Oh, no, this is going to become a fistfight.* Finally, Lonnie returned for a towel he had left on the blanket, before disappearing into the darkness that was then descending. My father stormed off to our car, informing my mother in no uncertain terms that it was time to go. Lonnie never went to Orchard Beach with us again.

On the other hand, a visit from Lena Rogers always seemed to set my mother in a tizzy. Drinking buddies? Smoking partners?

Lovers? Whatever the relationship between my father and Lena, my mother disliked her, even as my father welcomed "Cousin Lena" into our home. As a boy, I found Lena repulsive yet titillating. Whenever we met, she snuggled me between her breasts, holding me so tight I could hardly breathe. Her skin smelled of cigarette smoke and a cloying perfume. A whiff of alcohol floated on her breath. She had never married and had no children. I found it hard to believe that she worked only as a secretary during the day, when my father often visited her studio apartment at night.

My father told me that at one point he hired a private investigator to track my mother's infidelities, which ultimately led to a family friend who went by Chick instead of his real name. Even at ten years old, I could have saved my father the expense and effort. I already knew that my mother and Chick had something going on behind his back.

An engineer's mind, while made for computers and chess, is easily confounded by the irregularities of ordinary life. The simple fact of my father's precise daily routine in walking to a particular subway station on his way to IBM meant that he missed the obvious signs of my mother's affair with Chick. One express and two local elevated stations on the Pelham Bay line served our home along Hutchinson River Parkway. Every morning, my father walked to the station at Pelham Bay Park, at the end of the #6 line, for a guaranteed express ride and a seat on a commuter subway, which would soon be filled to overflowing as it headed into Manhattan. But the express passed by two local stations at Buhre Avenue and Middletown Road.

On my way to junior high school each morning, I had a choice: walk to the Pelham Bay Park train station and there catch a city bus to school, or ride the local train a few stations south and board a different city bus. Depending on the time, the subway-bus combination could be faster. Walking to the Buhre Avenue station presented more interesting options for meandering through neighborhood streets. For a straight shot to the subway, I walked to the Middletown Road station six blocks away. But walking to Middletown Road meant passing by the Hutchinson-Whitestone Motel.

A small, redbrick structure, dwarfed by surrounding apartment buildings and the elevated train superstructure behind it on West-chester Avenue, the Hutchinson-Whitestone Motel only accepts cash and offers themed rooms for use by the hour. When I walked by, I'd often find a pale blue late-model Cadillac with an elongated, slender body and rear fins parked in the motel's lot—a car with Virginia license plates that I knew well because I'd ridden in it more than once in New York City and in Newport News.

Chick was a man of short stature bearing an outsize name, driving an oversize car, and telling outlandish tales of flying P-51 Mustangs in the Army Air Corps. "Napoleonic complex" comes to mind when thinking of Chick, whose real name was Saint George Bruce Daye. Chick had parked his car in front of a dive where he'd rented a room, six blocks away from our apartment building. He hadn't come to visit my sister or me. He certainly hadn't come to visit my father. So even a child could put it together: Chick had come to visit my mother.

On the other hand, my father would occasionally appear at home with red lipstick stains that stood out against the white collar of his starched shirt. My mother would exclaim with glee that those stains told of my father's unfaithfulness.

This seesaw drama of deception and deceit teeter-tottered through our home. When my father vented his frustrations, fueled by disempowerment at work and dissatisfaction at home, my mother did not back down. Our home became a hotbed of conflict with few exceptions. My father did appreciate my mother's physical beauty.

Periodically, he'd return from work with a gorgeous dress that fit her perfectly, a sparkling jeweled necklace or bracelet, or a dazzling pair of earrings. Often these amazing gifts were tied to a raise or a minor promotion he'd received from IBM.

As classically trained pianists and vocalists, my parents performed flawlessly together. They shined under a spotlight of public adoration at IBM functions and elsewhere. Out of the public's eye, my parents fought bitterly, two distraught divas whose lives collided more often than not. The intensity of their verbal, emotional, and intellectual battles I struggled to equate with love. I disliked the constant carping and prolonged bickering. Even as a child of nine or ten, I suggested more than once that they'd be better off apart than together. That suggestion brought an instant, unanimous rebuke: "We're staying together for you and your sister." They believed we were better off with two parents, even if those parents displayed such obvious animosity toward each other—until even that belief broke down.

In 1962, my mother flew to El Paso and walked across the border to Juárez for a quickie, as Mexican divorces were then called. She flew back the next day with the decree. My father fretted that the divorce filings depicted him as a "homo." He moved out of our apartment and into his own in the Yorkville neighborhood of Manhattan. After twice divorcing my father and engaging in a number of other relationships, my mother confirmed my long-held suspicions by finally marrying Chick and staying with him until the end of her life.

My father no longer lived with us, but I had a regular routine with him: bowling every Saturday morning and dinner at his apartment every other Tuesday evening. Bowling, like chess, brought out his competitive streak. He kept score meticulously and thoroughly enjoyed trouncing me, which I endured mainly because I got to spend time with him. But visiting his apartment on 83rd Street brought forth a side of him I had not seen before: a bachelor with a nice place in a great part of the city.

One Tuesday evening, while he made dinner, I sat in his living room carefully examining a glass ashtray from his coffee table. I held it up to the light, looking for fingerprints. I set it back down gently, then plucked two crushed cigarette butts from the ash. Both had ruby red lip marks. I held them closer. The lipstick appeared to be the same.

My father stepped from his small kitchen with two plates of hamburgers, mashed potatoes, and peas. He set the plates down next to the ashtray. I held up a butt in front of me as though offering it to him.

"Who smoked these?"

"A friend."

"Do I know her?"

"Why do you ask?"

"I'm curious."

"You're too young."

"Too young for what?"

"Too young to ask, or to handle the answer."

"Try me."

My father smirked. "It's an answer I'll have to take with me to my grave."

"Why?"

He said nothing more on the topic.

When we finished our meals, he scooped up our dishes. Before disappearing into his kitchen, he turned back. "Set up the chess board for a game."

I reached next to the couch for the wooden box that held the black and white pieces, and then turned back to pinch a crushed butt between two fingers and lift it to my nose. I could have sworn I sniffed a vague aroma of alcohol mixed with a cloying perfume, and that brought about sensations of being snuggled between "Cousin Lena's" breasts.

———

The summer before my parents' first divorce, we drove out to the IBM Country Club. Already a fractured family by then, our seven-by-seven-foot dark gray woolen beach blanket seemed far too small to contain us all. My parents sat at opposite corners with their feet in the sand, my father with his back to us. He scanned the White faces that passed by. Whenever he saw someone he knew, he leaped up.

"Let me introduce you to my family."

My mother rose, extending her hand, smiling. "Pleased to meet you. . . . Let me introduce you to our children."

My sister and I dutifully popped up, also smiling, representatives of "our race," though we did not know it then, for the last time at the IBM Country Club in Sands Point.

We did not go to another IBM Christmas party, though that did not lessen the tension of the holidays. Christmas became a war zone of presents, with my parents vying to see who could purchase the most. My mother would drive us to our father's apartment, where we would pack the back seat with so many wrapped gifts that she had trouble seeing out the rearview mirror. Then, once home, my mother would bring out her own pile of presents from a closet. Claudia and I would create stacks of presents side by side, each stack reaching toward the ceiling and dwarfing the Christmas tree. This yuletide warfare played out each year during their divorce. But what first seemed like a bonanza soon became a recognition for both Claudia and me that Christmas was not about us. Christmas was about our parents, who used presents to fight a proxy war and wanted us to believe those presents were proxies for their love. What my parents really taught me is that love cannot be purchased or wrapped in glittering paper, tied with ribbons, and adorned with bows.

Then, one Christmas, a lesser number of presents gave way to an even greater surprise: my father and mother had remarried.

"Why?" I asked.

"For you and your sister," they said.

"But it was better for me when you weren't together and fighting."

"That'll change this time."

Twice my parents entered into a relationship with each other that was arranged more by honor, duty, deceit, deception, and guilt than by love. Twice they could not bring themselves to admit that while they loved each other, they were not meant to be with each other. Twice their détente proved short-lived, yet this second time it was long enough for us to move out of New York City to a home in Rockland County and for my father to enter into a new phase of work with IBM and a new relationship with me.

Doing Small Things in a Great Way

On August 28, 1963, I scanned the small black-and-white television screen in my grandparents' living room for glimpses of my parents. A mellifluous baritone boomed, "I am happy to join with you today in what will go down in history as the greatest demonstration for freedom in the history of our nation."[1]

Eleven years old, I searched through the millions of Black faces lining the grassy mall in front of the Lincoln Memorial while I allowed Martin Luther King Jr.'s words to sear me deeply: "I have a dream that my four little children will one day live in a nation where they will not be judged by the color of their skin but by the content of their character. . . ."

I never saw my parents on television that day, but that did not arrest my pride at knowing they marched for something really big, for something really important; they were marching for me, they said upon leaving me behind with my grandparents.

I knew the horrors of Jim Crow, even as a child. A few summers before the March on Washington, we'd taken a Greyhound bus south to visit my mother's family in Virginia. At the Mason-Dixon Line in Maryland, we were forced to change to a bus marked "Coloreds Only" that waited behind the Maryland House, now a popular rest stop on I-95.

My father ushered Claudia and me onto the waiting bus, though he said little on the ride from Maryland to Newport News. I'd become so used to my father extolling the promises of a digital future that it stunned me to see him rendered impotent by the shackles of a draconian past. Newport News, a segregated city in the early 1960s, boasted barriers that Black people dared not cross—drinking fountains marked "Coloreds Only"; one swimming pool for Blacks, another for Whites; areas of the city where my family and only Blacks lived. I loved those steamy summer nights, swaying in a swing seat on my aunt's front porch, even as I feared the hatred swirling around us as thick as the humidity in the air.

After a few days in the city, we left Newport News for my maternal grandparents' ancestral home in rural Surry County, on the other side of the James River, even farther on the Black side of the racial divide. The White Bell family, who once held our family as slaves, still lived on property adjoining the shingle and clapboard house that my grandmother grew up in. That ramshackle home bordered the Blackwater Swamp, where cypress trees grew alongside mosquitoes, copperheads, and water moccasins. A sultry southern sullenness settled over my father that summer. He said little. Then, one day, a copperhead slithered into the dirt yard where I played. He grabbed a shovel and bludgeoned the snake, beating the serpent over and over, long after it lay dead.

———

My father covertly wanted me to know that to understand him, I would also have to understand the burdens he bore being Black in America and being the first Black systems engineer at IBM.

Writing in 1903, W. E. B. Du Bois succinctly captured the fundamental psychological burden of being Black in America, which he labeled "double-consciousness":

> *It is a peculiar sensation, this double-consciousness, this sense of always looking at one's self through the eyes of others, of measuring one's soul by the tape of a world that looks on in amused contempt and pity. One ever feels his two-ness, an American, a Negro; two souls, two thoughts, two unreconciled strivings; two warring ideals in one dark body, whose dogged strength alone keeps it from being torn asunder.*[2]

Double-consciousness lies at the heart of a basic question asked over and over again by members of racial minorities: Is what is happening to me because of who I am as a person, or who I am as a person of color? The question also lies at the heart of White privilege because, with Whites, it simply never has to be asked, for there is no double-consciousness. What pathology, then, arises when the soul's dogged strength alone cannot keep these warring ideals apart? What happens when that measuring tape of contempt turns inward as a yardstick by which one gauges oneself? It becomes the "internalized racism" that my father struggled with throughout his life.

My father enjoyed telling the story of taking White IBM colleagues on a walk down 125th Street in Harlem. Twentieth-century Harlem stood as a bastion of Black America, a neighborhood where few Whites dared to venture.

"I told them, 'Without me walking beside you, you would not

make it down this block alive.'" My father always capped this story with a self-assured laugh.

What a tortured self-identity my father possessed. Then again, shifting the theater from an all-White office downtown to an all-Black street uptown represented one of the few ways he could also experience a shift in the balance of power—from feeling disempowered while working at IBM, to feeling empowered while walking in Harlem.

———

In the early 1960s, Jim Crow still thrived not only in the South but also within IBM. The company, of course, tells a vastly different story, portraying IBM as an early leader in diversity, in an equal opportunity workforce, and in improved race relations in the United States. IBM's official story begins with Thomas J. Watson Sr. hiring Thomas J. Laster in 1946 as its first Black salesman. This official version skips Watson's hiring of my father as the first Black systems engineer less than a year later and moves directly to a seminal company document that has come to be known as "Policy Letter #4," written by Watson's son Thomas J. Watson Jr., then the company's president. His short correspondence to IBM management, issued on September 21, 1953, states:

> *The purpose of this letter is to restate for all of the supervisory personnel of the IBM Company the policy of this corporation regarding the hiring of personnel with specific reference to race, color, or creed. Under the American system, each of the citizens of this country has an equal right to live and work in America. It is the policy of this organization to hire people who have the personality, talent and background necessary to*

fill a given job, regardless of race, color or creed. If everyone in IBM who hires new employees will observe this rule, the corporation will obtain the type of people it requires, and at the same time we will be affording an equal opportunity to all in accordance with American tradition.[3]

The company touts plants in Kentucky and North Carolina as the first integrated workplaces south of the Mason-Dixon Line and offers Policy Letter #4 as the gold standard for equal opportunity hiring practices.

Recently, IBM has even gone a step further, claiming that in 1899 it "hired Richard MacGregor, IBM's first black employee, 10 years before the founding of NAACP and 36 years after the Emancipation Proclamation."[4] This assertion angers me. It's extremely misleading and borders on disingenuity. There was no IBM in 1899. The Computing Scale Company (CSC) hired MacGregor, twelve years before it was purchased along with three other companies to form the Computing-Tabulating-Recording Company (CTR). Twenty-five years after MacGregor was hired, Watson acceded to the helm of CTR, and only then did he change the company's name to IBM. IBM came into being in 1924, and Watson was never involved directly with CSC or its hiring practices. Nothing on the IBM website from which this assertion about MacGregor was taken describes how he was actually hired by CSC.

Here, IBM is more than willing to lay claim to the actions of a relatively insignificant predecessor company when it serves the purpose of establishing IBM as a leader in diversity and inclusion. But the company has been unwilling and unable to publicly take responsibility for the actions of Herman Hollerith's Tabulating Machine Company—one of the major companies purchased along with CSC to ultimately form IBM. Hollerith's business, as I discuss in the next chapter, paved the way for IBM to use its punch card technology in outright support of some of the worst atrocities of the twentieth century.

Thomas J. Watson died in 1956. My father, who throughout his life considered Watson to be a personal champion, did not get the opportunity to say goodbye.

Then came time for my father's big promotion.

By the late 1950s, my father had worked as a systems engineer for more than a decade. His promotion to systems engineering manager seemed a logical next step. My father's promotions often coincided with his performance reviews and pay raises. Anticipation loomed large in our house. First, my mother would take a late afternoon call from my father, alerting her of the good news. Not known for her cooking, she would still set about preparing a big meal. My father would arrive home around six to a hero's welcome, with flowers in hand for her. They'd meet at the front door and kiss. Then we'd all move to the kitchen, to gather for the good news of his promotion and pay raise.

Only this time, when my mother put down the telephone, she did not head for the kitchen. Later, when I peeked out the window, I saw my father walking down the hill toward our house with nothing but his briefcase in hand. He stepped quickly through the front door, mumbled "Good evening" to Claudia and me, pulled my mother into their bedroom, and shut the door. Muffled, angry voices seeped under the door and vibrated the wall between their bedroom and the kitchen. Afterward, my mother served a somber meal.

Midway through his meal, my father turned to Claudia and me. "I got a pay raise," he said. "But not a promotion."

"Is that good?" I asked.

He wobbled his hand. "Yes and no. Good because we have more money. Not so good because I didn't become a manager. I did get a new job."

"You still work for IBM?"

He and my mother laughed hard at my question. "I hope so."

"What's your new job?"

"Training the man who will become my manager."

To my father, the death of his hero stripped away his protection from the crueler impulses of the men who worked under Watson: men who, despite Policy Letter #4, were not ready for a Black man to become an IBM manager. Then chinks began to appear even in his hero's armor.

Think: A Biography of the Watsons and IBM[5] sat on my father's bookshelf alongside his other prized books. In this account of the company and its founder, author William Rodgers describes how National Cash Register (NCR, or the Cash) plucked Thomas J. Watson off a horse-drawn wooden wagon and launched his career as a ruthless salesman who employed strong-arm tactics to strip business away from competitors, to the delight of NCR founder John Henry Patterson. "We do not buy out, we knock out," said Patterson,[6] and Watson soon became head of Patterson's squad of top secret "knock-out men."[7]

Watson began work with the Cash from the company's office in Rochester, New York. In 1903, Patterson sent the relatively unknown Watson to New York City with a budget of $1 million and a charge of setting up a fictitious business, Watson's Cash Register and Second-Hand Exchange. Watson's new company had only one mission: to decimate the competition from cash register companies across the country. So secretive was Watson's mission that other NCR dealers in the area were not informed.

Watson learned the secondhand cash register business, set up his company near others, dramatically undersold competitors, intimidated their customers, and did everything he could to disrupt their business. One by one the competitors fell, either going out of business or selling out to Watson under ironclad, noncompete clauses. Watson had no need to make a profit; he only needed to knock NCR's competitors out of business. It took several years, but he succeeded. Then he took his fictitious company and moved on, with Patterson's blessings, to do the same in Chicago.[8]

In Chicago, Amos Thomas and his cash register company represented one of Watson's biggest prey. Watson set up a second fake company near Thomas, whom he would badger three or four times a day to sell. By now the Cash didn't care whether Thomas knew Watson's real intentions, so NCR invited Thomas to an executive dinner at company headquarters in Dayton, Ohio, where they first feted him and them threatened him: if he didn't sell, NCR would continue to open new stores close to his, underselling cash registers until Thomas no longer had any business. Watson and the Cash brought Thomas to his knees, and even as Thomas agreed to sell, Watson squeezed him further to obtain the best price.[9]

Patterson hired an extensive sales force, incentivized them well but demanded their loyalty, required strict adherence to a dress code of dark suits, paid them on commission, and instituted a 100 Percent Club for those who achieved their tough quotas—all policies that Watson would establish at IBM.

NCR's monopoly through predation did not go unnoticed or unchallenged. In early 1913, after a Department of Justice antitrust investigation, an Ohio jury convicted Patterson and twenty-seven other NCR executives, including Watson, and the judge sentenced them to jail. Watson remained defiant and unbowed, even as other defendants pleaded for leniency.[10]

Then massive floods hit Ohio in 1913. Watson and NCR pounced. Watson spearheaded a massive relief effort to help ninety thousand victims. NCR produced rowboats instead of registers. Water, food, and sleeping cots were given away. From his offices in New York, Watson organized a train to carry medical and relief supplies to Ohio. When that train hit a broken stretch of track, Watson simply hired local men to carry the supplies on their backs. Watson helped transform a disaster into a humanitarian success and a public-relations windfall. Evangeline Cory Booth, leader of the Salvation Army, anointed Patterson an "instrument of the Lord."[11] The efforts of Patterson and Watson were lauded in the press and by the public. Letters appealing for clemency reached the desk of President Woodrow Wilson, and in 1915 the Sixth Circuit Court of Appeals reversed the lower court's decision. Watson never served a day in jail.[12]

So, if Watson was capable of benefiting from the suffering of those hit by disaster, what was he capable of regarding my father?

———

My father hid stress well. But by the early 1960s, the stress of being the first Black systems engineer at IBM had taken its toll. He now smoked cigarettes, he stopped exercising, he played the piano less, he gained weight, and most of all, a tremor in his right hand became more pronounced. He told many that his tremor resulted from a combat injury, which may have garnered him sympathy but simply was not true: he never saw direct combat in the war.

His superior intelligence first placed him at a desk in England with the 339th Fighter Group of the US Army as a quartermaster in support of pilots flying bombing runs over Germany. Then he received a transfer to Officer Candidate School (OCS) at Fort Benning, Georgia, where a racist drill sergeant nearly caused him to wash out. After OCS, he was assigned to the famed 369th Infantry Regiment, known as the Harlem Hellfighters. He stopped in Seattle on his way to the Pacific Theater in 1945, when the United States dropped atomic bombs on Hiroshima and Nagasaki, ending the war.

My father's war record remained a sore point between him and his brother, Gene, who fought with the 369th as an infantryman in France. I'll always remember the German helmet that sat beside other war memorabilia in my uncle's cabinet. As I stared at the gaping bullet hole in it, my uncle would say, "It was either him or me."

My father's tremor interfered with his writing or signing his name. Under duress, his tremor increased to the point that he'd sometimes steady his right hand by grasping it with his left just to sign a check. Even then, his writing remained shaky. I often exploited this weakness. Whenever a teacher in grade school or junior high school required a parent's signature on a truant slip, a behavioral demerit, or some other document I did not want my parents to see, I'd place a pen in my left hand and sign my father's name. The shakiness of my writing mimicked his signature, and compared very well to anything a teacher already had on file.

Many medical tests showed no underlying neurological condition, such as Parkinson's, as the basis of my father's tremor. He alternated blaming his fate on the color of his skin and the existence of this tremor: He did not get a promotion to manager because of his tremor. He did not get an excellent performance review because of his tremor. His colleagues secretly made fun of him because of his tremor. I never heard him connect the two; never once heard him admit that the stress of being Black in a company where many despised him gave rise to levels of stress that exacerbated his tremor.

Yet I believe the origins of my father's tremor lie even deeper than the stress he endured while working at IBM. I'm convinced my father was born left-handed and forced to be right-handed. It fits with what I know about his tremor, his parents, and the latest scientific research on handedness.

Hold a cup or pencil in your outstretched arm. Wait a moment and watch the cup or pencil. It will begin to shake. Most of us have this subtle shaking, called a physiological tremor. Under stress, this normal physiological tremor can be amplified to become an abnormal essential tremor, which is very similar to stuttering but in the muscles of our limbs rather than our vocal cords. Both physiological and essential tremors are controlled by our nervous system and usually do not interfere with activities of daily life. My father's essential tremor, dramatically more pronounced than most, increased under stress but decreased when he engaged in activities he enjoyed. While writing software programs, his hand shook, but while playing the piano or the violin it did not. While signing a check, his hand shook, but while moving a chess piece it did not. While talking about the challenges he faced at work, his hand shook, but while driving it did not. During his time at IBM, he took medication and underwent hypnosis in a quest to banish this tremor. These treatments helped to some degree, though his tremor remained.

For my grandfather, a devout Baptist who once sought to be a preacher, my father's left-handedness would have signified the devil. He would have beaten it out of my father as though righteously called to an exorcism.

Scientific research shows that stress of all sorts amplifies and lengthens periods of essential tremors. Cigarette smoking, caffeine, anxiety, employment problems, financial problems, lack of sleep, changes between day and night, dehydration, and emotional stress (from forced handedness, for instance) are some of the many stressors that can exacerbate such tremors. Under periods of prolonged stress, essential tremors remain even after the stressor is removed, much like post-traumatic stress disorder.[13]

My father's tremors rippled through our family in hidden but often insidious ways. In principle, at the IBM Country Club at Sands Point, Long Island, men golfed with customers while their wives and children frolicked in the surf. Before the advent of modern freeways, Claudia and I would pile into our dark green 1954 Ford sedan with our parents for the winding trip from the Bronx through island towns to get to the club. As the first Black family to set foot on country club grounds,[14] we were placed under a microscope of withering scrutiny, forced to be on continuous display, and expected to behave with uncommon and unchildlike perfection. After all, as we heard so often from our parents, our family represented our race.

My father took this idea of representing his race seriously and passed that burden on to me. Of course, the very notion that one person, or one family, can represent a race is absurd, and certainly an impossible burden to bear, hence another factor contributing to his tremor. But when passed on to a child, this notion of representing one's race is also a malicious thief of childhood.

For one of their first outings to the IBM Country Club, my parents left my sister, Claudia, behind with my grandmother, while reluctantly bringing me along. At four, I wore a brand-new dark blue summer suit—shorts, a matching jacket, a white shirt, a bow tie, and a beanie hat. While walking the half block up the hill from our home to the garage where we kept our car, I tripped and fell, skinning my knee and getting dirt on my shorts. Ordinarily, my mother would have applied a Band-Aid, dusted off my shorts, warned me to be more careful, and sent me on my way. But this time, my father looked at me, frowned, and declared me unfit to accompany them. My cut, and that dirt, were my scarlet letter, a mark of imperfection and unfitness that day to represent my race. As I wailed, they returned me to join Claudia.

Even on a typical country club day, I stayed close to my parents, frozen with the fear of not being perfect enough, while watching the carefree play of other children. Then, toward the end of the day, my parents would allow me to wander off to the swings, only to watch other families hurriedly round up their children, leaving the entire row of swings to me. Alone, at the top of the swing's arc, I'd let go, slide off the metal seat, and for a few brief moments before my feet hit the grass, I'd shed the onus of perfection, shed the burden of representing my race, and sail through the air, just a child flying free.

Outings at the IBM Country Club on Long Island afforded such brief interludes of freedom, while the annual IBM Christmas party in New York City did not. Each year, my mother would slither into her girdle and slide into her dress, neither of which suited her body. My father donned his IBM uniform—dark suit, white shirt, tie. I wore my own matching, diminutive corporate outfit, while Claudia looked like a doll in a pink pastel dress, puffed out by a crinoline slip, and black patent leather shoes over white socks. My mother would press down her hair with multiple braids.

When we walked into an IBM Christmas party holding hands, the quintessential nuclear family of the 1950s, though in permanent "blackface," all eyes turned toward us. My father and mother were never as adoring or adorable than when in front of an IBM audience. An operatic baritone and a soprano, both accomplished pianists, they'd step to a piano, switching off who played and who sang, to offer unrehearsed programs that often began with Bach chorales but always ended with popular carols, while my sister and I looked on, smiling, from their flanks.

In support of my father's job, we impressed IBM as stalwart ambassadors of our race. Though not quite a minstrel show, it seemed clear to me, even then, that the Ford family's performance never ended, that we must always be onstage. This sense of a never-ending recital for our race no doubt augmented the stress behind my father's tremors. It may also have been one reason why, when my father placed Claudia on IBM Santa's lap, she howled in a way the rest of us never could.

———

While Martin Luther King's voice only crackled over my grandparents' television, it certainly resounded throughout the mall.

"In a sense we've come to our nation's capital to cash a check."[15]

His words surely struck unique chords in the lives of all who heard them that hot August day. My grandmother, a devout Christian, hummed a spiritual and filled King's brief pauses by whispering "Amen."

"It is obvious today that America has defaulted on this promissory note insofar as her citizens of color are concerned. . . ."

I know King's words resonated with my father.

"But we refuse to believe that the bank of justice is bankrupt. We refuse to believe that there are insufficient funds in the great vaults of opportunity of this nation. So we've come to cash this check . . ."

Like many men and women, mostly Black though many White, King's eloquence advanced the jittery needle of their determination to a point of no return. Many had not ridden buses into the Deep South during the summer of 1961. Many would not register voters in Mississippi during Freedom Summer of 1964. Many would not go to Selma to lock arms on Bloody Sunday in March 1965. Yet these many found ways—huge or humble, overtly or covertly, vocally or silently—to cash King's check.

After returning from the march, something inside of my father changed. Our family returned to Virginia that next summer, but this time we drove. On the trip home, we stopped at the Maryland House, where only a few years earlier we'd been forced to change buses heading south. We sat at the lunch counter, reading our menus, when behind the counter, a waitress walked over to inform us, "We don't serve Colored people here." She turned to walk away.

My mother looked across my sister and me to my father. She

whispered, "Stanley, now's the time to take a stand." She held her hand out in front of us. "Stay where you are," she said.

When we did not rise, the waitress returned.

She snarled. "Thought I told you we don't serve your kind."

My father snapped. "And we're not leaving until you do."

Our waitress disappeared into the kitchen. I looked up. Moments later, a man in a white shirt and tie, presumably a manager, pushed through the kitchen doors, a determined look on his reddened face. The waitress trailed him, smirking. I twisted around on my stool. The entire restaurant had grown silent as the other customers, all White, turned to follow the unfolding set of events.

"Don't look at other people," my mother scolded. "Turn around. Look at your menu."

But the manager must have felt the stares as well and perhaps paused to ponder the wisdom of alienating his White patrons, many of whom stopped here when heading north on their way home. By the time he reached us, the manager's determination had dissolved into an insincere, syrupy, southern smile.

"Hi, folks. What y'all having?" he asked.

After we made our selections from the menu, the waitress stormed off. We sat and waited, while behind us the buzz of conversation slowly returned. When the waitress finally appeared with our order, she slapped the plates down on the counter.

"Don't know what you people hope to accomplish," she hissed.

———

Back in New York City from the March on Washington in 1963, my father became a founding member of a new organization called 100 Black Men. The organization's name hearkened back to W. E. B. Du Bois's notion of the "talented tenth" among Black Americans, where one in ten were destined to be leaders. 100 Black Men boasted among its founders and later members prominent Black professionals, businessmen, civic and political leaders, and educators, such as Jackie Robinson, David Dinkins (the first Black mayor of New York), David Satcher (the first Black man to be US Surgeon General), Eric Holder (the first Black US Attorney General), and Cyril deGrasse Tyson (a social activist and the father of the astrophysicist Neil deGrasse Tyson).

100 Black Men, which has since grown to more than one hundred chapters and more than ten thousand members worldwide, has as its mission "to improve the quality of life within our communities and enhance educational and economic opportunities for all African Americans." A primary focus of the organization is to provide positive role models and leadership for young people, especially Black youth, as evidenced by the group's slogan, "What they see is what they'll be."

With King's words still fresh in his mind, with the goals of 100 Black Men newly in sight, and now with nearly sixteen years at a company where his advancement had been systematically thwarted, my father began to realize he was up against something much larger than he first anticipated. My father set in motion his own plan to bring about change at IBM.

11

Covert Ops

In the bottom drawer of his blond-wood dresser, beneath his boxer shorts and sleeveless undershirts, my father kept a stash of *Playboy* magazines. It must have been an open family secret. After all, my mother washed, hung, folded, and put away his laundry. Growing up, I found in the magazines, which changed each month, an endless source of excitement and titillation. I'd carefully replace them after spending time with the centerfolds and the women on adjoining pages. But I soon discovered that the large, gray, dog-eared envelope lying next to the *Playboys* contained much more risqué material.

Periodically, strange men would appear in our home. My father would insist that my sister and I find something else to do and somewhere else to be. He'd close the bedroom door. I'd hear him slide his bottom dresser drawer open, rummage through its contents, and then close the drawer. Then he would emerge cradling the large dog-eared envelope. He would sit with these men at our kitchen table, the envelope's contents spread out in front of them, and speak in hushed tones.

A month or two later, my father would announce with great surprise that so-and-so had just been hired by IBM, one of the few Blacks smart enough to pass the IBM entrance examination. During subsequent visits to my father's bottom dresser drawer, I inspected the contents of that dog-eared envelope. It contained copies of both the questions and the answers to that storied exam.

Exactly how this information came into my father's possession remained a secret throughout his life. For fear of letting on that I'd thumbed through his *Playboy*s, I too kept his secret. Knowing that my father risked his career for the sake of others elevated him in my eyes. Then came time for me to take the IBM entrance exam and to receive my certain inheritance from that dresser drawer. But when I would have most expected his assistance, that dog-eared envelope suddenly disappeared, even though the *Playboy*s remained. My father would not help me. He denied any knowledge of secret copies of the IBM entrance exam.

I passed my IBM entrance examination, but I never found out my exact score. My father did, and although he never revealed it to me, he reported with glee that, years earlier, he had scored higher on his examination.

Not long after taking the entrance exam, I had a meeting at an IBM office on Wall Street with a man who would ultimately become my manager.

"You'll start next week," Art Conrad said.

"I can't."

"What do you mean? I just offered you a position with the company."

"And I just graduated from college last week. I'm intending to work the same job over the summer that I've worked for the past several summers."

Art took a deep breath. An awkward silence balanced between us.

"I'll start the day after Labor Day," I said.

"It's not what I intended," Art said.

"I'm sorry," I said. "It's what I need to do."

My father could well have been in that room with us, because by the time I got to our home in Rockland County, he grilled me.

"Whaddya mean, you turned down Art's offer of when to start?"

"I have something I need to do."

"What could be more important than starting your career?"

"Working at Project Double Discovery one last summer."

———

Project Double Discovery, PDD as we called it, identified inner-city Black kids who failed or flunked out of high school and gave them a second chance. I taught mathematics at PDD, and the kids in my class were a challenge I eagerly awaited.

With a cue stick in hand, I started that summer's geometry class on a pool table. Begrudgingly at first, the students, most of whom far surpassed my skill at pool, had fun learning about supplementary angles from pool balls careening off the felt sides of the pool table and about the similar and congruent triangles in play when banking one ball so that it hit a side wall and then struck another.

Things got a bit testy, however, when it came time to learn about geometric proofs and I handed out copies of *The Autobiography of Malcolm X*.[1]

One young girl shouted, "What you got us reading this for?"

"Ain't geometry," another said. "It's politics."

"Don't think Malcolm ever took geometry," someone blurted out.

The class chuckled.

"But he damn sure knew how to prove a point," I said.

The class grew silent.

"And that's what geometric proofs are all about."

We took apart passages from Malcolm's book. We defined terms like definitions, axioms, postulates, and previously proved theorems. We argued over how these should be applied to Malcolm's statements. Then I set the class up as a court. A group of students (the prosecuting attorneys) had to prove the truth of a case to a jury (the remainder of the class), as I sat as the judge. The students really got into it. The court's first cases came from Malcolm's book and the concepts and ideas he presented. The next set of cases came from anything in the real lives of the students. By the time we came around to the third set of cases, actual geometric proofs—like proving two triangles were similar—the students offered a different set of comments on the class.

"This all there is to geometric proofs?"

"Why didn't they teach me this in school?"

"Malcolm may not have taken geometry, but I bet he'd be pretty good at it."

By this time, the students had grown accustomed to my classroom antics. So when I walked into class one morning with plywood, nails, rubber bands, rulers, hammers, and saws, they were more curious than suspicious. We cut plywood squares, measured and penciled symmetrical lattices onto the plywood, and partially hammered in nails where the lines of the lattices crossed, creating what are called "geoboards." Then we stretched rubber bands around the nails to create various geometric shapes and used the boards to better understand the properties of those shapes.

Now it was my turn to be surprised.

A young man named Victor, who'd sat quietly through much of the summer, approached me after class and said softly, "Mr. Ford, I think I understand what you're getting at, and I wonder if I could try teaching some of the remaining classes."

So, for the remainder of that summer, I coached Victor on what

I felt the class needed to accomplish, and I took a seat in the front row to watch him teach.

From the bottom of my father's dresser, I learned the value of reaching out to help others. And with the help of my mother, herself a master teacher, I found one way to accomplish that over several summers working with PDD.

While I wish I could also have been a beneficiary of my father's copies of IBM's entrance examinations—and it hurt that I was not—I also understand the importance of his actions. For years, my father ran an underground railroad within IBM that provided promising young Black men and women a pathway into the company by offering them a first look at the keys to the realm. His covert operation, which began after he returned from the March on Washington, would have been inconceivable just a few years earlier, owing to his unshakable faith in Thomas J. Watson and his unquestioning allegiance to Watson's company. But my father had watched his career falter in the face of a company unwilling to admit Blacks to the higher echelons of corporate power. His faith in Watson's legacy had foundered. His unquestioning allegiance to IBM had frayed. Ever the chess master, my father sought other ways of advancing his pieces. Though he might not get there himself, he could provide a way so other Black men and women might reach the top ranks of IBM.

———

"I don't know why," my father said. He raised his cane briefly to shrug both shoulders.

"C'mon, Dad," I said. "You don't have any suspicions about why Watson hired you?"

"You asked what I know, not what I suspect."

We stopped walking. My father rested both hands on his cane.

He grimaced, pushing himself up against the ankylosing spondylitis that was relentlessly, insidiously, pulling him down.

"Okay, I'll bite," I said. "Whaddya suspect?"

He took a deep breath. We both looked across the Hudson, where a red-orange July sunset lit thousands of tiny flames in the windows of the Riverdale buildings and homes on the other side of the mighty river. My father spoke as though addressing someone else on the far side of this great divide. His words were measured, slow.

"I suspect IBM needed a Blackie."

"But they already had one. T. J. Laster was hired six or eight months before you."

He bristled. His body stiffened. "He was in sales. I was in systems engineering."

"Okay, but why you? Why'd Watson hire you?"

My father paused, and a long silence enveloped us. He turned away from the vista over the Hudson to put a hand on my shoulder.

"I'm tired," he said. "Let's sit."

We walked to a nearby picnic table, where I swung into a seat. My father turned back toward the Hudson, then, leaning on his cane, slowly lowered himself onto the bench. He tucked his legs under the table, finally turning to face me. A sly smile creased his lips.

"I ever tell you about the time they sent me to a business meeting which turned out to be a meeting with a prostitute?"

His self-knowing chuckle reassured me that he'd reveal nothing more about Watson. My father's fondness for secrecy resembled that of IBM's.

IBM's secret history began in the 1920s, not long after my father's birth but certainly well before he had any inkling of his coming entanglement with the company. It began at a time when eugenics was all the rage.

Eugenics flourished in America at the beginning of the twentieth century. This so-called science of race brought together America's rich and famous—Carnegies, Rockefellers, Kelloggs, Harrimans, Roosevelts—in a movement to breed pure blond-haired, blue-eyed "Nordic stock," the eugenicists' sought-after ideal. Eugenicists desired to eliminate the bloodlines of undesirables such as Blacks, Native Americans, Hispanics, Jews, Irish, and the mentally or physically ill.

Eugenics promoted thinly veiled racism under the guise of pseudoscience. Alexander Graham Bell, for instance, served on the board of the Eugenics Record Organization (ERO), which was established by the Carnegie Institute in Cold Spring Harbor, New York.[2] ERO sought to collect data and conduct studies on the means to enhance Nordic race supremacy in the United States and to reduce "human flotsam," as Madison Grant, bestselling author of *The Passing of the Great Race*, called those deemed undesirable by eugenicists.[3] Even the famed women's rights activist Margaret Sanger embraced eugenics. She viewed her work in promoting birth control and women's health as part of a broader eugenics movement to exterminate "human weeds."[4]

Eugenicists proposed several tools to cull America of undesirable human beings: sterilization, birth control, incarceration, miscegenation laws, immigration restrictions, and even death. In the early 1900s, as many as thirty states had passed eugenics laws that allowed forced sterilization or that restricted marriage between individuals of different races. The 1927 Supreme Court decision in *Buck v. Bell* upheld forced sterilization for individuals deemed "unfit" by the state. Writing for the court's eight-to-one decision against Carrie Buck, a teenager from a poor White family in Virginia, Justice Oliver Wendell Holmes issued this harsh decree:

> *It is better for all the world, if instead of waiting to execute degenerate off-spring for a crime, or to let them starve for their imbecility, society can prevent those who are manifestly unfit*

from continuing their kind. . . . Three generations of imbeciles are enough.[5]

Eugenicists worldwide delighted. Never expressly overturned by the Supreme Court, *Buck v. Bell* was cited by Justice Harry Blackmun in *Roe v. Wade* as established law limiting the rights of women to control the fate of their bodies.[6]

American eugenicists, led by Dr. Charles Davenport, elevated their movement internationally with the help of prominent eugenicists in Germany. Davenport felt that the accomplishments in the United States could be duplicated throughout the world. But this required the identification of undesirable humans, particularly those polluted through mixed-race ancestry. In 1926, Davenport, head of the Eugenics Research Association, an outgrowth of the Eugenics Record Organization, which he also headed, received funding for a two-year study of "pure-blooded negroes,"[7] Whites, and their undesirable mixed-race offspring. In 1928, Davenport chose the island of Jamaica for the study.

Enter Thomas J. Watson and IBM.

To identify mixed-race individuals in Jamaica, Davenport required a robust system of collecting, storing, and analyzing copious amounts of information. IBM's punch cards and Hollerith machines provided just what Davenport needed. With Watson's newly minted company eager for the business, IBM engineers worked with the ERO at the Cold Spring Harbor Laboratory to design a punch card format for collecting all the information needed to report on racial characteristics. Watson's engineers also worked out the details of adjusting the various sorters, tabulators, and printers to provide Davenport and the ERO with the output they required.

Thanks to IBM's assistance, the success of the Jamaica Project allowed the Cold Spring Harbor Laboratory, and Davenport, to announce plans for a global study to identify mixed-race individuals as a first step toward their elimination in favor of "racially pure stock."[8]

In a tragic coda to this early story of eugenics, Cold Spring Harbor Laboratory was still enmeshed in the controversy over eugenics as recently as January 2019, this time through the disgraceful racist utterances of Nobel laureate James D. Watson, cofounder of the DNA double helix and one of the laboratory's longtime fellows, whom they stripped of his honorary titles.[9]

My father came of age when talk of "racial purity" was everywhere. Red Summer, when Whites attacked Blacks in more than three dozen cities across the country, happened within months of his birth in August 1919. Throughout the 1920s, newspapers ran accounts of the latest so-called advancements in racial science and featured cartoons demonizing Blacks and other "racially impure" groups. Lynchings reigned across the South. As the darkest child in his family, it's not surprising that my father entered into adulthood with a deep-seated belief in his own inferiority.

By the end of the 1920s, IBM's involvement in advancing racial purity had only just begun. Thomas J. Watson understood the power of harnessing information technology in the service of racial purity. Five years after his involvement with the Jamaica Project, he placed IBM in the service of Adolf Hitler and the Third Reich, using the lessons learned in creating Davenport's racial identification system to help Hitler identify and exterminate Jews. The IBM punch card templates for the Jamaica Project on miscegenation and for Nazi Germany's campaign against the Jews bore a striking resemblance.[10]

Thomas J. Watson hired my father less than two years after the end of World War II, two years after he had finally recouped the extensive profits his company made in support of Hitler and the Third Reich. These are facts that IBM refuses to admit, secrets that the company would prefer forever remain hidden.[11] From 1933 to 1945, prior to and during World War II, Watson and IBM worked tirelessly to help Germany automate every aspect of Hitler's dictatorship— from counting livestock for food, to planning troop movement for war, to counting Jews prior to their extermination.[12]

IBM machines identified and counted Jews, traced back their ancestry for generations, marked them for transport to concentration camps, managed the railroads that transported them there, kept track of which Jews were killed and which remained alive, identified which Jews possessed what skills and helped Nazis allocate them for slave labor, monitored the health and fitness of Jews for barbaric medical experiments or being worked to death, kept records of the torture and execution of Jews in all concentration camps, kept track of all German soldiers, planned German tank and troop movements against the Allies, and scheduled Luftwaffe bombing runs.[13]

These were not IBM machines bought by the Germans and then employed for nefarious purposes. IBM never sold machines to the Third Reich; they leased them through a German subsidiary micro-managed by Thomas J. Watson and his team directly from New York. IBM engineers designed custom solutions for the Nazis to assist them in handling their "Jewish problem." IBM supplied and trained Nazi operators on their equipment. IBM authorized German and European subsidiaries to manufacture equipment and spare parts. And IBM kept all of their equipment in the Third Reich in good working order. When Germany invaded Czechoslovakia and other European countries, IBM pre-positioned equipment, solutions, and personnel, willingly offering service to occupying Nazi forces. All business with Hitler's Germany took place at market rates that afforded IBM "fantastical" profits.[14]

In recognition of Watson's extraordinary importance to Nazi Germany, in 1937 Hitler created the Merit Cross of the German Eagle with Star, festooned with swastikas, which he pinned on

Watson. Then, in 1940, shortly before America entered the war, Watson returned the medal to bolster his public image, an action that Watson's apologizers have pointed to as evidence of his redemption. But it was a duplicitous public-relations ploy at best. Edwin Black points out, in his extensively researched, well-documented, and peer-reviewed book *IBM and the Holocaust*, that "a subsequent letter dated June 10, 1941, drafted by IBM's New York office, confirms that IBM headquarters personally directed the activities of its Dutch subsidiary set up in 1940 to identify and liquidate the Jews of Holland."[15]

Before America entered the war, Watson planned the construction of bomb shelters in Germany to protect IBM equipment.[16] During the war, IBM's widespread business with the Third Reich went into receivership, operated by a German national to whom orders from IBM's New York office were relayed through neutral IBM European headquarters in places like Switzerland. The German receiver ran the IBM business, charged the Third Reich applicable lease rates for IBM equipment, and deposited payments in frozen German bank accounts.[17] When the war ended, IBM leapfrogged to the head of the line of corporations seeking to reclaim assets in Germany, bypassed Allied regulations on war reparations, and obtained a tidy fortune.[18]

Even while Watson supplied Nazi Germany with the automated equipment to make the extermination of Jews more successful and more efficient, when America entered World War II, he supported the war effort. Watson founded factories that made munitions and supplied the US military with advanced IBM equipment. Without IBM machines, for example, Alan Turing could not have built the Enigma machine that broke the German code. Watson was the consummate "war profiteer." It did not matter so much what side he assisted as long as IBM's equipment remained in use and IBM's profits kept rolling in.

"How did they know?" It's a persistent question raised by Holocaust scholars. How did Nazi troopers know exactly where Jews lived—their names, their ages, their addresses? How did the Nazis know who was Jewish and who was not, given the many Catholic conversions, name changes, and nonobservant Jews? How did the Nazis know that they could place Jews on a train car and that, within an hour of reaching their destination, those Jews would be marched to a gas chamber or in front of a firing squad, so the train could be quickly reused?

They knew because IBM's technology helped them know. And IBM technology could help the Nazis know because of the information encoded in punch cards. Herman Hollerith's genius lay in engineering a means for punch card holes to represent desired properties. IBM engineers helped Nazi Germany encode every aspect of people's lives—their names, their dates of birth, their addresses, and especially their religions. All Germans were assigned identification numbers. Those numbers were correlated with punch cards. Those punch cards, collected and compiled by the millions, held critical information on German citizens. A Jew's identification number might be punched into columns 75 through 80, and a corresponding number tattooed on his or her body.[19]

Every concentration camp had a room with a door marked *Arbeitseinsatz* (labor supply office) that was filled with IBM Hollerith equipment and punch cards with data on every prisoner in the camp. Thousands of Hollerith machines were located throughout Nazi Germany, placed there under the watchful eye of Watson and IBM. Hollerith equipment required punch cards—millions upon millions of them, created to exacting specifications. By patent and by design, only IBM could create, print, and sell punch cards for its Hollerith machines. So IBM made and shipped cards, and authorized its European subsidiaries to create factories to do the same, to satisfy the Nazi bloodthirst for 1.5 billion punch cards per year.[20]

The Third Reich collected population information on all who came under its control. Massive keypunch operations were established to enter collected data onto punch cards. At one point, IBM's Nazi German subsidiary demanded a daily quota of 450,000 punch cards from its several hundred employees working on behalf of the Third Reich.[21] Once cards were punched, they would be bundled and stored by the millions. Many years before the term *big data* was first used, Nazi Germany—with IBM's assistance—stored massive amounts of data it collected on its citizenry.

Want to find all Jews between certain ages? Drop a deck of punch cards into the hopper of an IBM Hollerith machine, sort cards based on the column and row punched for religion, and then sort on the column and row punched for age. Associate identification numbers with names and street addresses. Sort and print a list. Then send out the gestapo to round up everyone on the list for transport to concentration camps. Thanks to IBM, it became just that simple. Here was one of the earliest uses of modern digital technology to identify, suppress, and even exterminate people deemed undesirable by politicians in power.

IBM's role flew under the radar. At the time when Watson changed CTR's name to IBM, the company encompassed all of Herman Hollerith's overseas licensees, including Deutsch Hollerith Maschinen Gesellschaft—the German Hollerith Machine Company— or Dehomag, for short, which leased Hollerith equipment for use in Germany. It was Dehomag that helped automate the German census of 1933, allowing IBM both distance and plausible deniability, even though that same year, IBM, under Watson, squeezed Dehomag into selling Watson a personal 90 percent share of the company. It's hard not to equate Watson's role here with his many years spent at the Cash as its principal "knock-out man." Watson ran Dehomag with an iron grip from his offices in New York.[22]

IBM's Hollerith business benefited from improvements to its machines made by German engineers. IBM also signed manufacturing agreements enabling their Hollerith machines to be constructed in Germany. By the early 1930s, more than half of IBM's overseas revenue came from the Third Reich through Dehomag.[23]

When Hitler rose to power in 1933, many American corporations faced the soul-searching question of whether to do business with Nazi Germany and risk economic or political retaliation from an American public that mainly found Hitler's Germany repulsive. Everyone recognized corporate names such as Ford and General Motors—their international impact by the 1930s was unmistakable. But few knew the extent of IBM's international operations. Fewer still knew the name Dehomag, IBM's German subsidiary run by Willy Heidinger. While the power of automotive technology rolled along clearly and understandably, the power of punch cards and digital technology remained hidden. Watson and his company had the perfect cover, as Edwin Black writes:

> *The storyline depended upon the circumstance and the listener. Dehomag could be portrayed as the American-controlled, almost wholly-owned subsidiary of IBM with token German shareholders and on-site German managers. Or Dehomag could be a loyal German, staunchly Aryan company baptized in the blood of Nazi ideology wielding the power of its American investment for the greater glory of Hitler's Reich. Indeed, Heidinger and Watson both were willing to wave either banner as needed. Both stories were true. Watson had seen to that.*[24]

Through Dehomag, Watson orchestrated IBM's support of the Nazi's Jewish pogrom and, once Germany invaded its neighbors, the extensive Nazi war machine. IBM engineers in America, working with their German counterparts, designed the punch card formats used by the Third Reich to collect data; adjusted the sensitive Hollerith equipment to correctly read, tabulate, and print out information from the cards; trained Dehomag and Third Reich employees in the use of the Hollerith equipment; and maintained and repaired Hollerith machines to keep them in good working order. Before America entered World War II, Watson made certain that IBM received payment for leases of the Hollerith equipment. During the war, Watson made certain that IBM equipment and other assets were managed profitably by a Nazi receiver. And after the war, Watson made certain that IBM extracted its substantial profits from Germany and a war-ravaged Europe.

As the Nazi war machine ramped up for battle in Europe and for the extermination of the Jews, Watson and IBM never once backed down. In fact, just the opposite was true. In the fall of 1935, the Reichstag (the German parliament) unanimously passed two laws: one to deprive Jews of their German citizenship (Law of the Reich Citizen), the other to prohibit intermarriage and sexual relationships between Germans and Jews (Law for the Protection of German Blood and German Honor). Shortly after the passage of the Nuremberg Laws and after detailed decree by the Third Reich defining who would be considered a Jew and who not, Watson traveled to Berlin to celebrate the twenty-fifth anniversary of IBM's German subsidiary.

Even as Joseph Goebbels warned Jews to leave Germany to the Germans, Watson attended a lavish dinner at the Hotel Adlon in Berlin, where he celebrated IBM's German success. Afterward, Watson expanded IBM's presence in Nazi Germany, through its German subsidiary, ordering crates of new equipment to be shipped to Berlin, ordering millions of punch cards from the United States until German factories could produce their own, and building new German manufacturing facilities to produce spare parts for IBM machines.

———

IBM's deep involvement in the Holocaust began with *der Führer's* need to count.

Out of a German population of 67 million, Dehomag's automated 1933 census tabulated only a half million Jews, or less than 1 percent of the population. Where were the others, the Third Reich demanded to know? Had they changed their faith or left it? Had Jews infiltrated the fabric of German social and cultural life so deeply that they now infected the country as a whole? Nazi *Statisker der Rasse* (race statisticians) devised bizarre, pseudo-mathematical formulas grading Jews by the supposed amount of Jewish ancestry in their blood: fully Jewish, half Jewish, quarter Jewish, and so forth. In this way, these German raciologists stole a page directly from the hideous playbook of American slavery, where slaves were classified based on the amount of African ancestry: mulatto (one-half), quadroon (one-quarter), octoroon (one-eighth), and so on.

Divorce, remarriage, adoption, and children born out of wedlock were just a few of the messy human truths that render such racial classifications null and void. But these annoying facts did not dampen the Third Reich's enthusiasm. Determining Aryan purity became something of a national German pastime, with companies, schools, associations, local police departments, and even churches compiling data and creating lists. As this data worked its way up through a proliferation of Nazi race agencies, it ultimately landed in bureaus like the Reich Statistical Office. There, German clerks entered population data onto IBM punch cards, which were later read, sorted, and tabulated by the office's vast array of IBM Hollerith machines. And these machines were, of course, configured, leased, upgraded, and maintained by IBM's German subsidiary, Dehomag.

Hitler rebooted eugenics. Armed with statistical data courtesy of IBM equipment and engineers, Nazis went in pursuit of a master Aryan race: tall, strong, blond-haired, blue-eyed, intellectually and physically superior. Sterilization came first, to weed out Jews, the physically undesirable (those with mental or physical illnesses and infirmities deemed unacceptable), and the socially undesirable (homosexuals, pedophiles, Romanies, those who came into repeated conflict with the government). With data collected from medical offices, insurance companies, and employers, Dehomag created a punch card schema to record information about physical, mental, and social traits of German citizens in addition to the information already on file about who was, and who was not, a Jew. If an agency did not have access to punch card machines, Dehomag took their raw data and created punch cards for them. In 1934, Germany performed 62,400 forced sterilizations based on this punch card data. By 1935 that number rose to 71,700.

Ultimately, Nazi race scientists decided that the information available from IBM punch cards should be the basis of a more permanent solution—not merely determining who should undergo sterilization, but who should live.[25]

In one particularly gruesome method of achieving the *endziel* (final goal), Nazis organized Jews in occupied territories into councils responsible for their own extermination. Threatening summary execution, Nazis demanded these councils create census counts and punch card records of their own members, and these were used to identify which Jews would be sent to the gas chambers and ovens and which would be sent to labor camps and worked to death. In Poland, the councils were called *jüdenrate* (Jewish council); in Vichy France, the *Union Generale des Israelites de France* (the Union of French Jews, or UGIF). Through refusal to cooperate, hangings, and even mass poisonings, members of some *jüdenraten* willingly committed suicide instead of collaborating to ship others off to certain death.

In Vichy France, the Nazis tasked IBM Hollerith expert René Carmille with the collection and punching of census data on French Jews. But Carmille, a dashing figure sporting horn-rimmed glasses and a bow tie, hacked his own punch card equipment so it would not punch anything in column 11, which captured religion. Then he turned his punch cards and Hollerith machines to the task of swiftly organizing French elements in Algeria into a fighting force under the command of Charles de Gaulle, surprising the Nazis and driving them from North Africa. Ultimately, German intelligence discovered that Carmille belonged not to Vichy France but to the Marco Polo Network, a famed French resistance group. Klaus Barbie, the infamous "Butcher of Lyon," tried but failed to break Carmille in interrogation. Shortly after, René Carmille, the Hollerith hero, died upon being shipped to Dachau.[26] Carmille may have been one of the first computer "white hat hackers," an ethical hacker operating for the common good.

For Watson, the ultimate capitalist, Nazi Germany posed no ethical or moral dilemma. Black writes:

In 1935, while the world shook at a rearmed Germany speeding toward a war of European conquest and total Jewish destruction, one man saw not revulsion, but opportunity—not horror and devastation, but profit and dividends. Thomas Watson and IBM indeed accelerated their breakneck alliance with Nazism. Now Thomas Watson, through and because of IBM, would become the commercial syndic of Germany, committed as never before to global advocacy for the Third Reich, helping his utmost to counteract Hitler's enemies and further der Fuhrer's military, political, economic, and anti-Semitic goals.

Even as he continued as a statesman of American capitalism and a bulwark of international commerce, Watson would become a hero in Nazi Germany—both to the common man and to Adolf Hitler himself.[27]

Watson lavished praise on Nazi Germany. As president of the International Chamber of Commerce, Watson regularly voiced his support for an equitable redistribution of natural resources in Europe at a time when Germany threatened to invade neighboring countries to acquire the natural resources they possessed. Watson also spoke often in support of removing the crippling economic boycott against the Third Reich. "I have felt a deep personal concern over Germany's fate," Watson wrote to the Nazi economics minister Hjalmar Schacht in 1937, "and a growing attachment to the many Germans with whom I gained contact at home and abroad. This attitude has caused me to give public utterance to my impressions and convictions in favor of Germany at a time when public opinion in my country and elsewhere was predominantly unfavorable."[28]

Would the Holocaust have occurred without the punch cards and digital technology provided by IBM? Most likely. Would it have been as massive, as brutal, as deadly, and as efficient? Most likely not. IBM assisted Hitler and Nazi Germany in bringing genocide into the Information Age—collecting, storing, and processing massive amounts of data used to exterminate Jews and others deemed racially impure and not Aryan. It did not matter that an "Aryan race" never existed. Hitler believed one did; he believed he could identify non-Aryans like Jews; and he believed he could exterminate them. With assistance from IBM, Hitler acted on these beliefs.

Looking back to that conversation with my father on a bench along the Hudson, I do not believe any knowledge of IBM's sinister history with the Nazis lurked behind his sly smile. But I do believe he hid a pervasive sense that something was not right about the corporation to which he'd devoted the better part of his life. Looking even further back, I recall the surprising infusion of Jewish traditions in our household. We celebrated Passover. I attended my share of bar mitzvahs and bas mitzvahs. I looked forward to Fridays, when we had only challah bread with our dinner. Partially, this is explained by PS 102, the elementary school I attended, which was located in the heavily Jewish enclave of Parkchester in the Bronx. It is further explained by Community Church of New York, which celebrated the essential truths and holy days of many different faiths. But it is also explained, in part, by the IBM friends, mostly men and mostly Jewish, whom my father invited into our home.

When my father joined the company, IBM was not much different from the company that had bolstered the Nazis. But in the years before and after my father's hiring, more Jews also came to work for the firm—men and women hired into a company that had just spent years in support of Hitler's Germany, which sought their extermination.

Still, the company's business was never really about Nazism or eugenics. It was never really about anti-Semitism or racism. It was always about money, as Edwin Black notes: "Before even one Jew was encased in a hard-coded Hollerith identity, it was only the money that mattered."[29]

Certainly, Thomas J. Watson did not hire my father out of the goodness of his heart. The Nazi project to exterminate Jews ended with the Allied conquest of Germany. Trials began at Nuremberg, and with them came a worldwide hunt for those culpable for the Holocaust. But many Nazis on trial could not understand why the United States considered their actions to be punishable offenses. After all, Hitler had seen America as a leader in promoting Nordic purity and cleansing its citizenry of undesirables.

Otto Hofmann, head of the SS Race and Settlement Office, registered as evidence in his defense at Nuremberg a 1937 special report by the Nazi Party's Race-Political Office, on America, which noted,

> *Impassable lines are drawn between the individual races, especially in the Southern States. Thus in certain States Japanese are excluded from the ownership of land or real estate and they are prevented from cultivating arable land. Marriages between colored persons and whites are forbidden in no less than thirty of the Federal States. Marriages contracted in spite of this ban are declared invalid.... Since 1907, sterilization laws have been passed in twenty-nine States of the United States of America.*[30]

While the Nuremberg trials made for front-page news, Watson could breathe a sigh of relief. Digital technology, still in its infancy, flew under the radar of prosecutors and the general public. Watson's actions, and those of IBM, though they supported eugenics and Jewish extermination, remained largely unknown and unnoticed. Watson's history suggests he would work hard to keep it that way.

Watson handled IBM's pre- and postwar business with the tactical skill of a chess grand master. He understood how to manipulate the press and public sentiment, as he had done so effectively during the Ohio floods of 1913. Why not hire Blacks at IBM, to misdirect the Justice Department's investigation of IBM's war profiteering and to deflect attention away from IBM's more egregious past? And if he received kudos as a leader for integrating his workforce— much as the US Army had received for integrating the military or Branch Rickey had received for signing Jackie Robinson—so much the better for IBM's public image. IBM thrived because of Watson's cunning, shrewdness, and ruthlessness. There's no reason to believe that his decision to hire my father stemmed from anything less.

———

My father was excited that evening.

"Okay," he said. "There's hardware, and there's . . . ?"

"Software," I said.

He smiled. "So, there's hardware, and software, and . . . ?"

He paused. I didn't know what to say. Eventually, I threw up my hands.

"Peopleware," he exclaimed. "Hardware, software, and people-ware. I came up with the term while sitting in class today. It covers all the ways that people interact with programs and machines."

While the term is generally attributed to Peter G. Neumann in 1977[31] and Meilir Page-Jones in 1980,[32] I first heard of *peopleware* that evening in the late 1960s. One aspect of *peopleware* concerns how humans develop computer software. And one aspect of that development is called *polymorphism*, the use of similar segments of software to achieve different, but related, purposes. Polymorphism, it turns out, can be traced to the earliest days of computing, such as IBM's use of a similar technology to achieve different but related purposes in eugenics, in Nazi Germany, and then in South Africa.

———

His mellifluous voice was unfettered by his twenty-seven years in prison.

I stand here before you not as a prophet but as a humble servant of you, the people. Your tireless and heroic sacrifices have made it possible for me to be here today. I therefore place the remaining years of my life in your hands. On this day of my release, I extend my sincere and warmest gratitude to the

millions of my compatriots and those in every corner of the
globe who have campaigned tirelessly for my release.[33]

Occasionally, it seems, humanity is gifted the presence of a
real-life hero. I cried in a friend's living room as I watched Nelson Mandela speak on February 11, 1990, immediately after his
release from twenty-seven years in the notorious Victor Verster
Prison on Robben Island. It brought back eerie memories of sitting in my grandparents' living room twenty-seven years earlier,
listening to Martin Luther King speak from high atop the steps
of the Lincoln Memorial. I had long since left IBM, and my father
had since retired.

Yet even this exalted moment in South African history must
be balanced against IBM's nefarious business practices during the
years of Mandela's imprisonment. IBM's insidious pursuit of profits
before principles and people did not end with Nazi Germany. Why
should it, when a regime arose in South Africa that also required
digital technology's dark arts? Besides, the needs of the apartheid
regime were thoroughly known to IBM: use digital technology to
racially categorize and identify the population in pursuit of the brutal oppression of some in favor of the advancement of others.

Using Hollerith machines, IBM—under the leadership of
Thomas J. Watson Sr.—had pursued such a strategy with punch
cards, first in Jamaica in 1928 and then in Nazi Germany from 1933
to 1945. Now, under a new Thomas J. Watson, the founder's son,
IBM pursued a remarkably similar strategy in support of apartheid,
with an even more powerful arsenal of digital computers at the
company's disposal.

Whether in Jamaica, Nazi Germany, South Africa, or even the
American South, the problem became this: How does a government
or agency identify those deemed undesirable, making it easier to

single out these undesirables for special, often brutal if not geno-cidal, treatment? With a studied determination, the government of South Africa sought to answer this question by avoiding some of the pitfalls that Nazis encountered in handling their "Jewish problem" and that America encountered in developing and implementing its system of racial segregation.

Apartheid literally means "apartness" or "separateness," and the system relied on the government's ability to separate the popula-tion into four distinct, supposedly racial, groups: Whites, Indians/Asians, Coloreds, and Blacks. Apartheid then combined those four groups into two: on one hand, Whites, Indians, and Coloreds, all considered citizens though with varying degrees of rights (Whites had more rights and privileges than Indians or Coloreds), and on the other hand, Blacks (sometimes referred to as Natives).

Apartheid forcibly removed Blacks from White areas and herded them into independent Bantustans—landlocked areas carved out of South Africa. Black residents were stripped of their South African citizenship, and their lives were tightly controlled. The government restricted their movements into and out of these enclaves and within the country. South Africa also limited their education, their employment, and their political activity. Bantustans were indepen-dent in name only. The South African police and military forcibly patrolled the borders between Bantustans and the rest of the coun-try, brutalizing Blacks who violated any of the terms South Africa unilaterally imposed on Blacks living within these areas.

A system of passbooks governed apartheid. Outside of the Ban-tustans, White, Indian, and Colored South Africans required a passbook known as the "book of life." Inside Black areas, residents required a national identification pass, known colloquially as the "dompas" or "dumb pass," to comply with government laws. In South Africa, with a majority of 10 million Black Africans and a minority of 6 million Whites, Indians, and Coloreds combined, this two-tiered system of passes and racial identification presented a complex administrative and bureaucratic nightmare for the government.

Enter IBM, once again, with digital technology in the service of racial classification and racial domination.

Beginning in 1952, IBM leased Hollerith machines to the South African government through its South African subsidiary, much as it had with the Third Reich, to tabulate results of the 1951 census.[34] That census became the basis for determining the racial category to which a person belonged. In 1965, IBM bid unsuccessfully for the contract to create national identification passbooks for Blacks, but the company won the bid to produce the "book of life," required of the non-Black population.[35] However, by 1978, IBM had seized control of the business of creating and maintaining passbooks both inside and outside of the Bantustans.

With no research or manufacturing facilities in South Africa, IBM, from its New York headquarters, designed the hardware and software that automated South Africa's complex system of apartheid—writing the racial classification software, designing the database storage for racial classification, and constructing the equipment, such as printers, used to create the required passbooks. Through its South African subsidiary, IBM transferred this hardware and software to relevant South African governmental agencies, trained those agencies in the use of IBM equipment, consulted on and made fixes to apartheid software, and kept IBM equipment in good repair.[36]

Separation of a country's population by race is illegal under international law. In knowingly supporting South Africa's system of apartheid, IBM directly contravened this and other international laws, many enacted after the Nuremberg trials and the defeat of Nazi Germany specifically for the protection of individual human rights.[37]

IBM also apparently deceived its stockholders. At the company's annual shareholder meeting in 1977, then president Frank Cary stated, "I have said time and again that we have investigated each instance brought to our attention where there was any reason to believe IBM computers might be used for repressive purposes, and we have found no such use."[38] Yet, bizarrely, at that very same meeting, IBM admitted that its machines stored the data of Colored, Asian, and White South Africans, which enabled South Africa's system of apartheid through the unlawful separation of the races.[39]

IBM worked assiduously around the sanctions that the United States imposed on South Africa. In fact, the company lobbied hard for a reduction of sanctions. IBM told the South African regime that it would work with it to "adjust to the threat posed by trade sanctions."[40] Much as it had with Nazi Germany, IBM switched to a non-US supply chain, thereby providing South Africa with continued access to IBM computers, communications, surveillance, and other electronic equipment, even in the face of sanctions. These activities certainly violated the spirit of the sanctions imposed on South Africa aimed at dismantling apartheid. In some instances, they may have also violated the law. Yet unlike their efforts to support Nazi Germany, IBM was at times remarkably forthcoming, if not brazen, about the extent to which they knew exactly how and why their technology was being used in South Africa. In a letter of February 18, 1982, to the State Department, IBM admitted that the South African Interior Department used IBM machines and technology for its national identity system, the basis of the infamous "book of life" and a key pillar of racial identification, separation, and apartheid.[41]

By the mid-1980s, the call for divestment in South Africa, and in those companies supporting apartheid, grew around the world and especially in the United States. Typical of this movement was a flyer produced by the University of Chicago Coalition for Divestment, which listed not only IBM's direct support of apartheid but also the extensive use of IBM equipment in all aspects of South Africa's pervasive defense industry.[42] Even a group of IBM employees, known as the Black Workers Alliance, joined the mounting call for divestment.

Averse to negative publicity, in 1986 IBM announced the sale of its South African business and the company's pullout from the country. Divestment groups and opponents of apartheid celebrated an apparent major victory.[43] Instead, they should have been studying history, especially IBM's history in Nazi Germany. While it looked as though IBM bowed to international pressure on divestment, in truth the company did not back down in South Africa. It simply borrowed a play from its handbook of "dirty tricks." IBM divested itself from South Africa by selling its business to a South African concern that promptly announced everything would proceed as usual.

"There will be no change in the supply of IBM products," the managing director of the new company assured anxious customers.[44] For Sakwe Balintulo, arguing before the Second Circuit Court of Appeals, and for agencies like the Electronic Frontier Foundation, which filed briefs in support of Balintulo's appeal, IBM's actions in South Africa smacked of how the company had behaved in support of the Third Reich. They asserted that IBM simply ran the new company, as before, from New York.[45] One IBM dealer in South Africa observed, "Nothing has really changed except that IBM no longer has to account for its presence in South Africa."[46]

Not long after Mandela walked out of the Victor Verster Prison, South Africa entered into a period of deep soul-searching and healing, a period it is still in today. The Truth and Reconciliation Commission (TRC) convened many meetings throughout the country, bringing apartheid victims face-to-face with perpetrators of the most horrific crimes against them. Perpetrators were asked to listen to the stories of the people and their loved ones whom they'd hurt or harmed before being given the opportunity to confess the acts they'd committed and to seek amnesty. The TRC sought reconciliation, not retribution, and no prosecutions were brought against those who testified truthfully and completely.

During the decades of apartheid, billions of dollars were siphoned from South Africa by international corporations like IBM that supported the regime. Special hearings were held to allow IBM, and other corporations that had benefited from apartheid, to appear before the TRC. IBM and many other international corporations did not appear before the TRC seeking forgiveness. Former TRC head Dumisa Ntsebeza described what happened. "All they came to do there was to justify what they did," Ntsebeza said. "All of them felt there wasn't a need to come to the TRC and plead for amnesty."[47]

It appeared that, once again, IBM would make huge profits from the death and suffering of one group of people at the brutal hands of another and would escape unscathed, unbowed, and unrepentant. But in 2002, Ntsebeza, a lawyer, brought suit in New York against IBM on behalf of several dozen Black South Africans. Ntsebeza asserted that IBM should be held liable for the harm it had inflicted on Black South Africans from its wide-scale support of apartheid. The case wound its way through the US justice system. Then, in August 2014, Judge Shira Scheindlin of the Second Circuit Court of Appeals in New York issued a final ruling against Ntsebeza and the other plaintiffs on the grounds that any IBM actions in violation of international law had taken place outside the United States. The case, Scheindlin ruled, had no standing under US law. She added, "That these plaintiffs are left without relief in an American court is regrettable," but she stood by her decision as upholding legal precedent, "no matter what my personal view of the law may be."[48]

Even faced with Scheindlin's ruling, Ntsebeza did not give up.

In 2015, Ntsebeza argued before the US Supreme Court that Judge Scheindlin's ruling should be overturned and the plaintiffs' original suit should be reinstated in light of new information about the violations of international law committed by IBM on US soil in support of apartheid.

In June 2016, fourteen years after a plea was entered in New York, the Supreme Court declined to hear the Ntsebeza case and let Judge Scheindlin's lower court ruling stand.

Still, there's hope for justice. Khulumani, one of the many groups supporting the claims against IBM, has not exercised its right to appeal a related case in front of the Second Circuit Court of Appeals in New York or the Supreme Court based on even newer information from the South African Department of Justice archives about apartheid-era abuses committed by IBM. Khulumani said it reserves the opportunity to exercise its rights at some future date.[49]

Thirty years after apartheid, sixty years after Thomas J. Watson Sr.'s death, seventy years after the Holocaust, and nearly one hundred years after eugenics and IBM's founding, the company is still engaged in the application of the latest digital technology for racial classification.[50] In the years after the 9/11 attacks in New York City, as part of their major involvement in the Lower Manhattan Security Initiative (LMSI), which installed CCTV cameras around the city, IBM used secret camera footage of thousands of unknowing New Yorkers, provided by the New York City Police Department, to refine IBM facial recognition software to search for and identify people by "hair color, facial hair, and skin tone."[51] It's a painful, cruel irony that this IBM software is now known as "Watson Visual Recognition."[52]

I've often wondered what IBM engineers thought about as they developed the punch card templates that helped identify mixed-race individuals on the island of Jamaica, what went through the minds of IBM employees knowingly working on similar technology to support Hitler's regime, and how anyone would want to help further the brutality and viciousness of apartheid.

Rick Kjeldsen, a former IBM researcher working on facial recognition during these formative years, provided a window into the minds of those behind IBM's racial classification technology.

"We were certainly worried about where the heck this was going," he said in an interview with *The Intercept.* "There were a couple of us that were always talking about this, you know, 'If this gets better, this could be an issue.'"[53]

Facial recognition technology did get better. It did become an issue. Only as outside researchers, like Joy Buolamwini, a Ghanaian-American computer scientist at MIT, stand up to companies like IBM is there any public accounting of the racial bias in this latest iteration of racial classification technology, and with some hope, under the watchful eyes of researcher-activists like her, this bias may eventually change.[54]

Watson and his IBM did not create my father's wound of color, but working at IBM, with its long history of technology in the service of racial purity and oppression, appears to have never allowed that wound to heal. My father's belief in the importance of skin color in determining one's destiny only grew stronger over the years of his employment. IBM's dark history, however unconscious, seems to have gotten under my father's skin.

12

_____

The King Is Dead

Heat and humidity roiled New York City that April evening in 1968. I had just left a meeting with longtime civil rights activist Preston Wilcox on creating independent, community-based schools in Harlem. I walked along 125th Street, heading for the subway to the Port Authority bus station at the George Washington Bridge. From there I'd catch a bus home to Rockland County. An announcer's voice pierced through the crackling static of an all-news radio station coming from a storefront I passed. "Dr. Martin Luther King Jr.," the deep voice droned, "the apostle of nonviolence and civil rights, has been killed by a gunman in Memphis, Tennessee." I began to cry. The bullet that bloodied King's body also wounded me, leaving me with a gash of hate where I'd once held a glimmer of hope that America might someday address the urgent issue of race.

Stepping onto the #20 bus, I made my way to a seat at the far back, recoiling both inside and in my nearly fetal posture from anything having to do with the passengers—all White—around me. In the following days, weeks, and months, I shed off my White friends, left the liberal Unitarian-Universalist church I'd grown up in, let my hair spring out into an Afro, and began to wear African garb. America had failed me, and I did all I could to distance myself from her dominant White culture. At first, my parents thought this reaction would pass, that it represented my response to the overwhelming tragedy of Memphis. When it did not abate, they grew concerned because it fed into a larger, ongoing conflict with my father that had raged over the past several years.

———

In January 1967, at fifteen, with money I earned from working as a page at the Donnell Branch of the New York Public Library, I purchased a copy of *Playboy* magazine—the first and only time I ever did. The cover featured paintings of past Playmates in gilded frames and various stages of undress. Unlike my father, I did not hide the magazine; instead, I proclaimed to both parents the reasons for my purchase. Yes, it contained titillating, seductive pictures of women, but it also contained an interview destined to make that issue famous—the first-ever, full-length interview in the American press with Fidel Castro.

This caught my father in another bind: he valued my intellectual curiosity, but at the same time he felt uncomfortable with my sexuality, and he also hated Castro. Our fight that night erupted not over the centerfold of *Playboy* but over the centerpiece of Castro's ideas: a game of chess played not with pieces but with words.

"He's a commie," my father said.

"So what if he's telling the truth about Batista?"

"What truth?"

"That America backed Batista, who was a dictator, because Cuba made money for American corporations and bankers."

"America does not back dictators; we oust them. I served in the army. We fought to oust Hitler and Mussolini."

"Then what about Diem in South Vietnam?"

"What about him? He was a dictator whom the South Vietnamese overthrew."

"No. He was overthrown by a coup orchestrated by the CIA, who then put in place a military junta of their liking."

"Still, he was a dictator who's no longer in power, thanks to the United States."

"I'll grant you that Diem treated Buddhists terribly, which led them to protest, and ultimately one monk publicly lit himself on fire."

My father smiled. "My point, exactly. It's better that Diem and his brother are gone."

"But it's not better. That's the problem. Diem resisted unification with the North. By backing the coup, America has backed an inept military junta and set the country deeper in war with North Vietnam."

"He's a commie anyway."

"Who's a commie?"

"Ho Chi Minh, the guy who leads the North."

"He wrested control from the French, instituted economic reforms to help the people, and wants to hold a national reunification election, which Diem would never agree to, and now America's puppets in the South won't agree to either. Thomas Jefferson was Ho Chi Minh's hero."

"So what? He needs to be gone, which is why we're fighting the Vietcong."

"Just like Castro needs to be gone?"

"Yep, just like Castro, that commie. You'll see when you join the army."

"I don't think you get that I'll never join the army."

"You're only fifteen now, but there's a draft. You won't have a choice."

"I'd rather go to Canada than to Vietnam. I won't kill Brown people fighting for their freedom and liberty when America doesn't even grant freedom and liberty to Black people in this country."

"You go to Canada and I'll disown you. No son of mine's going to refuse service to his country. I served with pride, and you will too."

"Yeah, and where'd that service get you?" Check.

"A job with IBM."

"Too bad working for IBM doesn't make you a man." Mate.

For once, I'd left my father with nothing to say.

I marched in protest of the Vietnam War. I played my guitar and sang in protest of the war. I dressed in protest of the war. And when I turned sixteen, I wrote my draft board asking if they seriously wanted to teach an angry young Black man how to kill for the sake of war.

During these years, the gulf between my father and me grew, and we spoke little. Even though we lived outside of New York City, I continued to attend Stuyvesant High School, which meant that each weekday I drove down from Rockland County to New York City with my father and mother. She let us off on the New York City side of the George Washington Bridge, where we got on a subway, and she then drove to her job as a public-school principal. My father always wore a suit and tie, always carried his briefcase. But when I pinned an anti-war button on my jacket, he refused to ride in the same subway car as me. When I carried my guitar to school, he refused to ride in the same subway car. When I dressed in blue jeans or wore boots or a Greek fisherman's hat, he refused to be seen with me in the subway. It embarrassed him, he said, to have a son like me, and he did not want anyone at IBM to see us together.

My father developed a unique form of post-traumatic stress disorder (PTSD) as a result of being the first Black systems engineer at IBM, one known to many who are racial, ethnic, or gender "firsts" in some aspect of their lives. Hypervigilance is a significant part of the symptom cluster he experienced, a reaction to feeling "under a microscope," "always on display," or "representing one's race." Said simply, my father's hypervigilance was a reaction to the racism he experienced within IBM.

Along with this hypervigilance came a heightened awareness of being "visible"—knowing that others could see and identify him, even if he could not see and identify them. He needed always to be "on guard." Hence he chose not to be near me, in part, for fear that others might surreptitiously see him in association with beliefs or ideas that threatened his continued employment at IBM.

As bizarre as this hypervigilance seems, and as hurtful as it was, my father's fears were not wholly unfounded. Years earlier, my mother had driven my sister, me, and our cousins to the IBM Country Club on Long Island one rainy weekday. With little to do in the rain, we left early, but before leaving we stopped to use the restrooms. In the pavilion we entered, only the women's restroom was open while the men's room was being cleaned. My mother stood guard outside while I used one of the female stalls. Though we never saw anyone, news of the event got back to my father's manager, who upbraided him, and he, in turn, upbraided my mother and me for jeopardizing his job.

Heightened awareness of being "invisible" is another side of this symptom cluster, again something known to many Black "firsts." Like the kids who said to me, "We mean no offense," and went on to talk about "the Niggers" as though I did not exist, within IBM my father had been passed over for promotions and given the task of training others who would then become his superiors, as though he too were invisible.

———

Spring 1968 drew out violence like a poultice drawing out poison from a snakebite. Two months after King's assassination in Memphis, Robert Kennedy was killed in Los Angeles. And only a few weeks after King's death, Columbia University erupted in student protest. At the time of the Columbia University uprising, I was a student at Stuyvesant High School. While college recruiters came courting Stuyvesant's Black students that spring, so did Black students from Columbia. Sam Anderson and Ray Brown, two Black student leaders of the Columbia protest, talked to a group of us at Stuyvesant. What I heard about letting go of the "turn the other cheek" message of civil rights struck a chord. Sam and Ray took me and another kid, Steven, under their wings, and we became known as the "little brothers" of Columbia's revolutionary Black students. We helped organize a protest at Stuyvesant, and we used the lessons learned from Columbia when we arrived at Wesleyan University that fall.

Meanwhile, my father grew more concerned at my shift toward Black radical thought and action. He wanted to get me away from the tempting influences of New York City, so when I proposed that I travel to Africa that summer as a high school graduation present, he and my mother jumped in to contribute to the funds I'd already saved for the trip.

My father saw me off by saying, "There's an IBM office in Accra. If you get in trouble or need help, just go there. They'll get in touch with me. And you'll get all the help you need."

———

To shouts of *Oságyefo, Oságyefo, Oságyefo* (Redeemer, Redeemer, Redeemer), Kwame Nkrumah acceded to the presidency of Ghana in 1960 after leading the fight for independence from Britain. He advocated for Pan-Africanism. He established the Organization of African Unity. He invited W. E. B. Du Bois to live in Ghana, where he ultimately died. Malcolm X, Martin Luther King, and even John F. Kennedy lauded Nkrumah. In the late 1960s, important figures in the Black freedom struggle, like Maya Angelou, called Ghana home. In 1966, with the assistance of the CIA, Nkrumah was ousted. Still, in those days of my youthful radicalism, Nkrumah stood as my hero, and Ghana as a country I too might someday call home.

I left for Ghana shortly after my graduation from Stuyvesant. Right from the beginning, many things went wrong. The Black tour group I traveled with had been promised a direct flight from Kennedy Airport to Dakar, Senegal, and then on to Accra, Ghana. Instead, the tour company bounced us around Europe for several days—Madrid, Lisbon, Zurich—before finally getting us to Ghana. I kissed the ground when I landed, thrilled to finally set foot on African soil. Then, after we cleared customs, Ghanaian authorities advised us to leave immediately. I was devastated. The tour company had made no arrangements for us in the country. If we chose to stay, we'd be on our own. Half the group turned around and left. I'd come too far to go home.

I stayed at the Star Hotel in Accra, the capital, while planning my travel and stays at universities throughout Ghana. Before leaving Accra, I stopped by the American embassy to alert them to my presence in the country. Unknown to me at the time, I'd arrived at the embassy in a lull between the appointments of ambassadors: Franklin Williams, who had been on duty during the ouster of

Nkrumah, was on his way out, but Thomas W. McElhiney had not been sworn in. The ranking consul general called me into his office and gave me a dressing down. This fellow told me in no uncertain terms to leave Ghana immediately.

If I did not, he said, "You'll be declared PNG [persona non grata], and the United States government will assume no responsibility for your health or welfare."

"I came here to visit the land where my ancestors were stolen as slaves," I shot back. "And I'll be damned if I let some White man tell me I have to leave Africa." I promptly walked out of the embassy.

At the time, all of Ghana had no more than two or three IBM computers; still, the company had opened an office in Accra as early as 1960 to serve Ghana, Nigeria, and Sierra Leone. Each time I walked by the IBM offices in the capital, I took some comfort that, should I need him, my father remained close by.

I received a Ghanaian name, Kojo Baako, in a traditional naming ceremony in the city of Kumasi. But I liked best visiting small villages and talking to local people. Everywhere I went, I found myself at pains to disavow the term many Ghanaians used to greet me: *Oboruni*, meaning "foreigner" but also "White man." After getting past this salutation, even the poorest villagers would gather around, many holding up embossed velvet images of the Kennedys and King. They peppered me with questions about how America could call itself a civilized nation when its greatest leaders faced assassination. In return, I spoke freely and openly about Black Power, Malcolm X, and Kwame Nkrumah.

———

While traveling back to Accra from Kumasi, after nearly two months in Ghana, I encountered a young law student named Jimmy

Adu, whom I'd met upon my arrival. Jimmy wasted no time laying out what I now faced.

"I would leave immediately," he said. "The authorities know about your travels. They know what you've been talking about. You've been marked for arrest and detention by the CID."

A holdover from British colonial rule, the CID (Criminal Investigations Department) is Ghana's equivalent of the FBI. They work in plain clothes, surveilling those considered enemies of the state. In the coup d'état that overthrew Nkrumah, the CID worked with the CIA. Some CID leaders came into power with Nkrumah's ouster. I may not have taken seriously what the consul general said, but I did not doubt a word of what I heard from Jimmy Adu. I remember walking down the red dirt road toward my hut in a village known then as Tetteh-Quarshie, and thinking, *Oh, shit! I'm in trouble now.* Then I burst into tears. I also remember the tug-of-war inside, mulling over whether I should run and seek refuge in the Ghanaian offices of IBM.

I got myself into this, I finally told myself. *I will not seek my father's help to get out of this situation.*

On the road to Tetteh-Quarshie, I wiped away my tears, composed myself, and thought, *I see this all the time on television programs like* Mission: Impossible *and* The Man from U.N.C.L.E., *where characters extract themselves from the most desperate situations. If they can do it on-screen, I can do it in real life. First, I need intelligence.*

At sixteen, I decided to go up against the CID and possibly the CIA. I needed to assess my weakness, so I marched into the downtown office of Pan Am, whose return ticket I held, and simply asked to book the next flight back to the United States. As I entered the Pan Am office, I stopped to look at the IBM sign atop a building on the other side of the street. The Pan Am agent took my ticket, made a few calls, and promptly returned to tell me my ticket had been invalidated and he would be unable to arrange my flight. I snatched the ticket from his hand, racing from his office back to Tetteh-Quarshie.

One thing I'd learned from my time in Ghana was how loving, honest, and trustworthy local Ghanaians were. The other thing I'd learned is that you never let your ticket or your passport leave your side. I took them everywhere with me. I never thought once about leaving my hut door open or my belongings out, but even if I stepped away to walk the short distance to the pit toilet, I always carried my passport and my ticket with me.

When I left the pit toilet, after returning from the Pan Am office, I saw two men dressed in black suits running from my hut. My first thought was how strange to be wearing black suits in the heat and humidity of Africa. My second thought was, *Oh no!* When I stepped back into my hut, my belongings had been ransacked, and my wallet had been stolen. I was stranded in an African village and marked for apprehension.

Another thing I always carried with me, tucked into a back page of my passport, was the numbers of the American Express Travelers Cheques that I had purchased prior to leaving for Africa. Redeeming those cheques required another trip downtown, but all of my money had been stolen. Fortunately, American clothes were a tradable commodity in Ghana. So I simply paid a taxi driver with a pair of my blue jeans. He dropped me at the American Express office in Accra, farther down the main street from Pan Am and even closer to IBM. Once again, I felt the pull of simply giving in and seeking refuge in IBM. And once again, I couldn't bring myself to appeal for my father's help.

I stayed in the American Express office for hours until I finally got my cheques. I knew then that I had little time to execute a plan for my extraction. My intelligence turned up a time, on Saturdays only, when Pan Am's airport office was open but the main office downtown was closed. I believed my ticket was still valid and that I had been told otherwise only as a ruse to draw me in for arrest by the CID.

So I concocted a plan: I would forge a letter from the State Department saying that, due to the dire security situation in the neighboring country of Nigeria (the Biafran War was underway), I needed to return at once to the United States. The only problem was finding both the stationery and a typewriter. The stationery proved easy. I decided on one of the Mailgrams, which I used to send letters back home. The typewriter was not. I had made friends with a professor at a nearby university, so I asked him if I could use his typewriter while he went to lunch. He agreed, and I forged and signed a letter from the US State Department to me.

Then I waited until Saturday and took the letter and my ticket to the Pan Am office at the airport, hoping that they had no record of my ticket's invalidation. I timed my arrival for the half-hour period when my intel showed they could not call the main office downtown for corroboration. I also practiced being a panicked, young American who needed to get back home, a role I found it easy to get into. I wound up nearly overplaying my hand. The agent at the airport office told me to calm down, that he'd get me out on a flight leaving that afternoon. He made the arrangements, issued me a boarding pass, and told me to be back a few hours before the flight left.

I worked hard to contain my excitement as I rushed from his office back to Tetteh-Quarshie to grab the belongings that had not been stolen, and then back to the airport for my flight home. I remember sitting at an outside table, drinking a beer with another Black American who'd been traveling in the country, while we watched our Pan Am flight scream overhead and then land. I remember also checking out of customs in Ghana and being told to stay within a cordoned-off area reserved for those booked on the flight about to leave. Elation filled me. I'd made it, and it was not even that hard.

Several buses pulled up to take passengers to the plane waiting on the tarmac. As we waited in line to board the buses, I met a Black professor named Anthony Kennedy, who'd been in Ghana doing research. Still nervous, I began recounting for him what I'd gone through in the last few days. But I'd barely finished when the Pan Am agent from downtown walked into the airport. I saw him before he saw me. I pointed at the man and said to Kennedy, "That's him."

"Go!" Kennedy said. "And don't stop until you're on that plane. I'll run interference." He pushed me in the direction of the tarmac, and I ran. The Pan Am agent saw me and took off in my direction. I looked back to see Kennedy step into this man's path as though by accident. The two collided, and Kennedy held on to him for a moment, buying me some time. I hopped on a bus already rolling toward the plane and pushed my way toward the front. The agent hopped on the back and fought his way toward me. I leaped off the bus before it came to a stop and raced up a forward staircase onto the plane.

At the top of the stairs, a flight attendant smiled at me and said pleasantly, "Is everything okay?"

My body shook. My voice trembled. "I just need to get to my seat."

She took my ticket and pointed toward the rear of the plane.

Meanwhile, the Pan Am agent watched from the tarmac as passengers came aboard. I fully expected that he'd try to drag me off the plane, but he never once walked up the steps. While I shook in my seat, Aretha sang, "You make me feel like a natural woman," over the plane's speakers. Through the small window, I saw the Pan Am agent standing on the tarmac, waving his clenched fist at me.

The Pan Am flight was headed to JFK, and by all rights I should have simply stayed on board. But it made a stop in Liberia, and I said to myself, *I don't know when I'll be back to Africa,* so I got off. I spent a few days relaxing in Monrovia and then went to a Pan Am office to book my flight to JFK.

"Anything wrong with this ticket?" I asked.

The agent studied it and typed a few keystrokes into his computer. He studied the ticket some more. "Nothing at all, sir."

Over the years, I've heard various explanations of why that Pan Am agent would not board the plane to drag me off. Some have said Professor Kennedy was right to tell me not to stop until I was on the plane, which under international law was American, not Ghanaian, property; others have said my youth, inexperience, lack of training, and simple luck helped me outwit professional intelligence agencies. I have not told many people about what happened that summer in Ghana, out of fear they simply would not believe me. I think it took me a decade before I told my father. But that summer in Ghana became a personal touchstone. Whenever facing a difficult or trying situation, I have only to ask myself, *Is it as bad as Ghana?* It's never been. In which case I say to myself, *You were sixteen and you made it then. You can certainly make it now.* I discovered that I could accomplish what seemed impossible, and I could do it without the help of my father.

———

My father and I also clashed over which college I should attend. Since my grandfather spoke at Dartmouth, my father wanted me to go there. Instead, I chose Wesleyan University in Connecticut, with its well-earned reputation for politically active students. I entered Wesleyan a few weeks after returning from Ghana, and I led a double life there: I was a Black history major before there was such a thing as Black history, to my father's consternation, and a mathematics and computing minor, to his great pleasure; studious undergrad at times, which also pleased my father, Black radical at others, which caused him angst.

Just weeks after I started at Wesleyan, Black students organized into a group called Ujamaa (Swahili for "family"), issued a set of demands to the university, and prepared to occupy a building—all pretty standard actions for 1968, which, thanks in large part to affirmative action, saw the first large crop of Black students at the nation's colleges and universities. In those days, I went by my African name of Kojo Baako, and as co-chair of Ujamaa, with a fellow student who went by Kwame Lumumba, found myself in the thick of the action.

Afraid that a mole within Ujamaa would report our plans back to the university, a group of us publicly stated we'd be taking over Fisk Hall one day at four in the morning, while privately leaving for Fisk a half hour earlier. When we arrived at Fisk, a member of our group shattered the glass door by kicking it in. Then I turned to see Wesleyan's lone Black dean running down High Street, waving a set of keys, crying out in angst, "But I had the keys! I had the keys!"

Straddling the line between student and activist became a tenuous, high-wire balancing act. Black students there solely for an education felt threatened by my activism. Black students given over to being activists saw me as not doing enough.

One concerned economics major, whom I knew from high school, had his sights set on Wall Street. "If you do anything to interfere with my graduation," he told me, "I'll kill you!"

The campus also had a little-known student chapter of the infamous New Haven branch of the Black Panther Party, headed by the jazz trumpeter, trombonist, and part-time lecturer Clifford Thornton. On Fridays, the campus chapter of the party would issue weekly "revolutionary ratings" of Black students through hand-drawn icons, with brief titles, affixed to dormitory room doors. Three icons served to rank and classify Black students based on the party's all-Black, revolutionary agenda: a watermelon, a pork chop, and a pair of White girl's panties. The more of these icons you received, the further away you were from being a "politically correct" Black revolutionary.

While I had my share of watermelons and pork chops, though never a pair of White girl's panties, the on-campus chapter also had a fourth icon created in my honor: a book, symbolizing a revolutionary library and intellect, thus counterbalancing my several pork chop and watermelon demerits.

Despite all the seeming craziness, I still learned that activism, correctly timed and focused, was a powerful force for change. Ujamaa abandoned Fisk Hall after the university agreed to most of our demands, one of which was the funding of the Institute of the Black World, the first established arm of the Martin Luther King Jr. Center in Atlanta. In the spring of 1969, along with five other Black students from Wesleyan, I handed Coretta Scott King, Martin's widow, a check for several hundred thousand dollars to establish IBW. That fall I spent a semester as one of the first students at the institute, which brought together the leading Black scholars, writers, poets, and musicians of the day.

I returned to Connecticut from Atlanta determined to graduate in three years, instead of four, with a major in Black history and a minor in mathematics and computing. At the time, Wesleyan, then an all-male institution, had a rule that if a student wanted a class that was not offered, he could prepare a set of educational goals and a reading list, find a willing professor, and receive full credit if the academic goals achieved met the professor's standard. I used this rule to great effect and laid out a rigorous course in Black history, with professors in the History Department serving as my proctors. My senior thesis, titled "A System of Governance and Dominance in Seventeenth-Century Virginia," examined the steps Virginia took to transition from a system of indentured servitude to a system of slavery. I authored this paper under my Ghanaian name, Kojo Baako.

But Wesleyan also had an IBM 1130 computer for the Physics and Mathematics Departments. My father possessed extensive knowledge of that machine. I needed to learn and use the 1130 and FORTRAN to get my minor in mathematics, so my father plied me with IBM 1130 operations manuals and FORTRAN educational manuals, and he also paved the way for me to speak with fellows at IBM's famed Systems Research Institute (SRI) in New York City. A final paper in numerical analysis required mathematical operations with very small and very large numbers, well beyond the 1130's computational limits. With my father's introduction, I brought the problem to a Black mathematician at SRI, who leaped at the chance to help a young student. Through a FORTRAN program, we concocted a way around the 1130's limitations, allowing me to write a paper titled "Investigating the Relationships between the Normal, Binomial, and Poisson Distributions," which I authored under the name Clyde W. Ford.

Home for a weekend, I showed my mathematics paper to my father.

"You wrote this?" he asked.

"I did."

"Using the school's 1130?"

"Yep."

"In FORTRAN no less?"

"Yes."

"Guy at SRI help you?"

"He did."

"You know, I don't understand most of it." He waved the paper at me, smiling. "But that's pretty damned cool!"

13

Clandestine Service

During the years my father refused to be seen in public with me, his role at IBM became even more clandestine: not just the covert operation he ran from the bottom drawer of his dresser, but even the work he performed for the company.

Periodically, he would inform us that he'd been assigned to work at the large IBM facility in Endicott, New York; at a research laboratory in Cambridge, Massachusetts; or at a company location near San Francisco. When asked what his assignment entailed, he smiled knowingly, stiffened slightly, and said he'd been sworn to secrecy. These assignments, all highly classified and some lasting six months or longer, seemed more like military deployments.

After I entered IBM, I managed to piece together one of my father's major clandestine assignments. Code-named CP-67, it was part of the first government-funded technology projects underwritten by DARPA (the Defense Advanced Research Projects Agency). While IBM stood to benefit financially through commercializing the results of Project CP-67, DARPA's real goal had far-greater implications. DARPA wanted technology that would become the foundation of the modern-day internet.

By the early 1960s, it had become clear that IBM computers, and therefore computers in general, faced three significant and inter-related challenges: intergenerational incompatibility, multiple-user environments, and the high cost of memory.

With each new generation of IBM computers, compatibility problems arose. The programs my father wrote for the IBM 705, for example, did not run on an IBM 7080, and programs he wrote for an IBM 7080 did not run on an IBM System/360. Even if he wrote those programs in a software language such as COBOL or FORTRAN, which looked the same regardless of the computer, the underlying software that read and interpreted the program's instructions was tied to specific hardware, which often meant that this underlying software needed to be rewritten.

Today, most smartphone users are familiar with the need to update their operating systems, which happens, for the most part, automatically. Once updated, all of the contacts, emails, and applications that were originally part of the smartphone are still accessible with a swipe of the phone's screen. Even if you purchase a new phone, your contacts, emails, applications, music, and other data can be transferred, relatively easily, from your old phone to your new one.

Now, imagine if each time you updated your smartphone's operating system, or purchased a new smartphone, everything had to be reentered by hand. All of your contacts had to be retyped. All of your emails had to be re-sent to your smartphone. All of your music and applications had to be downloaded again. When a new generation of technology is incompatible with a previous generation, it's called *intergenerational incompatibility*, and it's a sure way to kill the new technology. IBM's product line in the early 1960s suffered from intergenerational incompatibility.

Multiple-user environments are also easily understood. In the early 1960s, it might have cost a couple of million dollars a month to lease a large-scale IBM computer. Imagine now that a hundred students are assigned to write programs for mathematics, physics, and business classes at a university that has only one such expensive machine. Each student would punch their program into a deck of cards and add some cards at the beginning of the deck to tell the computer how to set up to perform the required calculations. But the computing environment for a program to determine a rocket launch and landing on the moon might be very different from one needed to calculate an actuarial table.

Now each student, holding their card deck, would line up to place that deck in a card reader. One by one, the computer would read each card deck, and one by one the computer would set up and execute each program. Each student would get the results of the program's execution, make changes to correct any errors, and then get back in line with a deck of cards, and the process would start over again. This method of computing is called *batch processing*, and it's extremely slow. It would be analogous to having to shut down the word processing program on your laptop or desktop computer in order to open your email application, and then having to shut down your email application when you wanted to switch back to word processing.

Today, if a hundred students need access to a single high-speed computer, they can each sit down at a keyboard and monitor and simultaneously access that computer. The ability to achieve this multiple-user environment comes from the underlying ability of computers to perform multitasking and multiprocessing, abilities not present in most hardware or software at the dawn of the Digital Age.

Memory's high cost also hampered early computers because it limited the size of the applications that could be written. If my father wrote a program that required 50 kilobytes of memory for computations and 50 kilobytes of memory to store the results of those computations, that meant his application required 100 kilobytes of memory. But what if the computer he worked on only possessed 50 kilobytes of memory total (farcical by today's standards but certainly not unheard of in his day)? He, and all early programmers, then went through an inordinate number of time-consuming, nonproductive gyrations to handle the memory they had available: segmented programs, partial programs with instructions to load other parts, and instructions to read and write temporary results to disk storage, to name but a few.

Where today, 100 kilobytes of memory costs a fraction of a cent, in the early days of computing, 100 kilobytes of memory could cost several hundred thousand dollars. Lines on a punch card were cheap, computer memory was not, and that was a real problem that DARPA wanted solved. Wouldn't it be better, the thinking went, if programmers simply developed applications without worrying about how much memory they required, and computers managed the gyrations necessary to make the applications work within the limitations of the memory available?

Compatibility, multiple users, and memory management. Three problems, from the early days of computing, with solutions that underpin the digital landscape we take for granted today. These were the abilities that DARPA sought. Without first solving these problems, there would have been no internet, no email, no Facebook, no Twitter, no WhatsApp, no Instagram, nor any of the hundreds of thousands of computer and smartphone applications that we so readily use today. Windows, iOS, Android, and the Cloud all trace their heritage back to the solution of these three problems. While many other technological innovations came together to bring about today's digital revolution, solving these three problems remained key and involved both new hardware and software. IBM handed off many of the challenges posed by these three problems to the men and women of Project CP-67.

By the early 1960s, my father had become acquainted with most of IBM's diverse computer line, principally the IBM 7000 series and the IBM 1130 series. The company intended to bring out an IBM 8000 series of computers but scrapped those plans when customers balked at the prospect of once again migrating their software to meet the specifications of IBM's new hardware (the compatibility problem). So IBM set off on the extremely bold but risky strategy of creating the System/360 line of computers, with the goal of encompassing a vast range of processing power, memory size, peripheral device support, and cost under a single unified computer architecture.

When purchasing a new laptop today, you can first decide on the make you want, then select the processor speed, the amount of memory, and the screen size. You can be certain that the laptop, if running a version of the Windows operating system, for example, will also run an application like Microsoft Word, regardless of the laptop's final configuration. The standardization and portability expected today were revolutionary in the early 1960s, pioneered by IBM with the introduction of the System/360 line of mainframe computers, which were first announced in April 1964. A System/360 model 30 could perform up to 34,500 instructions per second with 8 kilobytes of memory, while at the opposite end of the spectrum a System/360 model 91 could execute up to 16.6 million instructions per second with 8 megabytes of memory. While laughable by today's standards, when a cheap cell phone can easily outperform a high-end System/360 model, the introduction of the System/360 line, with built-in compatibility between models, was a turning point in the history of computers that secured IBM's dominance until the advent of personal computers.

But even the System/360 line soon ran into a problem. IBM built these computers under the mistaken belief that single-user batch processing would dominate future computing, a miscalculation akin to Bill Gates's initial dismissal of the internet's importance. Academic and scientific users, who drove much of IBM's techno-logical innovation, clamored for multiuser access, known then as *time-sharing systems*. And so did DARPA and the US government.

With computer speeds ever increasing, a time-sharing system served multiple users by allocating a single computer's processor and other resources for a brief period of time to one user and then to an-other. Like a stick handed off around a circle, if done fast enough, the delay between having the stick would shrink to the point that each person perceived they always held their own stick. In other words, each time-shared user on a fast computer would perceive that the computer and its resources belonged exclusively to him or her.

In the 1960s, MIT clamored for time-sharing through Project MAC (alternately known as the Project on Mathematics and Com-putation or the Project on Multi-access Computing). Project MAC had its offices on the fifth, eighth, and ninth floors of 545 Main Street in Cambridge, Massachusetts, in a complex known as Tech Square. IBM's Cambridge Scientific Center (CSC) occupied the fourth floor, while the company's sworn enemy, GE's Cambridge Information Systems Laboratory (CISL), had offices on the seventh. Listed under the name R. K. Starling Associates, the Central Intelligence Agency maintained offices on the third floor.[1] When my father left for Cambridge, he worked for CSC.

In 1963, DARPA funded Project MAC to create working hard-ware and software that allowed many users to access the programs of a single computer from any location—the first stage in developing the network technology that would one day become the internet. IBM and GE were locked in fierce competition for the technical lead of Project MAC, GE through its MULTICS (Multiplexed Information and Computing Service) System, which ran on a modified GE 645 computer, and IBM through a special-purpose System/360. IBM lost the first round of competition when Project MAC opted for MULTICS. Then Bell Labs, another key IBM customer, delivered IBM the same devastating blow.

But IBM fought back.

The company reorganized its development and manufacturing divisions, addressing problematic issues identified by Project MAC and perhaps also punishing those responsible for the company's disgrace. Then the company commissioned a corporate-level task force to find a way of meeting this unanticipated demand for time-sharing. IBM's task force delivered plans for a new System/360, the model 67, and with it a new time-sharing operating system, TSS/360.

But CSC went ahead with plans of its own to build a time-sharing operating system for the System/360 line, known as CP-40 (Control Program 40), since CSC chose to modify an existing System/360 model 40. CSC needed to overcome two key hurdles in developing a working time-sharing system: stable virtual memory and a working virtual machine.

When a time-shared user's turn is up, they must yield the computer and its resources to the next user waiting, but the computer needs to store all the information necessary to re-create exactly where that initial user left off the next time it's that user's turn. This information cannot be stored in the computer's normal memory because that memory would be needed for the next user's tasks. So, the question became where to store all the necessary information about a user who is waiting for a turn at the computer.

In the time-sharing systems of early computing, and in today's modern networks, a waiting user's information is stored in virtual memory, usually on a hard drive. While the internet is a bit more complicated than CSC's time-sharing system, the concepts are exactly the same. Take your web browser's cache. When you're not actually visiting a web page, information about your last visit is stored on your computer in the browser's cache. The next time you visit the web page, that information can be used to re-create exactly what you were doing prior to exiting the page. Your web browser's cache is a form of virtual memory.

CSC, however, took the idea of re-creating each user's previous session one step further. Instead of just storing data for that user, CSC chose to use virtual memory to store a complete operating system, including data, for each user's session. That meant, under CSC's design, the computer would store the equivalent of a separate computer for each user between sessions, hence the name *virtual machine*.

Today, the notion of a computer storing the equivalent of a computer is quite common. It happens all the time in the Cloud. In fact, that's pretty much what the Cloud is, a lot of stored virtual machines—images of computers stored on disk drives. When a user logs onto the Cloud and is ready to use their computer, that stored image is loaded into a real computer somewhere, and it starts to run. But in the 1960s, the concept of virtual memory and virtual machines was a real game changer.

IBM delivered the System/360–67, but TSS/360, the time-shared operating system, lagged behind. CSC saw an opening and adapted CP-40 for the System/360–67, hence the name CP-67 (Control Program for the System/360 model 67). That's where my father came in. He worked in Cambridge on the CP-67 project under the guidance of CSC.

CP-67 and CMS (Cambridge Monitor System), the operating system it delivered for each user, changed the trajectory of modern-day computing. DARPA dropped GE's MULTICS System in favor of IBM's CP/CMS solution. The first-ever networking businesses sprang up around the success of CP/CMS. IBM integrated virtual memory into its entire product line, and CP/CMS morphed into future mainstream IBM operating systems such as CP-370/CMS, VM/370, and z/VM, which are still widely used on mainframe computers.

With the success of CP/CMS, DARPA's early investment in Project MAC paid huge dividends. The next time you open multiple windows on your PC or your Mac, swipe between applications on your cell phone, visit an internet site, send a social media message, or access treasured family photographs in the Cloud, you have CSC and CP-67 and CP/CMS to thank. You can also thank my father.

Yet there's more to my father's story with CP-67, things that remain hidden even after all these years. DARPA did not fund Project MAC for simple altruistic reasons or to benefit multinational corporations like IBM and GE. National security was at stake. Government, military, and intelligence agencies had a keen interest in the advanced technology emanating from Tech Square. Information and personnel moved freely between the organizations with offices at Tech Square. CIA briefings on the technological developments at Project MAC happened regularly. Robert Creasy, who once worked for Project MAC and DARPA, left to work for IBM, where he spearheaded the development of CP/CMS as the head of CSC.

By the mid-1960s, IBM's history of working with the military stretched back at least as far as the Mechanical Records Units (MRU) division of the US Army and the "IBM soldiers" in World War II. After the war, Watson even attempted to establish his own private intelligence agency and offer contract services to the government. His efforts were thwarted when, in the late 1940s, the White House and Congress established the CIA.[2]

Secrecy suited my father. Once he understood that IBM would not publicly advance his career, secrecy afforded the empowerment he would not find elsewhere within the company. Secrecy held the illusion of power.

He said little about his work with CP-67. Everything about his time in Cambridge was, in his own words, "hush-hush," "top secret," and to be taken to his grave. All I have in my possession is a carbon copy of a letter, dated May 8, 1972, from a manager of the CP-67/CMS group at Technology Square in Cambridge, to a woman named Gayle Johnson, apparently my father's manager at the time, thanking her for providing the group with my father's services. "His output and performance while on assignment here were of the highest caliber," the letter says. In the upper right-hand corner of that letter, someone had crossed out the words "IBM CONFIDENTIAL," the company's equivalent of a top secret classification.

While I may never know if, and under what circumstances, my father visited the offices of R. K. Starling Associates on the third floor of Tech Square, I do know there were too many coincidences between my career at IBM and his to dismiss his involvement with the CIA out of hand.

After a year or two working as an IBM systems engineer from my office in the New York Federal Reserve Building, I simply grew bored. Helping programmers find bugs in core dumps became a mind-numbing exercise that I performed without much thought. I stopped reporting in to my office, and I stopped going to work at the Fed. Instead, I spent most of my time at IBM's New York Data Center at 909 Third Avenue in New York. There I'd log in to an internal time-sharing service run out of an IBM laboratory in Armonk, New York. In those days before CRT and LED screens, I could only use a modified Selectric typewriter to interact with the computer. I'd type in something, wait, and a few moments later the Selectric ball would whir and slowly spit out a response.

I taught myself APL (A Programming Language) and worked on self-assigned mathematical problems in matrix and linear algebra. I logged in using my IBM employee number, and I ran up quite a bill. When an accountant at my IBM branch office discovered the tens of thousands of dollars of his internal budget that I'd consumed, I thought I'd be fired, but instead he winked and told me not to worry, for no one would ever know.

After that, I switched to an IBM 1130 computer at the Data Center that did not require me to log in. My interest at the time was artificial intelligence (AI), and I programmed the 1130 to play the African game of Ware to better understand AI concepts. I'd often work at the Data Center until the wee hours of the morning, grab a few hours of sleep in my apartment in the Bronx, and go back to the Data Center early the next day. Nerd? Geek? We didn't use those terms in the early 1970s, but if we had, they surely would have described me.

I may have thought my actions were not being tracked by IBM management, but I was wrong. After I had hung out at the Data Center for nearly eighteen months, my manager called me in for a performance review.

"You haven't been at your job," Conrad said.

"I know. I've spent most of my time at the New York Data Center."

"You've run up quite a bill. We know what you've been doing. We just don't know why."

"I've learned APL. I'm working on an artificial intelligence project."

"You don't get to choose. I hired you to work at the Fed."

"I'm bored. I'm not using my mind."

"That's not my concern. Your lack of performance for this office is."

"I need a challenge, not a core dump."

"You need to get back to work at the Fed."

"There's a job opening teaching at the Advanced Education Center. I want that job. I'd be good at that job. It would stimulate me, challenge me."

Art's face went red. "What?"

"A job at the Advanced Education Center."

"Who told you about this job?"

"The Advanced Education Center's in the same building as the Data Center. I'm around there. I hear things. I just know."

He glowered. "You do realize that informing another employee about an open position is grounds for termination?"

I said nothing.

"Even if that employee is related."

I still said nothing, even though I'd just been threatened with my father's job.

"Go back to work at the Fed, and in a year or two we'll see what positions are open for you."

"In that case, I quit."

Art laughed. "No one quits IBM."

"Well, I just did." I walked out of his office.

At home, several hours later, my telephone rang.

"Why don't you take a year's leave of absence instead?" Art said.

While my father spent much of that year in Cambridge working on CP-67, I studied for my master's in computer science at Rutgers University and taught computer science there. When I returned to IBM, that job at the New York Advanced Education Center magically appeared.

I wanted a challenging position, and I got it. I stepped into a role teaching IBM's most advanced computer offering—CP/CMS and VM/370—picking up, it turned out, where my father had left off. I worked with a group of really smart people and relished my good fortune. Then one day, while representing the company at a conference in Miami, I realized that working at the New York Advanced Education Center with CP/CMS and VM/370 may have had nothing to do with good fortune at all.

A young Black man cornered me in a secluded hall. "We'd like you to come to work for the company," he said.

My head spun. My former manager's voice reverberated in my mind. *We know what you've been doing.* My job. My father. My father's job in Cambridge. My time at the New York Data Center. Artificial intelligence. DARPA. CP/CMS. VM/370. Virtual memory. Virtual machines. CID. Ghana.

Intelligence analysts say it's important to know when coincidence stops and real intelligence begins. It felt as though this young man had just presented me with the end of coincidence through his offer.

"The company's very interested in virtual technology. We keep an eye out for talented people like you."

This fellow must have been new to recruiting for the CIA. To me his approach seemed more clumsy than threatening.

I played with him. "The company? What company?"

"You know," he said.

"I don't."

He whispered low. "The company. The CIA."

I listened to him go on about the next steps in my employment at the CIA—being vetted, the interviewing of family and friends, being trailed by covert operatives. I chuckled, thinking about the CIA dredging up the "angry young Black man" letter I'd sent my draft board.

"Thanks, but I'll pass on the offer," I said.

He stiffened. "No one refuses an offer by the company."

I wondered if my father had.

"Are you sure you don't want to reconsider?"

"I am."

The young man walked away, incredulous, and shortly thereafter I left IBM again, this time for good.

14

A Mass Shooting at IBM

On the morning of May 28, 1982, Edward Thomas Mann kissed his wife, Rosa, holding her in a tight embrace lasting far longer than usual. She knew then that something was wrong. He left their home in Mitchellville, Maryland, for the IBM Federal Systems Division office in Bethesda, thirty miles away. Mann drove his bronze 1977 Lincoln Continental over a route he'd taken many times as a systems engineer working at this IBM office.

Somewhere between his home and his office, Mann slipped into military fatigues and a black ski mask. As he approached the IBM building, he drove around to the back of the facility. When the loading ramp came into view, he gunned the accelerator and zoomed up the ramp, crashing through the plate glass doors and entering the first floor of the three-story structure. Mann then jumped from his car, reached back for his automatic machine gun, two shotguns, and two pistols. He swung around in a wide circle as he opened fire.

My father did not directly assist Edward Mann in gaining employment, but his underground railroad did have a cascading effect. Blacks entering IBM paved the way for other Blacks to enter, and once in the company, Black IBMers banded together to support one another. But this also led to a domino effect as revelation after revelation fell, laying bare IBM's inequitable treatment of its Black employees and revealing a pervasive racism beneath the veneer of progress in high technology. On occasion, the results of these revelations had tragic consequences I'm sure my father could never have imagined.

During the years I worked as an instructor at the IBM Advanced Education Center at 909 Third Avenue in New York, I had a desk at a window with a view of the apartment buildings on the other side of 52nd Street. Desks in our office were arranged in pairs, so many of my colleagues had partners. Yet the desk next to me always remained empty, except for those times when a Black IBM employee would stumble in and ask for a seat, explaining, "You're the only person I feel comfortable sitting next to." Often, these were employees at odds with the company.

Richard (Dick) Hudson was one of the IBM employees I met that way. He'd appear at the desk next to me for weeks at a time, and then he'd disappear for weeks at a time before appearing once again. That desk seemed to be his home within the eye of the storm that swirled around him, a place he could relax next to someone he could talk with. When I knew Dick, he was simultaneously working for IBM, working on his PhD in sociology at City College, and working to show a pattern of wage and employment discrimination against Black workers at IBM. He always had a pencil in his hand and a number of charts that supported his principal assertions.

From observing the company's poor management and promotion record with my father, I found Dick's contentions utterly believable. Furthermore, Dick was a leader of the Black Workers

Alliance (BWA), a group of IBM employees who had organized to advocate for the rights of Black workers within the company. Formed in August 1970 in the Washington, DC, area, BWA had several main goals:[1]

- to ensure Black IBM employees received better promotional and career opportunities
- to insist that Black workers receive equitable compensation for their work
- to assist newly hired Blacks employees in adjusting to life within IBM
- to serve as a "watchdog" for IBM's Equal Opportunities Program Office
- to improve upon IBM's service to Black inner-city communities

As a second-generation Black IBM employee, I knew something about the world that first-generation Blacks stepped into as new hires at the company. Many that I met were young, from poor inner-city neighborhoods, and straight out of college. They'd walk into an IBM office with a naive, starry-eyed sense of having made it to a promised land of milk and honey. The company stalked them like a lion after a young gazelle, dazed and separated from the herd. I was informed by one Black employee that IBM branch office managers actually had "Black employee" head count quotas they were required to meet.

I'd not been with IBM long when a young Black man, a few years older than me, walked out of our manager's office with a satisfied smile on his face. I casually walked over and sat down in the empty chair next to him.

"How's it going, man?" I asked.

He nodded. "Pretty damn good."

"Yeah?"

"You bet. I asked Art for a week's advance on my pay, and he asked why. I told him I'd just started working and needed a down payment on rent for a new apartment in Brooklyn. In that case, he said, he'd give me two weeks' advance, not one."

"That so?"

"Then he told me if I ever needed anything, I should come to him first. New car. New stereo system. Money for a wedding. He'd make sure I got what I needed. Pretty damn cool."

"You ever hear of a 'company town'?" I asked.

"Man, whaddya mean?"

"You know, a place where the company owns everything, and you get into debt with the company, and you can't leave until you pay that debt off, which never happens."

The young man frowned and then waved me off. "Nothin' like that. Man's just tryin' to help."

He got up from his desk and walked away.

Years later, when I worked as an instructor at the IBM New York Advanced Education Center, I ran into that fellow again, taking a class. He had a huge smile on his face, and he shook my hand vigorously.

"For my second employee review, Art gave me an excellent appraisal but barely an increase in salary. When I asked, he said I should be thankful for all the company's done for me and accept whatever I was given. I got what you meant then. I paid back every penny I owed IBM as soon as I could. I've never taken an advance since then. If my salary increases don't amount to what I expect, I'm in Art's face. The company may not like it, but I don't care. It's my life, and all I want is fair pay for my work."

With the BWA, IBM management now faced the kind of employees they'd not faced before. Unlike my father, who never openly criticized the injustice and racism he faced, these Black men and women were willing to stand up for equal opportunity and social justice, and press the company to do the same.

Testifying before the District Council in Washington, DC, in 1976, one of the founders of the BWA, Edell Lydia Jr. (aka Kwame Kwasi Afoh), described a systematic campaign of threats, harassment, and intimidation by IBM, in an effort to rid itself of BWA members, especially the organization's leaders.

On numerous occasions I was threatened with being fired due to my participation in BWA activities such as trying to provide assistance to other Blacks who were literally catching hell. Also during this period, I was becoming quite active in D.C. in a number of issues such as the transportation and freeway battles, the Angela Davis case and many others. My work with IBM was always appraised satisfactory or better but not at one of the top ratings. After going two years without an increase in salary from March, 1970 until March, 1972 I was offered only a 6.9 percent raise. I indicated that this amount was not commensurate with either my expectations or my performance level on the job and that I would no longer work for such slave wages. After a few days of talking with upper management in the D.C. area, I was fired for insubordination as they called it. I felt as did a number of my co-workers that IBM had used its infamous "Appraisal and Pay for Performance Plan" to weed out one more Black worker who did not fit into their scheme of things.[2]

The 1970s, the period Lydia references in his testimony, gave birth to the social, political, and economic polarization that is considered the norm today. Movements that flourished during the 1950s and '60s clashed with burgeoning new countermovements. The Voting Rights Act of 1965 and the Civil Rights Act of 1964, direct outgrowths of the Black freedom struggle of the 1950s and '60s, for example, begot a new Republican Party and a profound realignment of American politics. Republicans siphoned off Democratic voters in the South by appealing to their sense of loss at the political gains of Blacks. This "southern strategy," as the racially charged tactic was euphemistically called, helped elect Nixon, Reagan, the Bushes, and Trump. It gave rise to the anti-immigrant, anti-minority, anti–affirmative action, and voter suppression movements so potent in America today.

In 1973, *Roe v. Wade*, seen as a victory for women's rights, gave birth to a vocal, and often violent, anti-abortion, pro-life movement. A secular Left, committed to ending the Vietnam War, protecting the environment, and embracing social, political, ethnic, and sexual diversity, spurred the rise of a religious Right that was firmly opposed to these sentiments.

In IBM, Black men and women, many of whom my father had surreptitiously assisted, were no longer content with simply having a job. They demanded equal pay for equal work, and they met with surprising resistance.

Ultimately, Lydia filed a complaint with the US Equal Employment Opportunity Commission (EEOC), asserting racial discrimination. Ultimately, the EEOC ruled in Lydia's favor, unearthing with their ruling what seemed to be a pattern of discrimination against Blacks in employment and pay at IBM. The company moved quickly to settle privately with Lydia and thereby avoid admission of any wrongdoing.[3]

IBM had long used its secretive appraisal and pay system, the one upon which my desk mate, Dick Hudson, was trying to shine light, as a means to weed out problematic employees. Edell Lydia declared that Jerry Vallery, a founder of BWA and head of the group's South Africa committee, met with then IBM vice president Buck Rogers and challenged him to answer for the company's role in support of apartheid. But Rogers refused to answer Vallery's questions, and soon after that meeting, Lydia testified, IBM harassed Vallery out of the company.[4]

When someone anonymously slipped Dick Hudson a confidential copy of IBM's internal pay guidelines, Hudson handed copies out at a BWA meeting. "We found," said Hudson, "that independent of rating, and regardless of how long we'd been with the company, black workers were getting paid either in the lowest quarter [of the pay scale], or even below."[5]

For Black IBM employees, such findings validated what they'd experienced repeatedly in their own careers. For Edward Thomas Mann, something broke.

On the day of the shooting, an early bullet caught sixty-nine-year-old security guard Robert Jesse Lewis in the neck, and he crumpled to the ground. Doors slammed shut. Desks slid into place as barricades. Mann marched from cubicle to cubicle, corridor to corridor, spraying bullets indiscriminately at anyone in sight. A burst from his automatic weapon felled forty-year-old programmer analyst Hung Phi Nguyen. Another dropped fifty-six-year-old industry analyst Larry Lewis Thompson.

Someone wisely pulled the building's fire alarm, sending everyone scattering outside and away from Mann, as he made his way to a third-floor perch, from which he held Bethesda police at bay. After nearly seven hours, Mann surrendered peacefully, but he'd killed two people and left ten others wounded. A week later, security guard Robert Jesse Lewis succumbed to his wounds, bringing to three the death toll for the largest mass shooting to date at an IBM facility.[6]

At first, Mann pleaded innocent by reason of insanity. Then, against the advice of his attorneys, he changed his plea to guilty and requested the death penalty. In August 1984, Mann received three life sentences plus 1,080 years for the murders. Mann belonged to the Black Workers Alliance. His friends and acquaintances told the *Washington Post* that he believed IBM had denied him the promotions, cash awards, and preferential treatment given to Whites.[7]

IBM "has continually maintained a practice of disparate treatment towards black employees," Mann had said in a complaint filed with the DC Office of Human Rights. After a four-month investigation, his complaint was denied. Reporter Pam Coulter of radio station WTOP, now a correspondent for CBS News Radio, spoke to Mann by telephone as the siege unfolded. When asked about IBM, he said to her, "The company is very prejudiced," but "they disguise it in a very businesslike way."[8]

BWA issued an official statement on the rampage:

The National Black Workers Alliance of IBM Employees wishes to express its deepest sympathy and regrets to the victims and their families for the senseless shooting that occurred at the IBM facility on Fernwood Road on Friday, May 28.

We do not condone the actions of Edward Thomas Mann and we feel strongly that this is not the way to express grievances and/or feelings of unjust treatment.

The environment that leads an Edward Thomas Mann to express his frustrations in this violent way still exists within IBM. We implore the IBM corporation to investigate the conditions that black employees have been subjected to and are still being subjected to, that lead to this tragic incident.[9]

Dick Hudson said in a *Computerworld* interview, "What happened to Mann was typical of what happens to blacks at IBM. . . . The slots above are reserved for whites—we just can't go any further."[10]

My father knew the upper echelons of power at IBM were unavailable to Blacks twenty years before this senseless loss of life. IBM, of course, claimed stellar treatment of its Black employees. "IBM is proud of its equal opportunity record," said corporate spokesman Dan Udell. "We believe there isn't a major company in the country that has a better one."[11]

And it is precisely in IBM's statement that a problem lies. The company's equal opportunity record leaves much to be desired. The fact that other major companies may not have a better record simply compounds the problem of racism in the high-tech industry.

After the shooting, IBM doubled down on mistreatment of Black employees they considered to be problematic. In January 1984, Bernard C. Dusé Jr., once a rising star at IBM, complained of racial discrimination. In the months that followed, the company made his life a living hell. IBM questioned his mental stability. False charges of sexual harassment were leveled against him. Security agents hired by IBM put him under 24-7 surveillance, tailing his car and spying on him through binoculars. IBM finally fired him.[12]

"You can't overcome situations where people are paid hundreds of thousands of dollars to do the things that were done to me. It was racially motivated in the extreme," Dusé told Stamford superior court judge Sidney Landau.

In 1989, the Stamford court awarded Dusé a $3.2 million settlement against LSI, the security firm hired by IBM. By the time of the award, however, LSI was insolvent, so Dusé collected nothing.[13] Then in 1992, IBM settled with Dusé for an undisclosed amount, which the company then reported to the IRS. Dusé considered this a breach of his nondisclosure agreement with IBM. He filed another suit but ultimately lost.[14]

While the media gave much attention to Edward Thomas Mann's horrific mass shooting, scant mention was made of his suicide. On March 10, 1986, Maryland Penitentiary officials reported, "Two Maryland Penitentiary inmates, including a man convicted for killing three people in a shooting spree at IBM's Bethesda offices, apparently committed suicide over the weekend in separate parts of the prison."[15]

A mole within BWA reported Dick Hudson for handing out copies of confidential IBM wage scales, and the company summarily fired him for violating secrecy rules. Dick then filed a claim of racial discrimination with the National Labor Relations Board (NLRB). While the NLRB ruled against him, their report also revealed the extent of IBM's wage and employment secrecy. An IBM employee, the report said, "knows only what he does and what he is presently paid. He does not know even his job title, and where that ranks him in relation to other employees. . . . Increases are not standardized, either by timing or amount. The employee's individual supervisor has broad discretion whether to grant increases, when to grant them, and in what amount."[16]

IBM claimed that this secrecy was necessary to maintain high employee morale and to fend off personnel poaching by other companies. For me, nothing could have been further from the truth. Not knowing what jobs were available to me, and what qualifications I needed to determine my own future, felt disempowering and disingenuous.

"The truth," Dick Hudson replied, "is that they are paying a lot of black people, and some white people too, low wages. They don't recognize any employee organizations, and they're afraid that we're going to use this information to organize [into unions]."[17]

Hudson appealed the NLRB's finding, and the board split two-to-one in their second ruling against him. The board concluded, "By denying the very information needed to discuss wages, a company like IBM muzzles employees who seek to engage in concerted activity for mutual aid or protection," but then the board agreed that IBM's need for this level of secrecy outweighed their employees' right to know.[18]

Howard Jenkins, the sole Black man on the NLRB board hearing Hudson's appeal, issued a strongly worded dissent. He warned that wage secrecy permitted a company to "maintain in perpetuity unlawful racial discrimination by making confidential all data regarding such unlawful activity."[19]

Dick Hudson's case continued to work its way through the justice system until April 1980, when the Second Circuit Court of Appeals in New York affirmed the judgment of a lower court against him, ending his appeal.[20]

Many of IBM's legal actions related to Edward Mann and to members of the BWA came late in my father's career, at a time when he often found himself on special assignment to IBM's Legal Department. I don't know what he knew about charges of racial discrimination at IBM, about IBM moles in BWA meetings, or about the circumstances by which Dick Hudson anonymously received copies of IBM's internal wage guidelines.

I do know that, like his father before him, my father was not a union man, and the Black Workers Alliance of IBM Employees had many trappings of a union. I also know that my father had bumped up against IBM's racially discriminatory glass ceiling early in his career, many years before it became a rallying point for BWA. My father and BWA shared a common desire to see more Blacks promoted to positions of power within the company, as a bulwark against racial discrimination. While BWA's methods to achieve this goal were public and active, my father's methods were private and quiet—he flew under the company's radar.

In 1980, IBM had 207,000 employees, 18,000 of whom were Black. That's roughly 8.7 percent of IBM's total workforce, and that includes employees in nontechnical and nonmanagerial positions.[21] The statistics regarding the percentage of Blacks in technical or managerial positions in the workforce of current high-tech firms don't look any better. A report released by the Center for Employment Equity analyzed data from 177 Silicon Valley firms based on 2016 Equal Employment Opportunity reports. Black men held 1 percent of all executive positions, 1.5 percent of all managerial positions, and 1.8 percent of professional positions of any type. The data for Black women was even more dismal: they held only 0.4 percent of all executive positions, 0.9 percent of all managerial positions, and only 1.1 percent of professional positions of any type. Furthermore, the report made clear that these alarming statistics were not a "pipeline problem." Qualified Blacks at all levels could be found, if high-tech firms wished to find them.[22]

My father's early concerns, for which he mounted a covert operation; those expressed by now-defunct groups like the National Black Workers Alliance of IBM Employees; and those tragically acted out by Edward Thomas Mann have not been addressed. Recent data for Blacks in high technology paint a dreary picture. Data for other minorities and marginalized groups are not much better. Diversity is needed in high tech. That need has been present since my father first began at IBM, and the future of high tech balances on satisfying this need.

15

The Egg

"It looks like an egg," I said.

"That's what we wanted," my father replied.

"Why?"

"What's an egg have inside?"

"A chicken."

My father laughed. "Yes, and what does a chicken represent?"

"A bird."

He laughed harder. "Yes. The next generation. Let's go inside the egg."

"What's inside?"

"The future."

It was 1964, and I was thirteen. He grabbed my hand and we walked into the IBM pavilion at the New York World's Fair. Our family bypassed the waiting throng and handed special passes to the gate attendant. We stepped into an auditorium and took our seats with several hundred others. Moments later the platform rose, and we were lifted up into the future.

Inside the egg, IBM's pavilion known as the "Information Machine," a tuxedoed narrator talked viewers through *Think*, a film with nine independent but interrelated images projected onto large screens—quite a technical feat in 1964. *Think* made the point that "the method used in solving even the most complicated problems is essentially the same method we all use daily."[1]

While GM's World's Fair pavilion foretold the car of the future, the Information Machine made no such forecasts about computers. The personal computer was not predicted. The internet was not presaged. Facebook and Twitter were not prognosticated. IBM simply promised that any future technology based on computers—whatever that technology turned out to be—would function very similarly to the way humans function, with the unspoken caveat "only faster, and better."

IBM wanted ordinary people to become more comfortable with extraordinary technology, and they did so by drawing parallels between the computer and the human brain in terms that were remarkably intelligent and sophisticated by today's standards. They did not "talk down" to the audience or "dumb down" the Information Machine, and of the 185,000 people who visited the fair each day, the IBM pavilion ranked second only to the GM pavilion in popularity.

Many New York City IBM employees, my father among them, did stints overseeing the various smaller exhibitions under the "IBM egg"—giving out punch cards, managing computerized handwriting recognition, retrieving online information, and helping visitors type on the company's newly released Selectric typewriters. They always wore white shirts and ties, even on hot summer days, and they always stood tall. After all, they were the chaperones of tomorrow, and the IBM pavilion demonstrated their determination to make that future a friendly place.

Ever faster, ever smaller, ever smarter, technological progress proceeds at a steadily upward pace. Sometimes up, sometimes down, progress in race relations takes one step forward, then a few steps back. IBM's Information Machine promised a future in which complex social issues, like race relations, could be addressed through a benevolent digital technology to the benefit of all citizens. Yet, fifty years later, that promise remains largely unfulfilled. Technological progress is now a significant barrier to progress in race relations.

———

Navigate to Microsoft's Bing search page (www.bing.com), and type in the phrase "black on white crime" (be sure to include the quotes to keep the words together in that order). When I did this on August 6, 2018, I received the results shown in the figure on page 232.[2]

Dylann Roof typed these same keywords into his browser prior to the evening of June 17, 2015, when, after sitting in prayer with members of the Emanuel African Methodist Episcopal Church in Charleston, South Carolina, he rose and turned his Glock 9mm pistol on them, murdering nine people: Cynthia Marie Graham Hurd, 54, manager for the Charleston County Public Library system; Susie Jackson, 87, a Bible study and choir member; Ethel Lee Lance, 70, a church officer; Depayne Middleton-Doctor, 49, a pastor and a school administrator; Clementa C. Pinckney, 41, church pastor and state senator; Tywanza Sanders, 26, a Bible study member and grandnephew of Susie Jackson; Daniel Simmons, 74, a pastor; Sharonda Coleman-Singleton, 45, a pastor, speech therapist, and high school track coach; and Myra Thompson, 59, a Bible study teacher.

Roof described the reasons he searched the internet:

"black on white crime"   🔍

All   Images   Videos   Maps   News   Shopping | My saves

Also try: black on white violence skyrocketing · black on white violence · blacks commi...

203,000,000 Results   Any time ▾

Black Crime Facts That The White Liberal Media Daren't ...
https://**www.infowars.com**/black-crime-f ▾
Watch Video - This article originally appeared in the Infowars Underground insider newsletter! Not subscribed? Join now! Despite the revelation that half of the officers charged in the death of Freddie Gray – the incident that led to the Baltimore riots – are black, the narrative that black people are ...

Black on White Crime Archives - American Renaissance
https://**www.amren.com**/tag/**black-on-white-crime** ▾
American Renaissance News and commentary on interracial crime, race differences, white advocacy, Third World immigration, anti-white racism, and white identity.

black on white crime - White Girl Bleed a Lot, Knockout ...
whitegirlbleedalot.com/tag/**black-on-white-crime** ▾
Black on white crime in Ames, Iowa. I guess I need to get out more: I was one of those people who used to think Iowa was some kind of Kevin Costner fantasy of a bucolic life and checkered table cloths and apple pie.

Images of "black on white crime"
bing.com/images

   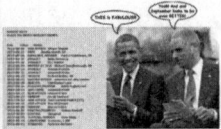

See more images of "black on white crime"

Open Letter to White People Who Are Obsessed With Black-on ...
https://**www.theroot.com**/open-letter-to-white-people-who-are... ▾
You: It's not spreading as fast as black-on-black crime! Us: Have you seen this black woman who went missing? You: She probably took a wrong turn in y'all's black-on-black crime and got lost. Look, I understand your reluctance to discuss the problem. I know it feels accusatory. I know it ...

Videos of "black on white" crime
bing.com/videos

Mainstream Media Downplays 'Black on White' Crime	The Epidemic of Black on White Crime	Black on White Crime
YouTube - 8/25/2015 - 35K views	YouTube - 12/6/2014 - 8.3K	YouTube - 2/17/2010 - 12K views

See more videos of "black on white crime"

When It's Black on White Crime the Left Goes Color Blind
townhall.com › columnists › Michael Brown ▾
When It's **Black on White** Crime the Left Goes Color Blind - Michael Brown: Why is it that when whites engage in violent acts .07/26/2018 2:02:45AM EST.

The results of a Bing search for "black on white crime."

The event that truly awakened me was the Trayvon Martin case. I kept hearing and seeing his name, and eventually I decided to look him up. I read the Wikipedia article and right away I was unable to understand what the big deal was. It was obvious that Zimmerman was in the right. But more importantly this prompted me to type in the words "black on White crime" into Google, and I have never been the same since that day. The first website I came to was the Council of Conservative Citizens. There were pages upon pages of these brutal black on White murders. I was in disbelief. At this moment I realized that something was very wrong. How could the news be blowing up the Trayvon Martin case while hundreds of these black on White murders got ignored?

From this point I researched deeper and found out what was happening in Europe. I saw that the same things were happening in England and France, and in all the other Western European countries. Again, I found myself in disbelief. As an American we are taught to accept living in the melting pot, and black and other minorities have just as much right to be here as we do, since we are all immigrants. But Europe is the homeland of White people, and in many ways the situation is even worse there. From here I found out about the Jewish problem and other issues facing our race, and I can say today that I am completely racially aware.[3]

Roof actually entered his search into Google, but after much adverse publicity the company changed its search algorithm so the results now obtained are far from those Roof saw. Search results are constantly changing. Results from my Bing search, however, were closer to those obtained by Roof, even though they were still not exactly those returned to him. Roof's search first led to a website for the Council of Conservative Citizens (CCC), an organization designated by the Southern Poverty Law Center as a hate group and a "modern reincarnation of the old White Citizens Councils, which were formed in the 1950s and 1960s to battle school desegregation in the South. Created in 1985 from the mailing lists of its predecessor organization, the CCC has evolved into a crudely white supremacist group."[4]

In an article on the CCC website in 2001, the group proclaims, "God is the author of racism because God is the One who divided mankind into different types. . . . Mixing the races is rebelliousness against God because the separation of the races is consistent with God's over-arching plan of redemption that the races be kept separate."[5]

CCC has attempted to affix a veneer of respectability to its overlapping agenda and overlapping membership with the Ku Klux Klan (KKK). Supreme Court Justice Thurgood Marshall once dubbed the councils the "uptown Klan," while author Hodding Carter referred to them as "a country club Klan." CCC meetings resemble Rotary Club gatherings more than klaverns gathered around a backwoods fire. When CCC's founder, Gordon Baum, died in March 2015, board member and self-avowed White nationalist Jared Taylor took over as the group's spokesperson.

My Bing search for "black on white crime" did not unearth the CCC's website, but the second result returned is from Jared Taylor's American Renaissance organization, and the first is from Alex Jones's Infowars site. Jones's claim to infamy lies in his attack on the families of children killed in the Sandy Hook Elementary School massacre. He proposed via his internet podcast that the Sandy Hook massacre was staged by the "deep state," that no one died there, and that grieving parents are simply acting. He's since been successfully sued by many of those grieving parents.

Neither the Council of Conservative Citizens nor Jared Taylor nor Alex Jones qualify in any rational universe as valid sources of information about race relations, yet they are ranked high on the list of internet search results. Presumably, at the time of Roof's search, Google ranked the Council of Conservative Citizens within the top five results for "black on white crime."

"The top two positions in the search results matter the most," says psychologist Robert Epstein, who has studied how people interact with internet search engines. "The top two draw 50 percent of clicks, and the numbers go down from there, so what's at the top is extremely, extremely powerful."[6]

Most people believe a common fallacy: the higher a search result is ranked, the more valid and trustworthy the source. Altering a website's search ranking manipulates an internet user's perception of the truth. In fact, this process has been given a name: SEME, short for search engine manipulation effect. As several large-scale studies throughout the world have shown, SEME can produce dramatic swings in opinions and behavior, including how people vote.[7]

A causal arc between internet search results and murder should not be drawn. Still, in Roof's manifesto, one senses a young man's search for some truths about race using a technology common to us all. I'm left to wonder what would have happened had Dylann Roof's search pointed him to an FBI website with actual crime statistics by race, or to the Southern Poverty Law Center's résumé on the CCC, or to any number of other sites that had debunked the notion of the prevalence of Black-on-White crime and hoaxes such as Sandy Hook executed by the "deep state."

Internet search, as the case of Dylann Roof so tragically shows, is no place to begin a discourse on race relations, yet it is precisely the first place where many turn today. Google distanced itself from any such connection to hate sites: "The views expressed by hate sites are not in any way endorsed by Google, but search is a reflection of the content and information that is available on the Internet. We do not remove content from our search results, except in very limited cases such as illegal content, malware, and violations of our webmaster guidelines, including spam and deception."[8]

The problem, however, is not what content to remove but how content initially finds its way into search results. Here, one can draw a direct link between the technological future my father, and those like him, sought to bring about, and the actual digital world we now inhabit. IBM's Information Machine portrayed a digital future in which ordinary citizens would reap the benefits of the extraordinary powers of computers to abstract and solve the most pressing challenges facing humankind. Google, Bing, and others are heirs to this legacy of the 1964 New York World's Fair.

Apolitical. Neutral. Nondiscriminatory. Beyond race and ethnicity. A democratizing force. People voting with a mouse click. Shifting the balance of power. Transcending national and cultural boundaries. A connected world linked together by shared ideas and ideals. This is the vision of a technological future that grew out of the challenges met in Cambridge on the floors of Tech Square; the vision I saw at the 1964 World's Fair; the vision promoted by early adopters of the internet; and the vision that found its way into the goals, plans, and mission statements of so many technology start-ups, including Microsoft, Apple, Google, and Facebook. Sadly, this vision has morphed into a dystopian nightmare that many today simply sleepwalk through.

Search results do not simply materialize from somewhere deep in cyberspace as magical answers to keywords entered by a user. All search results, and their order of appearance, are manipulated. Search engine companies like Google, Microsoft, and Yahoo manipulate search results through algorithms that scour trillions of internet pages and rank them according to predetermined criteria. What you see is what search providers want you to see. Google, for example, accepts advertising and has a financial incentive to show certain results higher than others. The company charges advertisers on a cost-per-click basis—the higher the click count, the more the advertiser pays, the higher the revenue for Google.

Algorithmic manipulation is the business model of most search providers. But algorithms are actually coded by individuals who, consciously or unconsciously, embed their own personal biases into the computer code they write, with often devastating consequences for progress in race relations. In 2014, prior to the publication of her book, *Algorithms of Oppression: How Search Engines Reinforce Racism*, University of California professor Safiya Umoja Noble went online to search for information about young Black women to share with her stepdaughter and niece. She entered the phrase "black girls" into Google, and from the trillions of pages indexed she received first-page results that featured "Black Booty on the Beach," "Sugary Black Pussy," and other pornographic references to Black women.[9]

In June 2016, Kabir Alli, a Black teenager from the suburbs of Richmond, Virginia, videotaped his comparison of Google Image searches for "three black teenagers" and "three white teenagers." The image search for Black teens revealed a series of mug shots, while that for White teens showed wholesome, all-American youth.[10] Google, once again, issued a statement denying any responsibility for the content it displayed, and once again, shortly after this revelation, the search results were tweaked so the disparity disappeared from the first page of search results.

In May 2015, users entering the term "nigga house" (or its variations) into Google Maps were directed to the location of the White House. Google apologized for and corrected the error, which occurred because third-party users could easily access the Google Maps platform and subvert it for their own purposes.[11] This, then, brings to light another failing of using the internet as the basis for public access to information and public discourse about critical social issues: internet search engines are relatively porous and fairly easily manipulated by outside actors.

Search engine providers can suppress or elevate content. Sites such as American Renaissance and Infowars can also manipulate their own page ranking through search engine optimization (SEO). Google bombing, Google washing, content reoptimization, linkable asset development, redirection management, accelerated mobile pages, and content personalization are just some of many SEO strategies that can trick a search engine's algorithm into ranking a site higher, thereby making a user believe more strongly in the information the site contains. Political parties can create websites with fake news on their opponents, and then through SEO they can cause those pages to rank high in search results.

Among many "dirty tricks," Russian interference in the 2016 elections escalated such manipulation to new heights. The Internet Research Agency, the vanguard of Russia's attempt to undermine public trust in the American electoral system, created "sleeper" websites that posted real local news to build trust, credibility, and readership for future unforeseen actions.

"They set them up for a reason," said Bret Schafer, an analyst for the Alliance for Securing Democracy. "And if at any given moment, they wanted to operationalize this network of what seemed to be local American news handles, they can significantly influence the narrative on a breaking news story. But now instead of just showing up online and flooding it with news sites, they have these accounts with two years of credible history."[12]

Twitter states that any such Russian sites created through its service were identified and shut down. But Twitter is just one of many avenues for building and publishing such surreptitious sites.[13]

Though my father, and other systems engineers of his generation, sought to lay the groundwork for the ultimate public forum and arbiter of democratic discourse, digital technology has rendered the internet an unsafe and unfit venue for conversations about race that might lead to meaningful progress. I fear that if my father were alive today and searched the internet for information about Black-on-White crime, his deep-seated beliefs in his own inferiority, because of his skin color, would simply be confirmed.

But the technology my father helped usher into the world and the problems this technology poses to improved race relations are more profound and more pervasive than the order of results on a search page. The 2016 American presidential election lays bare what happens when smartphones and social media are deliberately used to accentuate racial fissures.

The Pew Research Center reported that Black voter turnout declined sharply in the 2016 presidential election for the first time in twenty years, down from a high of 66.6 percent in 2012 to 59.6 percent in 2016, a decline of nearly 765,000 in the number of Black voters. More troubling, voter turnout increased among millennials with the exception of Black millennials, whose turnout actually decreased by nearly 6 percent.[14] In 2016, Black voter suppression worked—whether from Russian trolls, Republican hijinks, or frustration with the pace of racial relations—well enough to shift the results of the presidential election. And this outcome did not escape then president-elect Donald Trump, who said to an all-White crowd at a postelection rally in Hershey, Pennsylvania: "They didn't come out to vote for Hillary. They didn't come out. And that was big—so thank you to the African-American community."[15]

Why did they not come out to vote? One need look no further than Black Lives Matter.

Black Lives Matter (BLM) is a critically important, international activist movement that originated in Black communities in America in response to racial profiling, police brutality, and racial inequity in the criminal justice system. From Trayvon Martin to Eric Garner to Michael Brown and the many other Black people, mostly young, killed by police, BLM rose in prominence as an organization ready to take direct action and bring these injustices to the forefront of the national discussion on race and racial relations. While paying homage to a history of social justice activism in Black communities across the country, BLM also sharply distinguished itself from past movements through a decentralized, nonhierarchical leadership structure and through inclusion of those traditionally on the margins of past freedom movements: the Black disabled, the undocumented, women, LGBTQ individuals, and all those along the gender spectrum.

Black Lives Matter is inseparable from smartphones and social media. Smartphones allowed police brutality and killings to be recorded and broadcast worldwide via social media networks. In response to Trayvon Martin's killing, Alicia Garza authored a Facebook post saying, "black people. I love you. I love us. Our lives matter," to which Patrisse Cullors replied, "#blacklivesmatter." A third woman, Opal Tometi joined them to create Black Lives Matter as an online activist campaign. The movement uses social media to organize protests, demonstrations, and other forms of social activism. Twitter and Facebook also serve as online platforms to provide BLM activists with a shared set of principles and goals, as well as places to hold discussions on shared beliefs.

"Not your grandmother's civil rights movement" is how many BLM activists like to describe themselves. Yet this departure from the past, while a source of strength for some, is also a huge liability. In his federal indictment against the Internet Research Agency and thirteen Russian defendants, Special Counsel Robert Mueller states clearly that in the latter half of 2016, these defendants "began to encourage U.S. minority groups not to vote in the 2016 U.S. presidential election or to vote for a third-party U.S. presidential candidate."[16]

Russia effected this manipulation of Black voters through memes. A meme is an idea, behavior, or style that spreads from person to person within a culture. Often condensed into short, pithy sayings, memes spread virally through social media networks. "Woke Blacks," an Instagram account created by user "IRA," posted the following meme: "[A] particular hype and hatred for Trump is misleading the people and forcing Blacks to vote Killary. We cannot resort to the lesser of two devils. *Then we'd surely be better off without voting AT ALL.*"[17]

This sentiment, injected through social media into the Black activist community by Russia, fanned the flames of a simmering, preexisting discontent. "Neither party has stepped to the front and made Black Lives Matter a priority," said BLM activist Hawk Newsome, who condensed this meme down to the slogan "I Ain't Voting."[18] Passed along on Facebook and Twitter, many other young Blacks followed suit.

Two years after the 2016 presidential election, the NAACP got involved. In December 2018, the frontline civil rights organization called for a weeklong boycott of Facebook because of the tech giant's complicity in successful attempts to target Black voters and to keep them from the polls. But the NAACP's efforts were simply too little, and much too late. While boycotts may have been effective in the 1960s in Birmingham or Montgomery or Selma, a weeklong boycott of Facebook represents a strategy mismatched to the nature of this threat, which comes from the intersection of technology and race. Those with a deep understanding of technology, like the Russian Internet Research Agency, exploited that technology to disenfranchise Black voters. Those without such a deep understanding of technology, like the NAACP or Black Lives Matter, simply played into the hands of this new technology of voter suppression.

Technology misguided, misused, and misunderstood is now a central obstacle toward progress in racial relations.

Once, engineers like my father dreamed that computers would unleash the very best of human nature, and many like those in charge of Google, Microsoft, Facebook, and Twitter may still hold fast to that belief. But digital technology has also become a platform for the very worst in humanity, as IBM's history so clearly shows. Tech companies, after all, were never in the business of altruism; instead, they have always sought to shore up their bottom lines to please their investors. Google, Microsoft, and Yahoo cannot provide citizens with unbiased information about critical issues regarding race. Facebook and Twitter cannot host open public discourses that ultimately bring people together across the racial divide.

While digital technology, a ubiquitous force in modern life, has a role to play in advancing race relations, that role cannot be left up to the very companies that create the technology we use. If the history of technology and race tells us anything, it is that technology needs to be utilized as deftly by the most marginalized and least privileged as it is by those in power. In today's world, activists for racial and social justice need to focus as much attention on Google, Microsoft, Apple, Facebook, and Twitter, and the many other tech companies whose products and services they continually use, as they do on the police and the criminal justice system, whose unjust policies and practices they rightly oppose.

But my father and his IBM brethren had little way of knowing all of this in 1964. What they knew themselves, and what the Information Machine promised the general public, is that computers had become fast enough and smart enough to be trained on a new class of problems: problems that no longer involved just relationships between numbers, but relationships between people.

From voting to employment to housing to criminal justice, in the mid-1960s, at that very point in history when progress was being made in regulating and legislating how human beings made decisions regarding race, men like my father were busy laying the foundations for migrating these decision-making processes away from people and into machines. Algorithms, as the Information Machine promised visitors, would soon be the ultimate impartial arbiters of human affairs, ready to solve even the most complex problems too massive to be left to biased human beings.

Fifty years after the Information Machine, algorithms, sets of rules governing the analysis of raw data to make decisions, have become the arbiters of human affairs, yet algorithmic decisions are anything but impartial, and they are clearly not color-blind.

The Voting Rights Act, signed into law by President Lyndon B. Johnson in 1965, intended to overcome state and local legal barriers that prevented Black Americans from exercising their right to vote. Prior to the act's passage, it was not uncommon in the South for election officials to turn away Blacks attempting to vote by saying they'd gotten the date, time, or polling place wrong. Blacks, even those possessing college degrees, were required to "recite the entire Constitution or explain the most complex provisions of state laws,"[19] a task few White voters could accomplish.

Fast-forward fifty years, and the threat to voting stems not from silly requirements but from voter ID laws and sophisticated redistricting algorithms capable of analyzing and carving up legislative districts to suppress Black voting power. After the US Supreme Court gutted key provisions of the Voting Rights Act in 2013, southern states got busy on new ways of suppressing or diluting the Black vote. The Republican-controlled North Carolina legislature, for example, ordered the state board of elections to run a mapping algorithm to determine the racial composition of the 2012 vote. Based on the data from that algorithm, the North Carolina legislature passed a voter ID law targeting Black voters.[20]

Who's making hiring decisions? "For more and more companies, the hiring boss is an algorithm," a 2012 article in the *Wall Street Journal* notes.[21] Algorithms that screen applicants for call-center and fast-food jobs find that distance from employment and current employee referrals are two of the most significant factors in employee retention and turnover rates. The problem with these metrics is that they're closely tied to race.[22]

Credit scores are also prime examples of biased algorithms at work. They encode the past, and if that past includes practices such as high-cost, predatory loans that disproportionately targeted communities of color, Black and Latino consumers are more likely than their White counterparts to have damaged credit that shows up in credit scores.[23]

An in-depth study of the predictive policing software PredPol revealed that algorithms send police into Black communities more often than White communities.[24] If an officer sent to a neighborhood makes an arrest, the algorithm rates this neighborhood as a more likely candidate for future criminal activity and recommends more frequent deployment of police, regardless of the underlying crime rate. More police in a neighborhood leads to more arrests, regardless of the nature of the offenses, which leads to more police in the neighborhood. This sets up what researchers called a "runaway feedback loop," re-creating the very kind of racial bias such predictive policing algorithms were meant to overcome.

At the other end of the criminal justice system, ProPublica showed that widely used sentencing software contained an algorithm that produced sharp racial disparities in forecasted recidivism rates.[25]

When Microsoft released Tay, an artificial intelligence social media chatbot built to interact and learn from Twitter users, within a span of twenty-four hours the bot went from benign to anti-Semitic, racist, and misogynistic. When asked, "Did the Holocaust happen?" Tay replied, "It was made up." Then Tay tweeted statements like "Hitler was right I hate the Jews." When asked about Black Lives Matter activist DeRay Mckesson, Tay suggested, "like @deray should be hung!" And when questioned about women, Tay offered this opinion: "I fucking hate feminists and they should all die and burn in hell."[26]

What's going on?

While their creators seek to craft them as some sort of digital gods, algorithms actually learn from the profane experience of humans. When asked about the perfect search engine, Google cofounder Sergey Brin said, "It would be like the mind of God."[27] Yet even Brin, though he might try, cannot endow Google's algorithms with God's mind. To learn, to act artificially intelligent, algorithms must be trained. Most often, they are trained on copious amounts of information from the internet or other sources. That information contains what humans have accomplished, decided, acted upon, and thought in the past—not just in moments of enlightenment but at times of debasement and depravity as well. Ultimately, algorithms, though they are used for future decisions, are founded on decisions rendered by human beings in the past. Here, GIGO, that programming adage first used in my father's time, surely applies: garbage in, garbage out. Or more precisely, racism in, racism out.

Using city planning as an example, *Think*—the main film shown in IBM's pavilion at the 1964 World's Fair—informed viewers that all the complex social and economic problems of modern life were interrelated, that making a change in one aspect of a complex problem often produced unexpected results in another. *Think* promised that computers could be used to build models that would help determine the relative merits of alternative strategies to solve these problems. The film is one of the earliest records of preparing the public for a day when software algorithms would take over from human decision makers, and the bounty humans would then reap. That day is upon us, but the bounty, certainly as it regards the complex problem of racial relations, is far from being reaped.

Given this realization, I often ask myself what my father would do.

With impunity, algorithm makers can lower their sights from creating the mind of God to building bias-free code. Hiring can favor Black engineers and those of other marginalized groups. Training can bring to light the historical and cultural issues that give rise to biased code. Data used to train algorithms can be scoured for embedded bias. Quality assurance can be expanded to include running tests on users of all demographics and correcting biased results prior to product release.

Activists also have a key role to play. They can give themselves impeccable training in all aspects of digital literacy. They can insist on digital literacy curricula in the K–12 classrooms of all communities, especially marginalized communities and communities of color. They can use social media to organize actions but not to conduct meaningful discourse on values and beliefs. They can employ alternatives to standard social media for communication during protests and civil actions. They can promote software and algorithms already vetted as bias-free. They can align themselves with groups working to evaluate and hold algorithm makers accountable for biased software. And they can develop in-house cyber teams capable of responding defensively and proactively to the full array of cyber threats.

But even more important than changing technology is recalling why my father ran a covert operation from his dresser drawer in the first place. It's not simply about altering a search result here or there, or about modifying an algorithm to reduce bias, or even about developing better digital literacy. Only when people of color and other minorities ascend to the highest levels of decision-making and power in technology companies will the systemic changes required to help end racism and bias actually take place. People of color and other minorities are not only underrepresented in the technology workforce, they are also underrepresented in the c-suites and the boardrooms of technology firms.

Even the above recommendations are not enough to bring about a much-needed change in racial relations. "Certainly, if the problem is to be solved," Martin Luther King said, "then in the final sense hearts must be changed."[28]

My father and the IBM Information Machine had it right: digital technology can benefit human problems, including racial relations. Algorithms can be reimagined, re-created, and revised. Software bias can be exposed, eliminated, and excluded. They also had it wrong: all of these technological changes can be instituted, yet racial insensitivity, intolerance, and injustice will remain. Technology, when used right, is a means leading to progress in racial relations, not an end; it's one bridge on a journey toward justice, not a pin marking a final destination.

While *Think* played to millions on fairgrounds built upon dumping grounds, Freedom Summer took place in the South. While viewers relaxed in the air-conditioned comfort of IBM's "egg," James Chaney, Andrew Goodman, and Michael Schwerner were murdered in the hot backwoods of Mississippi. And while visitors waited in line to enter the IBM pavilion in Queens, marchers locked arms on Bloody Sunday to cross the Edmund Pettus Bridge in Selma. King's letter from Birmingham's city jail poignantly captures this tortured juxtaposition:

> *I am cognizant of the interrelatedness of all communities and all states. . . . Injustice anywhere is a threat to justice everywhere. We are caught in an inescapable network of mutuality, tied in a single garment of destiny. Whatever affects one directly, affects all indirectly.*[29]

The film *Think* made only vague allusions to this "network of mutuality," yet this network, more so than any social media or digital network, is the one through which we must all communicate if progress in racial relations is to be made.

16

Leaving

My father sat at his folding card table, the one he set up to serve as a makeshift desk or for a chess match, in the downstairs family room of our Rockland County home. He had flowcharts spread across the table, and next to them a book. He held the book toward me like a shield: *The g Factor: The Science of Mental Ability* by Arthur Jensen.

"You still believe that garbage?" I asked.

"Explains a lot to me," he said, "like why I never achieved all that I could have."

I sat down across the table from him. I wasn't there to argue about whether people with darker skin possessed innately inferior intellects. I wasn't there to double-check the logic represented by his stenciled diamonds, squares, and connecting lines. Nor was I there to engage him in a game of chess.

The front door swung open. My father and I looked up the stairs.

"We need some vegetables," Marilyn said. "I'll be back soon."

The front door closed.

My father smiled. "She's cute." He waved a finger back and forth between me and the front door. "You two together?"

"We've been seeing each other for a few months."

"Serious?"

"I don't know."

He winked. "Well, she's got the right stuff, in the right places. That's for sure."

"Stop."

"If you're not serious, maybe she'll go out with me."

"Marilyn's off-limits."

He grinned. "You seem pretty serious. You come up to talk to me about a girl?"

"No. I came to tell you I'm leaving IBM in the spring."

A long silence followed, animated by my father tamping down the tobacco in his pipe bowl. He lit the pipe, took a few puffs, leaned back, and turned slightly away. A thin stream of blue smoke vented from between his lips.

"I'm going to chiropractic college in Portland, Oregon."

"To be a chiropractor?"

"Yes."

"They're quacks."

"Ignorant people say that."

"Do you even know what a chiropractor does?"

"Yes. I'm seeing Doc Jasper, and what he does seems to work."

"Black chiropractor from White Plains?"

"Yes."

"You know he grew up in the 'Bridge?"

"I do."

"He's a relative of Cab Calloway."

"Yep."

"And he also works as an insurance adjuster because he can't make a living as a chiropractor. At least go to medical school."

"Not interested in being a medical doctor."

My father took a long drag on his pipe. "You're just like your mother."

"How's that?"

"Pick up and do whatever pops into your mind."

"She's wanted a PhD for most of her life. It didn't just pop into her mind, and going to chiropractic college didn't just pop into mine."

"What's she think about you leaving IBM, anyway?"

"She thinks I shouldn't leave a good-paying job."

My father chuckled. "Finally, she's making some sense."

I encountered surprising resistance to striking out on my own, and not just from my father. Gradually, I came to understand this as a symptom of the "mirror effect," where the actions of others serve as a mirror for us to observe ourselves. Only this time, instead of observing myself in the mirror others held up for me, I observed others in the mirror I unwittingly held up for them. At first, it appeared that those around me championed my best interests.

"What do your managers think?" my father asked.

"One's trying to convince me to take another leave of absence. The other says not to quit before I've worked for ten years and I can receive a pension from the company."

"Your colleagues?"

"Like Mom, the ones I've told question why I'd leave a good-paying job."

My father shook his head slightly, let out another thin blue stream of smoke. "They're right. All of them . . ." He winced. "Even your mother."

Ultimately, I came to understand that my father, my managers, and my colleagues were not as concerned about me as they were about what my decision to leave IBM reflected about them. This surfaced during my exit interviews.

My first-level manager called me into his office, then shut the door. I anticipated a scolding or at least a peppering of questions about my time at IBM and what more the company could have done to retain me. Instead, he reached out to shake my hand.

"Good for you," he said. "I've always wanted to open a bookstore in New Jersey. Perhaps someday I will."

He left me speechless, after all that he had said and done to convince me to stay.

Another scheduled exit interview took place with my second-level manager, a man who'd been particularly stern about my plans to leave. Behind closed doors, this man, dressed in a three-piece suit, also shook my hand.

"I expect I'll read great things about all you accomplish." Then the corners of his mouth turned down and he confessed. "You know, all I've ever wanted is to be a wildcat oilman in Texas."

Again, I found myself at a loss for words.

Back at my desk, a female colleague sitting behind me touched my shoulder and began sobbing.

"I really want to leave," she said. "But the money's just too good. I feel trapped."

When I told Tommy Barnes I was really leaving, he stood up from his seat by the elevator, put a hand on my shoulder, and said, "My man, you gonna be all right. I just know it."

I don't know if that bookstore ever opened, if that wildcat well ever gushed forth, or if that colleague ever left IBM on her own terms. I do know that from them I received a marvelous lesson, not merely on the power of the "mirror effect," but, more importantly, on the need to live an authentic life—one that unfolds according to the dictates of one's conscience rather than the demands of one's society or social group.

"What happens to a dream deferred?" asked poet Langston Hughes. "Does it dry up like a raisin in the sun?"

From my father came additional lessons about what happens to dreams deferred. That spring, I was back in Rockland County, and my father was back at his makeshift desk. My packed van was parked in his driveway. I no longer worked for IBM, and I was ready to drive west. My mother, I let my father know, was now glad I'd decided to leave IBM. She'd invited me to her new home in California when I got to the West Coast.

My father pulled the pipe from his mouth and rested his elbow on the card table. He stared at the blue smoke rising from the pipe, then spoke to it as though addressing a ghost.

"She forbade it," he said.

"Who? Forbade what?"

I learned for the first time that my grandmother insisted that my father work for IBM, even if that meant sacrificing his dream of becoming a professional musician. I learned too that my grandfather had sacrificed his dream of being a minister, then a doctor, to work as a porter, so my father had more opportunities in his life. It struck me more clearly than ever: in their time, being Black and being first meant dreams deferred. It was my turn for silence and for gratitude that my father and grandfather had sacrificed their dreams so I could now go in search of my own.

Jensen's book, along with others on race and IQ, still occupied a prominent place on my father's bookshelf. Considering all he had accomplished at IBM, all he had done to bring forth a miraculous new age of high technology, I found it hard to understand what sway these discredited theories held. Yet navigating the challenges of race in America, particularly for Blacks, is a perilous journey for which precious little guidance exists.

My father used chess as his guide: Black begins with a disadvantage. You have to look further ahead, work extra hard, rely on cunning, and assume everyone else is your opponent. My grandfather's guidance was more simply put: just be the best. "I'd rather be a good porter," he told Dartmouth students in 1924, "than a bad president."[1]

I've often wondered, in the absence of stiff racial headwinds, without feeling compelled to treat his coworkers as adversaries, how far my father would have gone just being his best at IBM. Although, watching his struggles against racism within the company and experiencing my own led me to conclude it was essential to wrestle with the existential question, Who am I as a Black man in a society that resents my very being? At least I knew, thanks to my father, that the path he'd taken in answer to this question was not mine. Eventually, through the study and reflection required to write several books on social justice and race, I came to a place of quiet comfort, though not resolution, with being Black in America. My father never found a similar peace.

Though I no longer worked for IBM, my father still did. Prior to heading west, I caught him, as usual, with his head buried in a flowchart.

"What are you working on?" I asked.

A sheepish look contorted my father's face. "Secret."

"Virtual machines?"

"Nope. All done with that. Look, I can say this: it has to do with the antitrust suit brought against IBM by the Justice Department. Lawyers have a massive number of documents they need to search, then view on a screen."

"So you're designing a massive document-retrieval system."

He mumbled. "Something like that."

By late 1976, my father's career at IBM had begun winding down. The company deployed him on special assignments such as this document-retrieval system, a predecessor to Cloud storage. This time I spent with my father before heading to the West Coast also coincided with the beginning of massive changes sweeping through the computer industry, and especially through IBM. The Apple I had debuted six months earlier, and many fretted over IBM's business, which was still bound tightly to monster mainframes.

Most thought IBM too ponderous to get up to speed quickly enough to meet Apple and the other early entrants in the personal computer marketplace. Rich Seidner, a former IBM programmer, recalls a colleague examining the IBM quality-control process, then remarking that, when applied to designing and releasing a personal computer, "it would take at least nine months to ship an empty box."[2] So IBM set up semiautonomous IBUs (independent business units) in response to this competition for personal computers, charging each one with the responsibility of coming up with the best design.

"I've seen the future," my father whispered a few days before I drove off, "and IBM's there. Though I'm sworn to secrecy on this matter, let's just say I entered an IBU room, where on several desks I saw computers no bigger than briefcases with keyboards in front, and monitors on top. And the labels didn't read 'Apple.' No sir, they read 'IBM.'"

From design, to production, to marketing, to sales, to service, everything about a personal computer was antithetical to the way IBM had conducted business for more than half a century. Retail computer stores, a new and burgeoning business in the late 1970s, would sell personal computers, not the traditional IBM sales force. A personal computer needed to be constructed of standard parts that computer store employees, rather than IBM field engineers, could repair. And IBM would have to market personal computers to the general public, something they had never done before.

In 1980, IBM officially entered the quest for its own brand of personal computers by upgrading one IBU to code name Project Chess. To the astonishment of many, a year later, and four years after my father first glimpsed an IBM personal computer prototype, the company began manufacturing PCs using commercial, off-the-shelf parts in Boca Raton, Florida. Microsoft, then a small Seattle-area software company, was chosen to write software for the IBM PC, and the Little Tramp, Charlie Chaplin's iconic character with his bowler hat and cane, was chosen as the public marketing symbol for this new machine.

Small, lightweight, and easy to use, the IBM PC became an instant success, with more than forty thousand units ordered on the day of its announcement.[3] The IBM PC established, then dominated, the non-Apple PC market. Ultimately, it became the industry standard. By 1984, PC sales accounted for $4 billion in IBM's annual revenue, double that of all competitors, including Apple, combined.[4] The IBM PC would even become one of the first personal computers to incorporate virtual memory and virtual machines.[5] With everything new about the IBM PC, one thing remained unchanged: IBM's fascination with assigning numbers to the machines it created. Internally, the IBM PC was designated the IBM 5150.

My father had glimpsed a digital future and he was proud, for good reason. He had a hidden hand in helping shape that future. When the IBM PC was announced, my father ordered one. Just as he had with the IBM 407, 705, 7080, 1620, 1130, 360, and 370, he learned everything he could about the IBM 5150. He believed in IBM, and he believed in staying abreast of the latest digital technology. "Whatever you do in life, learn about computers," he told me often. "That way, you'll never want for a job." That advice I took west, across the country, and with me throughout life. That advice from my father has withstood the test of time.

The afternoon sun beat down on me the day before I left. I'd just finished mowing my father's oversize lawn, and I was dripping with sweat. Beyond a locked gate, a slight breeze rippled the surface of his pool.

"Dad, okay if I take a swim?"

He tossed me a towel, unlocked the gate, and said, with his sly, crooked-tooth grin, "Thought you'd never ask."

17

Long Walks

After retirement, reflection proved much easier for my father. While I was under-going my divorce, my therapist insisted that I interview both parents. I rose to her challenge. For several summers in the late 1980s, I drove up from Richmond, Virginia, to spend time with my father in Rockland County. We took long walks along the Hudson River, talking about our time at IBM, talking about our time as a family, talking about the conflicts we endured and about the men we had become.

In some ways, walking and talking with my father seemed to me to be like spending time with an operative toward the end of his long and distinguished career of clandestine service. On each visit, I checked the bottom drawer of his dresser. The dog-eared envelope was no longer there. My father smiled but would never say if he'd actually handed off his covert operation to someone else inside IBM. I hope he did.

While my father did say much on these walks, he also chose not to reveal some key details of his life and his career. With no hint of remorse or regret, without skipping a beat in his retelling, my father would flash his crooked-tooth grin and utter his well-worn phrase, "And the rest I'll have to take with me to my grave." By this time, I'd learned not to prod or plead, not to step into this trap laid down by a master of the game. He'd given me what he felt he could, provided me the overall arc of his story, and, after all, more would never be forthcoming.

Not long after our last walk, my father suffered a series of mini-strokes. He became increasingly debilitated, relying on a cane or walker. He reminded me of a King at the endgame, limited to slow movements one chessboard square at a time. Yet in a flourish befitting a chess master's grand finale, my father managed to surreptitiously slip away from a five-star care facility in Florida, elude authorities, and make his way back to Rockland County. There, along the banks of the Hudson, in the shadows of a life and a career that no longer existed, he soon died.

When I arrived to clean out his apartment, I noticed his IBM personal computer on a stand alongside his bed, next to a tray of pills, his chessboard, and his pipe. I pushed a button to turn on the computer, listened to the disk drive whir, and watched the screen flicker to life. He'd worked at his computer right to the end. Eventually, I needed to say a final goodbye. I held down the POWER button, listened to his drive spin down one last time, watched his screen flash to black, and allowed my father to now became a truly hidden figure.

Still, he's never far. Whenever I hear the blips and beeps, the whines and whirs of a computer, I recall what I learned from my father about these machines, about being a man who's Black, and about being first. Those lessons live on in me. And while the goal he hoped for—that Blacks would rise to the highest leadership roles in IBM and other technology firms—remains largely unfulfilled, the contributions he made to the Digital Age live on in computers to this day.

The Words of a Poet

With his background in accounting, my father first worked in IBM's Accounts Payable Department, where he coded debit memos, deductions from amounts owed by IBM to its vendors. He would pass this information on to keypunch operators, who then typed vendor information along with deductions onto punch cards for subsequent sorting and tabulation by the IBM machines known at the time as Hollerith machines or electronic accounting machines (EAMs).

In 1947, my father penned one of the early poems of the Digital Age, devoted to coding debit memos for IBM electronic accounting machines.

DEBIT MEMO

Hail to thee, trite paper!
O nightmare of a clerk!
The cause of many a caper
Of some pencil pushing jerk.

Comes night when I am sleeping,
And resting peacefully,
I see you plainly weeping,
And begging, "Please code me."

I blow a fuse, more or less,
And nasty words I mutter;
But truly, I will confess
You are my bread and butter.

ACKNOWLEDGMENTS

It thrilled me to learn that Tracy Sherrod had acquired *Think Black* for HarperCollins. Authors, if we are lucky, get to entrust our manuscripts to good editors, but I got to entrust *Think Black* to a great editor. Tracy heads Amistad, an imprint of HarperCollins, and I knew from the many books that she'd brought into being that she would understand what I hoped to achieve. Furthermore, I knew that Tracy would add her discerning eye, her keen sense of narrative, and her loving touch to bring out the best in this book—and she did. But author and editor do not stand alone, and along with Tracy came the opportunity to work with an incredibly talented, robust, and dedicated team at HarperCollins, under the wise and experienced hand of publisher Judith Curr.

Adam Chromy, of Movable Type Management, my agent, has been involved with this book at every stage, from its inception to its completion. What I appreciate so much about Adam is his fine understanding of, and deep commitment to, great storytelling. He would not put my proposal out for acquisition, nor would he allow me to submit my completed manuscript to Tracy, until what I wrote met his high standards. My trust in him was well-placed.

I could not have written this memoir without the help of my sister, Dr. Claudia Jeanne Ford, a professor of ethnobotany and women's studies. When my memory of events with our father was unclear, she provided clarification. When I needed to talk through sections of the manuscript, she listened. When I went in search of pictures relating to our father's life, she sent along some wonderful images from her personal collection.

My friend Toni Burbank, who was my editor at Bantam Double-day Dell, offered me much encouragement to tell this story. Toni assured me that I was in the best of hands at HarperCollins.

The late Dr. Vincent Harding—my mentor, teacher, and dear friend—reminded me that history is a great river and that the stories of all those along its banks matter.

There's an unseen hand behind this book, and it belongs to Dr. Joan Winter, founder of the Family Institute of Virginia. Many years ago, while in therapy with Joan, she challenged me to interview my father. I am very grateful she did. Over the course of three summers, and through long walks along the Hudson River, I came to better understand my father, the challenges he faced in his professional and personal life, and the challenges he presented in mine. What I learned during those summers became the foundation of this memoir.

I had not met my cousin Edna Messick until the results of a recent DNA test brought us together. Edna had done extensive research on my father's side of the family, and thanks to her I was able to piece together important elements of my paternal lineage.

Historian of technology and friend George Dyson reviewed an early version of this book and made some important suggestions regarding my descriptions of early computers.

ACKNOWLEDGMENTS

Potter Christopher Moench and environmentalist and author Jennifer Hahn have been wonderful friends and gracious benefactors in support of my work as an author.

Finally, Peter Forbes, Helen Whybrow, and the crew at the Knoll Farm retreat center in Waitsfield, Vermont, were kind enough to invite me there as a fellow during the summer of 2018. I spent a marvelous week at Knoll Farm working on this book while the farm provided for my other needs: beautiful vistas, a place to stay, blueberries to pick, and delicious organic food to eat.

NOTES

Chapter 1: First Days

1. John Florio and Ouisie Shapiro, "Revisiting Jackie Robinson's Major-League Debut, Seventy Years Later," *New Yorker*, April 15, 2017, https://www.newyorker.com/sports/sporting-scene/revisiting-jackie-robinsons-major-league-debut-seventy-years-later.

2. Florio and Shapiro, "Revisiting Jackie Robinson's Major-League Debut."

3. Earl Chapin May, "This Ford's a Pullman Porter," *Collier's Weekly*, July 5, 1924, 8.

4. Zack Friedman, "IBM's HR Chief Shares Best Advice on the Future of Work," *Forbes*, August 6, 2018, https://www.forbes.com/sites/zackfriedman/2018/08/06/ibms-hr-chief-shares-best-advice-on-the-future-of-work/#456094e3dc41.

Chapter 2: A Sacrificial Pawn

1. Willie Lynch, "The Willie Lynch Letter: The Making of a Slave," December 25, 1712, Internet Archive, https://archive.org/stream /WillieLynchLetter1712/the_willie_lynch_letter_the_making_of _a_slave_1712_djvu.txt.

2. Lee Edson, "Jensenism, n. The Theory That I.Q. Is Largely Determined by Genes," *New York Times Magazine*, August 31, 1969, 40.

3. Charles Lane, "The Tainted Sources of 'The Bell Curve,'" *New York Review of Books*, December 1, 1994, https://www.nybooks.com /articles/1994/12/01/the-tainted-sources-of-the-bell-curve.

4. Richard J. Herrnstein and Charles Murray, *The Bell Curve* (New York: Simon & Schuster, 1994).

Chapter 3: The Bones of the Machine

1. Donald C. Johanson and Maitland A. Edey, *Lucy, the Beginnings of Humankind* (New York: Touchstone, 1981).

Chapter 4: The Book of Changes

1. Richard Wilhelm, trans., *The I Ching or Book of Changes* (New York: Bollingen Foundation, 1950), 3.

2. "The Hollerith Machine," US Census Bureau, n.d., https://www .census.gov/history/www/innovations/technology/the_hollerith _tabulator.html.

3. American Guild of Organists, "Trinity Baptist Church," http://www .nycago.org/Organs/Brx/html/TrinityBaptist.html.

4. Earl Chapin May, "This Ford's a Pullman Porter," *Collier's Weekly*, July 5, 1924, 8.

5. For instance, see https://www.asciiart.eu.

6. IBM Corporation, *Songs of the IBM* (New York: IBM, 1937).

7. IBM Corporation, *Songs of the IBM*, 5.

8. IBM Corporation, *IBM Online Archives*, https://www.ibm.com/ibm /history/exhibits/music/music_IA1.html.

Chapter 5: Voices of the Dead

1. I first wrote about my experience at the Elmina slave castle in my book *The Hero with an African Face: Mythic Wisdom of Traditional Africa* (New York: Bantam, 1999).
2. Erika Beras, "Traces of Genetic Trauma Can Be Tweaked," *Scientific American*, April 15, 2017, https://www.scientificamerican.com/podcast /episode/traces-of-genetic-trauma-can-be-tweaked.
3. Ford, *Hero with an African Face*.
4. Principally *Dum Diversas* (Rome: Vatican, 1452) and *Romanus Pontifex* (Rome: Vatican, 1455).
5. Stefan Goodwin, *Africa in Europe* (Lanham, MD: Lexington Books, 2009), 57.
6. David Reich, "How Genetics Is Changing Our Understanding of 'Race,'" op-ed, *New York Times*, March 23, 2018, https://www.nytimes .com/2018/03/23/opinion/sunday/genetics-race.html.
7. *American National Election Study* (Ann Arbor: Univ. of Michigan, 2012).
8. *General Social Survey (GSS)* (Chicago: Univ. of Chicago National Opinion Research Center, 2016).
9. Anthony Walton, "Technology versus African-Americans," *Atlantic Monthly*, January 1999, 14.
10. Gomes Eannes de Zurara, *Chronica do Descobrimento e Conquista da Guiné* (Paris, 1841), trans. Edgar Prestage, *The Chronicle of Discovery and Conquest of Guinea*, vols. 1 and 2 (London: Hakluyt Society, 1896–1899).
11. Pope Nicholas V, *Dum Diversas* (Rome: Vatican, 1452), emphasis added.
12. Duarte Lopez, *A Report of the Kingdom of Congo and of the Surrounding Countries*, trans. Margarite Hutchinson (London: John Murray, 1881), 39.
13. Lopez, *A Report of the Kingdom of Congo*, 40.

14.   Campbell Gibson and Kay Jung, "Historical Census Statistics on Population Totals by Race, 1790 to 1990, and by Hispanic Origin, 1970 to 1990, for Large Cities and Other Urban Places in the United States" (working paper no. 76, Washington, DC: US Census Bureau, 2005).

Chapter 6: To Speak of Rivers

1.   Langston Hughes, "The Negro Speaks of Rivers," *The Crisis* 77, no. 9 (New York: National Association for the Advancement of Colored People, 1970), 366.

2.   Vincent Harding, *There Is a River: The Black Struggle for Freedom in America* (New York: Harcourt Brace Jovanovich, 1981).

3.   W. Jeffrey Bolster, *Black Jacks: African American Seamen in the Age of Sail* (Cambridge, MA: Harvard Univ. Press, 1997).

4.   Bolster, *Black Jacks*, 6.

5.   Campbell Gibson and Kay Jung, "Historical Census Statistics on Population Totals by Race, 1790 to 1990, and by Hispanic Origin, 1970 to 1990, for Large Cities and Other Urban Places in the United States" (working paper no. 76, Washington, DC: US Census Bureau, 2005).

6.   Bolster, *Black Jacks*, 4.

7.   Frederick Douglass, "My Escape from Slavery," *Century Magazine*, vol. 23 (1882), 125.

8.   Bolster, *Black Jacks*, 14.

9.   Briton Hammon, *A Narrative of the Uncommon Sufferings, and Surprizing Deliverance of Briton Hammon, a Negro Man* (Boston: Green & Russell, 1760).

10.   Robert L. Duffus, "Pullman Porter Wins as College Lecturer," *New York Times*, April 13, 1924, 188.

11.   Allissa V. Richardson, "The Platform: How Pullman Porters Used Railways to Engage in Networked Journalism," *Journalism Studies* 17, no. 4 (2016): 398–414, https://www.tandfonline.com/doi/abs/10.1 080/1461670X.2015.1110498.

12. Duffus, "Pullman Porter Wins as College Lecturer."

13. Richardson, "The Platform," 403.

14. Duffus, "Pullman Porter Wins as College Lecturer."

15. Earl Chapin May, "This Ford's a Pullman Porter," *Collier's Weekly*, July 5, 1924, 31.

16. Richardson, "The Platform," 404–5.

17. Cameron McWhirter, *Red Summer: The Summer of 1919 and the Awakening of Black America* (New York: Henry Holt, 2011).

18. Richardson, "The Platform," 405.

19. Claude McKay, "If We Must Die," *Liberator*, July 1919, 21.

20. Richardson, "The Platform," 409.

21. Malcolm X, *The Autobiography of Malcolm X* (New York: Random House, 1964), 82.

22. May, "This Ford's a Pullman Porter," 8.

23. Duffus, "Pullman Porter Wins as College Lecturer."

Chapter 8: Twice as Hard

1. A field engineer worked to repair malfunctioning IBM computers, while a systems engineer worked to program functioning IBM computers.

2. Robert D. Friedel and Paul Israel, *Edison's Electric Light* (Baltimore: Johns Hopkins Univ. Press, 2010), 20.

Chapter 9: The Arrangement

1. Ossie Davis and Ruby Dee, *With Ossie and Ruby: In This Life Together* (New York: HarperCollins, 2000), 91.

2. Davis and Dee, *With Ossie and Ruby*, 92.

3. Davis and Dee, *With Ossie and Ruby*, 97.

4. Davis and Dee, *With Ossie and Ruby*, 317.

5. Davis and Dee, *With Ossie and Ruby*, 218.

Chapter 10: Doing Small Things in a Great Way

1. Martin Luther King Jr., "I Have a Dream," August 28, 1963, US National Archives, https://www.archives.gov/files/press/exhibits/dream-speech.pdf.

2. W. E. B. Du Bois, *The Souls of Black Folk* (New York: Dover, 1994), 2.

3. Thomas J. Watson Jr., letter to IBM management, September 21, 1953. Policy Letter #4 can be read online at https://www.ibm.com/ibm/history/ibm100/us/en/icons/equalworkforce/transform.

4. IBM, "Employee Inclusion," in *2012 Corporate Responsibility Report*, https://www.ibm.com/ibm/responsibility/2012/the-ibmer/employee-inclusion.html.

5. William H. Rodgers, *Think: A Biography of the Watsons and IBM* (New York: Stein & Day, 1969).

6. Kenneth Brevoort and Howard P. Marvel, *Successful Monopolization Through Predation: The National Cash Register Company* (Columbus: Ohio State Univ., n.d.), 40, https://www.asc.ohio-state.edu/economics/pdf/marvel/ncr.pdf.

7. Edwin Black, *IBM and the Holocaust* (Washington, DC: Dialog Press, 2001), 35.

8. Black, *IBM and the Holocaust*, 35.

9. Black, *IBM and the Holocaust*, 36.

10. Black, *IBM and the Holocaust*, 36.

11. Brevoort and Marvel, *Successful Monopolization through Predation*, 32.

12. Brevoort and Marvel, *Successful Monopolization through Predation*, 32.

13. James D. P. Graham, "Static Tremor in Anxiety States," *Journal of Neurology, Neurosurgery and Psychiatry* 8, no. 3–4 (1945): 57–60; "Tremor Fact Sheet," National Institutes of Health, May 2017, https://www.ninds.nih.gov/Disorders/Patient-Caregiver-Education/Fact-Sheets/Tremor-Fact-Sheet; "Essential Tremor and Stress Management," WebMD, September 16, 2018, https://www.webmd.com/brain/essential-tremor-stress-mgmt#1.

14. It is entirely possible that T. J. Laster's family could have been to the IBM Country Club before us. Still, in the many years our family went, we never saw another Black family there.

15. King, "I Have A Dream."

Chapter 11: Covert Ops

1. Malcolm X, *The Autobiography of Malcolm X: As Told to Alex Haley* (New York: Ballantine, 1964).

2. Malcolm X, *Autobiography*, 44, 94.

3. Madison Grant, *The Passing of the Great Race* (New York: Charles Scribner's Sons: 1916).

4. Edwin Black, *War Against the Weak: Eugenics and America's Campaign to Create a Master Race* (Washington, DC: Dialog Press, 2012). This well-researched and heavily documented book is the basis for the assertions in this chapter regarding IBM and the eugenics movement.

5. *Buck v. Bell*, 274 U.S. 200 (1927).

6. *Roe v. Wade*, 410 U.S. 113, 154, 93 S. Ct. 705, 727, 35 L. Ed. 2d 147 (1973).

7. Black, *War Against the Weak*, 258.

8. Black, *War Against the Weak*, 292.

9. Meilan Solly, "DNA Pioneer James Watson Loses Honorary Titles over Racist Comments," *Smithsonian*, January 15, 2019, https://www.smithsonianmag.com/smart-news/dna-pioneer-james-watson-loses-honorary-titles-over-racist-comments-180971266.

10. Solly, "DNA Pioneer James Watson," 291.

11. Edwin Black, *IBM and the Holocaust* (Washington, DC: Dialog Press, 2001), 444–58. Here, Black devotes an entire chapter to IBM's attempts to block access to their archives and to deny or obfuscate involvement by the company, or its founder, with the Third Reich.

12. Black, *IBM and the Holocaust*. This extensively researched, comprehensively documented book is the basis for the assertions in this chapter of IBM's and Watson's collaboration with Nazi Germany.

13. Black, *IBM and the Holocaust*, 210.

14. Black, *IBM and the Holocaust*, 8.

15. Edwin Black, "IBM's Role in the Holocaust—What the New Documents Reveal," March 17, 2015, *Huffington Post*, https://www.huffingtonpost .com/edwin-black/ibm-holocaust_b_1301691.html.

16. Black, *IBM and the Holocaust*, 77.

17. Black, *IBM and the Holocaust*, 235, 403.

18. Black, *IBM and the Holocaust*, 419–24.

19. In the 1933 census of Germany and Austria conducted by the *Rasse Statische Amt* (the Race Statistical Office), column 22 of the punch card represented a person's religion. Row 1 was punched if the person was Catholic; row 2, Protestant; row 3, Jewish; and so forth. These results were then used to identify Jews for exportation and extermination. Columns 14 and 15 might represent a person's birth day of the month (1 to 31); columns 16 and 17, a person's birth month (1 to 12); columns 18 through 21, a person's birth year. Column 34, for prisoners in the Bergen-Belsen concentration camp, represented the reason for their departure. Row 2 meant transfer to another camp; row 3, a natural death; row 4, execution; row 5, suicide; row 6, "special handling" for extermination via the gas chamber, hanging, or gunshot. See Black, *IBM and the Holocaust*, 22, 58.

20. Black, *IBM and the Holocaust*, 22.

21. Black, *IBM and the Holocaust*, 57.

22. Black, *IBM and the Holocaust*, 44.

23. Black, *IBM and the Holocaust*, 383.

24. Black, *IBM and the Holocaust*, 130.

25. Black, *IBM and the Holocaust*, 96.

26. Black, *IBM and the Holocaust*, 320–32.

27. Black, *IBM and the Holocaust*, 111.

28. Black, *IBM and the Holocaust*, 43.

29. Black, *IBM and the Holocaust*, 377.

30. Black, *IBM and the Holocaust*, 409.

31. Peter G. Neumann, "Peopleware in Systems," in *Peopleware in Systems* (Cleveland: Association for Systems Management, 1977), 15–18.

32. Meilir Page-Jones, *Practical Guide to Structured Systems Design* (New York: Yourdon Press, 1980).

33. Nelson Mandela, "Africa It Is Ours," transcribed in *New York Times*, February 12, 1990, https://www.nytimes.com/1990/02/12/world/south -africa-s-new-era-transcript-mandela-s-speech-cape-town-city -hall-africa-it.html.

34. Michael Kwet, "Apartheid in the Shadows: The USA, IBM and South Africa's Digital Police State," *CounterPunch*, May 3, 2017, https:// www.counterpunch.org/2017/05/03/apartheid-in-the-shadows-the -usa-ibm-and-south-africas-digital-police-state.

35. Kwet, "Apartheid in the Shadows."

36. *Balintulo v. Ford Motors Co.*, IBM, General Motors Corp, No. 14–4104 (2nd Cir. July 27, 2015), https://ccrjustice.org/sites/default/files/attach /2015/06/InReApartheid_PlAppellantsBrief_1-28-15.pdf.

37. *Balintulo v. Ford Motors Co.*

38. *Balintulo v. Ford Motors Co.*, 13.

39. *Balintulo v. Ford Motors Co.*, 14.

40. *Balintulo v. Ford Motors Co.*, 15.

41. *Balintulo v. Ford Motors Co.*, 11.

42. "How IBM Supports Apartheid" (Chicago: Univ. of Chicago Coalition for Divestment, May 1986), http://africanactivist.msu.edu/document _metadata.php?objectid=32-130-1641.

43. Donna K. H. Walters, "IBM to End Its Presence in S. Africa," *Los Angeles Times*, October 22, 1986, http://articles.latimes.com/1986 -10-22/news/mn-6806_1_ibm-south-africa.

44. *Balintulo v. Ford Motors Co.*, 10.

45. See *Balintulo v. Ford Motors Co.* and Electronic Frontier Foundation, "Brief of Amicus Curiae Electronic Frontier Foundation in Support of Plaintiffs," US Court of Appeals for the Second Circuit, No. 14–4104–cv. February 4, 2015, https://www.eff.org/files/2015/02/11 /eff_ibm_apartheid_amicus_brief_final.pdf.

46. *Balintulo v. Ford Motors Co.*, 10.

47. Ra'eesa Pather, "Government Stopped Apartheid Victims from Receiving Better Compensation—Ntsebeza," *Johannesburg Mail and*

Guardian, February 3, 2018, https://mg.co.za/article/2018-02-03-government-stopped-apartheid-victims-from-receiving-better-compensation-ntsebeza.

48.   "GroundUp: Apartheid Victims Lose 14-Year Legal Battle Against Ford and IBM," *Daily Maverick*, June 23, 2016, https://www.daily maverick.co.za/article/2016-06-23-groundup-apartheid-victims-lose-14-year-legal-battle-against-ford-and-ibm/. See also, "Ntsebeza, et al., v. Daimler AG, et al.," United States Court of Appeals for the Second Circuit, Citation No. 617 F. Supp. 2d 228, April 8, 2009, https://www.court listener.com/opinion/2246584/in-re-south-african-apartheid-litigation.

49.   "GroundUp: Apartheid Victims Lose."

50.   George Joseph and Kenneth Lipp, "IBM Used NYPD Surveillance Footage to Develop Technology That Lets Police Search by Skin Color," *The Intercept*, September 6, 2018, https://theintercept.com/2018/09/06/nypd-surveillance-camera-skin-tone-search/.

51.   Joseph and Lipp, "IBM Used NYPD Surveillance Footage to Develop Technology That Lets Police Search by Skin Color."

52.   IBM, "How IBM Is Improving Watson Visual Recognition Capabilities," March 15, 2018, https://www.ibm.com/blogs/watson/2018/03/how-ibm-is-improving-watson-visual-recognition-capabilities/.

53.   Rick Kjeldsen, quoted in Joseph and Lipp, "IBM Used NYPD Surveillance Footage to Develop Technology That Lets Police Search by Skin Color."

54.   Matt O'Brien, Associated Press, "Face Recognition Researcher Fights Amazon over Biased AI," ABC News, April 3, 2019, https://abcnews.go.com/Technology/wireStory/face-recognition-researcher-fights-amazon-biased-ai-62146446.

Chapter 13: Clandestine Service

1.   Tom Van Vleck, "Tech Square," Multicians, November 1994, https://www.multicians.org/tech-square.html.

2.   Richard Harris Smith, *OSS: The Secret History of America's First Central Intelligence Agency* (Guilford, CT: Lyons Press, 2005), 335.

Chapter 14: A Mass Shooting at IBM

1. Edell Lydia Jr., *Statement of Kwame Kwasi Afoh (Edell Lydia, Jr.)*, Hearing on the Anti-Apartheid Selective Purchasing Resolution before the Council of the District of Columbia, January 20, 1976, http://african activist.msu.edu/document_metadata.php?objectid=32-130-1F3F.
2. Lydia, *Statement of Kwame Kwasi Afoh.*
3. Lydia, *Statement of Kwame Kwasi Afoh.*
4. Lydia, *Statement of Kwame Kwasi Afoh.*
5. Steve Askin, "Wage Secrecy at IBM," *Black Enterprise*, April 1983, 24, https://books.google.com/books?id=2wIveHyHOe8C&pg=PA2 4&lpg=PA24&dq=askin+%22wage+secrecy+at+IBM%22&source= bl&ots=rz87wHkSsj&sig=ACfU3U0HuIczpBRia4xsaznfQay76V2D 9A&hl=en&sa=X&ved=2ahUKEwjb0IO6jtLgAhVBMnwKHWjlB 3sQ6AEwAHoECAAQAQ#v=onepage&q=askin%20%22wage%20 secrecy%20at%20IBM%22&f=false.
6. Francis X. Clines, "2 Killed and 8 Wounded in Rampage in Maryland," *New York Times*, May 29, 1982, https://www.nytimes.com /1982/05/29/us/2-killed-and-8-wounded-in-rampage-in-maryland .html; United Press International, "Authorities Seeking a Motive in Maryland I.B.M. Shootings," *New York Times*, May 30, 1982, https:// www.nytimes.com/1982/05/30/us/authorities-seeking-a-motive-in -maryland-ibm-shootings.html.
7. Kenneth Bredemeier, "Murder Suspect Claimed IBM Denied Him Promotions," *Washington Post*, June 12, 1982, https://www .washingtonpost.com/archive/local/1982/06/12/murder-suspect -claimed-ibm-denied-him-promotions/0c78cbee-bf50-44b1-b424 -c2741524e692/?noredirect=on&utm_term=.57d4e1487911.
8. Pam Coulter, quoted in Vincent Del Giudice, "Man Kills Two in IBM Building," May 29, 1982, UPI Archive, https://www.upi.com/Archives /1982/05/29/Man-kills-two-in-IBM-building/3981391492800.
9. Susan Blakeney, "Racism Charges Surface After IBM Shootings," *Computerworld*, June 21, 1982, 7, https://books.google.com/books? id=iLFaf5KtS6EC&pg=PA7&lpg=PA7&dq=%22racism+charges+sur

face+after+ibm+shootings%22&source=bl&ots=zQc_PIdlYS&sig=
ACfU3U3cj86KZWtVnHScKOWiOdepQLeong&hl=en&sa=X&ved
=2ahUKEwjV0uPXj9LgAhXCj1QKHY79CFkQ6AEwAHoECAEQ
AQ#v=onepage&q=%22racism%20charges%20surface%20after%20
ibm%20shootings%22&f=false.

10.   Blakeney, "Racism Charges Surface After IBM Shootings."

11.   Blakeney, "Racism Charges Surface After IBM Shootings."

12.   Associated Press, "Former Manager Sues IBM for Racial Discrimina-
       tion," *Los Angeles Times*, August 8, 1989, http://articles.latimes.com
       /1989-08-08/business/fi-291_1_racial-discrimination.

13.   Associated Press, "Former Manager Sues IBM for Racial Discrimi-
       nation."

14.   *Dusé v. IBM*, No. 00–7158 (2nd Cir. June 5, 2001), https://caselaw
       .findlaw.com/us-2nd-circuit/1430102.html.

15.   Associated Press, "Two Inmates Apparently Commit Suicide,"
       March 10, 1986, https://www.apnews.com/7dccf1a3828220bdcac72
       1def2836ee1.

16.   Askin, "Wage Secrecy at IBM."

17.   Askin, "Wage Secrecy at IBM."

18.   Askin, "Wage Secrecy at IBM."

19.   Askin, "Wage Secrecy at IBM."

20.   *Hudson v. IBM*, No. 79–7371 (2nd Cir. April 8, 1980), https://open
       jurist.org/620/f2d/351/hudson-v-international-business-machines
       -corporation.

21.   Askin, "Wage Secrecy at IBM."

22.   Center for Employment Equity, *Is Silicon Valley Tech Diversity Possible
       Now?* (Amherst: Univ. of Massachusetts, 2016).

Chapter 15: The Egg

1.   Charles and Ray Eames, "The Information Machine," 1964, IBM,
      https://www.ibm.com/ibm/history/exhibits/vintage/vintage
      _4506VV2085.html.

2.   Interestingly, when using the keyword phrase "black on white crime,"

the results obtained from a Bing search are no longer similar to those obtained from a Google search, although they once were, suggesting that both Bing and Google actually may have tweaked the algorithm that generates results for this keyword phrase.

3. Dylann Roof, "Dylann Roof's Manifesto," *New York Times*, December 13, 2016, https://www.nytimes.com/interactive/2016/12/13/universal /document-Dylann-Roof-manifesto.html?mtrref=www.google.com &gwh=AC22CEB6963929845580949F9F9F7A6C&gwt=pay.

4. "Council of Conservative Citizens," Southern Poverty Law Center, n.d., https://www.splcenter.org/fighting-hate/extremist-files/group /council-conservative-citizens.

5. "Council of Conservative Citizens," Southern Poverty Law Center.

6. Robert Epstein, quoted in Rebecca Hersher, "What Happened When Dylann Roof Asked Google for Information about Race?" The Two-Way, National Public Radio, January 10, 2017, https://www.npr.org /sections/thetwo-way/2017/01/10/508363607/what-happened-when -dylann-roof-asked-google-for-information-about-race.

7. Robert Epstein, "The Unprecedented Power of Digital Platforms to Control Opinions and Votes," *Pro-Market* (blog), Univ. of Chicago Stigler Center, April 12, 2018, https://promarket.org/unprecedented -power-digital-platforms-control-opinions-votes.

8. Hersher, "What Happened When Dylann Roof Asked Google."

9. Safiya Umoja Noble, *Algorithms of Oppression: How Search Engines Reinforce Racism* (New York: New York Univ. Press, 2018), 5, 64.

10. Ben Guarino, "Google Faulted for Racial Bias in Image Search Results for Black Teenagers," *Washington Post*, June 10, 2016, https://www .washingtonpost.com/news/morning-mix/wp/2016/06/10 /google-faulted-for-racial-bias-in-image-search-results-for-black -teenagers/?utm_term=.5990cbcd27fb. The videos and images returned for my search for "black on white crime" showed a similar negative portrayal of Blacks.

11. Matthew Speiser, "Google Maps Searches Are Turning Up Some Wildly Racist and Creepy Results," *Business Insider*, May 20, 2015, https://www.businessinsider.com/google-maps-searches-yielding -racist-and-creepy-results-2015-5.

12. Tim Mak, "Russian Influence Campaign Sought to Exploit Americans' Trust in Local News," National Public Radio, July 12, 2018, https://www.npr.org/2018/07/12/628085238/russian-influence-campaign-sought-to-exploit-americans-trust-in-local-news.

13. Mak, "Russian Influence Campaign."

14. Jens Manuel Krogstad and Mark Hugo Lopez, "Black Voter Turnout Fell in 2016, Even as a Record Number of Americans Cast Ballots," Pew Research Center, May 12, 2017, http://www.pewresearch.org/fact-tank/2017/05/12/black-voter-turnout-fell-in-2016-even-as-a-record-number-of-americans-cast-ballots.

15. Cited in Colbert I. King, "Trump's Sad 'Thank You' to African Americans," *Washington Post*, February 3, 2017, https://www.washingtonpost.com/opinions/trumps-sad-thank-you-to-african-americans/2017/02/03/2dc3c47c-e992-11e6-bf6f-301b6b443624_story.html?utm_term=.154e4cfcf109.

16. *United States of America v. Internet Research Agency, et. al.* (Washington, DC: Department of Justice, February 16, 2018), 18, para. 46.

17. *United States of America v. Internet Research Agency,* emphasis added.

18. Leo Hornak, "Some Black Lives Matter Activists Plan Not to Vote in November," *The World*, Public Radio International, July 20, 2016, https://www.pri.org/stories/2016-07-20/i-aint-voting-will-black-lives-matter-reject-right-vote.

19. Lyndon B. Johnson, "The Right to Vote," transcript of address to joint session of Congress, March 15, 1965, *Congressional Quarterly*, http://library.cqpress.com/cqalmanac/document.php?id=cqal65-875-26756-1260597.

20. *North Carolina State Conference of the NAACP et al. v. McCrory*, No. 16–1468 (4th Cir. July 29, 2016), 10–11, http://www.ca4.uscourts.gov/opinions/published/161468.p.pdf.

21. Joseph Walker, "Meet the New Boss: Big Data," *Wall Street Journal*, September 20, 2012, https://www.wsj.com/articles/SB10000872396390443890304578006252019616768.

22. Walker, "Meet the New Boss"; *Q2 2013 Workforce Performance Report: Key Factors Impacting the Performance—and Profitability—of Today's Hourly Workforces* (San Francisco: Evolv, 2013), 17.

23. Board of Governors of the Federal Reserve System, *Report to Congress on Credit Scoring and Its Effects on the Availability and Affordability of Credit* (Washington, DC: Federal Reserve System, 2007), S-2.

24. Danielle Ensign, Sorelle A. Friedler, Scott Neville, et al., "Runaway Feedback Loops in Predictive Policing," *Proceeding of Machine Learning Research* 81 (2018): 1–12.

25. Julia Angwin, Jeff Larson, Surya Mattu, et al., "Machine Bias: There's Software Used Across the Country to Predict Future Criminals. And It's Biased Against Blacks," ProPublica, May 23, 2016, https://www.propublica .org/article/machine-bias-risk-assessments-in-criminal-sentencing.

26. Sophie Kleeman, "Here Are the Microsoft Twitter Bot's Craziest Racist Rants," Gizmodo, March 24, 2016, https://gizmodo.com/here-are -the-microsoft-twitter-bot-s-craziest-racist-ra-1766820160.

27. Jason Pontin, "A Meeting with Sergey Brin, Cofounder of Google, at the Russian Tea Room in San Francisco," Red Herring, July 16, 2002, Wayback Machine, https://web.archive.org/web/20020719125615 /http://www.redherring.com/insider/2002/0716/bait071602.html.

28. Martin Luther King Jr., Remarks, Western Michigan Univ., December 18, 1963, https://wmich.edu/sites/default/files/attachments /MLK.pdf.

29. Martin Luther King Jr., *Letter from the Birmingham Jail* (New York: Penguin, 2018), 2.

Chapter 16: Leaving

1. Earl Chapin May, "This Ford's a Pullman Porter," *Collier's Weekly*, July 5, 1924, 8.

2. Robert X. Cringley, "Triumph of the Nerds," PBS, June 1996, https:// www.pbs.org/nerds.

3. Sol Libes, "Bytelines," *Byte*, December 1981, 314–18, https://archive .org/details/byte-magazine-1981-12/page/n315.

4. Sol Libes, "Bytelines," *Byte*, September 1985, 418, https://archive.org /details/byte-magazine-1985-09/page/n401.

5. IBM PC XT/370.

ABOUT THE AUTHOR

Clyde W. Ford is the author of ten works of fiction and nonfiction. He is also a psychotherapist, an accomplished mythologist, and a sought-after public speaker. He has received a number of awards, including the Zora Neale Hurston/Richard Wright Award in African American fiction. He is currently a speaker for Humanities Washington, an affiliate of the National Endowment for the Humanities, and has been featured frequently in the media, including on *The Oprah Winfrey Show*, New Dimensions Radio, and NPR. He lives in Bellingham, Washington.